Risto Uro is Lecturer in New Testament, University of Helsinki.

John Barclay and **Joel Marcus** are Lecturers in the Department of Biblical Studies, University of Glasgow.

John Riches is Professor of Divinity and Biblical Criticism, University of Glasgow.

Studies of the New Testament and Its World

Edited by

JOHN BARCLAY
JOEL MARCUS
and
JOHN RICHES

Thomas at the Crossroads

Thomas at the Crossroads

Essays on the *Gospel of Thomas*

Edited by
Risto Uro

T&T CLARK
EDINBURGH

T&T CLARK LTD
59 GEORGE STREET
EDINBURGH EH2 2LQ
SCOTLAND

ISBN 0 567 08607 0

British Library Cataloguing-in-Publication Data
A catalogue record for this book is available from the British Library

Typeset by Fakenham Photosetting Limited
Printed and bound in Great Britain by Bookcraft Ltd, Avon

Contents

Preface

This volume contains part of the results of a research project on the *Gospel of Thomas* funded by the Academy of Finland in 1993–5. The members of the project, Ismo Dunderberg, Antti Marjanen and Risto Uro, have been working in cooperation with the Institute of Antiquity and Christianity (Claremont Graduate University, CA) and its Associate Director, Jon Ma. Asgeirsson. The Consultation on *Thomas* Christianity, chaired by Asgeirsson, which took place within the Society of Biblical Literature in 1993–5 and was replaced by the Thomasine Working group in 1996, forms an important context for the research behind this publication as well. A few essays in this book were initially presented in these program units.

Some parts of the book have been published previously. Chapter 1 is a slightly revised and updated version of an article published in *Foundations & Facets Forum* 9.3–4 (1993) 305–29. Similarly, chapter 4 is a slightly revised and expanded version of a section in Marjanen, *The Woman Jesus Loved: Mary Magdalene in the Nag Hammadi Library and Related Documents* (NHMS 40; Leiden: E. J. Brill, 1996) 39–55. Chapter 6 incorporated portions from Uro, 'Asceticism and Anti-familial Language in the *Gospel of Thomas*' in H. Moxnes, ed., *Constructing Early Christian Families: Family as Social Reality and Metaphor* (London: Routledge, 1997) 216–34. We are grateful to Brill and Routledge for permitting the use of these materials in this book.

The subdivision of the sayings in the *Gospel of Thomas* follows the style established by the Westar Institute, which has been adopted, e.g., in J. S. Kloppenborg et al., *Q-Thomas Reader* (Sonoma: Polebridge Press, 1990).

Several persons have helped in getting the manuscript ready for publication. Ralph S. Carlson, Gary Denning, Patrick J. Hartin, and Margot Stout Whiting corrected the English of the Finnish contributors. Arto Järvinen and Juhana Saukkonen gave valuable help in technical editing. Joel Marcus, the editor of the present volume for the

Studies in the New Testament and Its World series, read the manuscript with care and suggested a great number of improvements. Countless discussions with other colleagues and, most importantly, between the contributors themselves, have created the fertile intellectual soil from which the ideas presented in this book have grown.

Risto Uro (Editor)

Contributors

Risto Uro is a Docent at the Department of Biblical Studies, University of Helsinki, and the director of a research project on 'Gnosticism and early Christian Culture' at the Academy of Finland. His publications include several studies on the Sayings Gospel Q and the *Gospel of Thomas*.

Ismo Dunderberg is a Senior Research Fellow at the Academy of Finland and a Docent at the Department of Biblical Studies, University of Helsinki. He has published several studies on the Gospel of John and Nag Hammadi writings. He is currently doing research on the creation myth in Valentinian Christianity.

Antti Marjanen is a Docent at the Department of Biblical Studies, University of Helsinki. He has published extensively on Gnosticism and the history of women in early Christianity, including *The Woman Jesus Loved: Mary Magdalene in the Nag Hammadi Library and Related Documents* (Leiden 1996).

Abbreviations

AAAbo	Acta Academiae Aboensis
AASF DHL	Annales Academiae Scientiarum Fennicae. Dissertationts humanarum litterarum
AB	Anchor Bible
ABD	*Anchor Bible Dictionary*
ALGHJ	Arbeiten zur Literatur und Geschichte des hellenistischen Judentums
ANRW	*Aufstieg und Niedergang der römischen Welt*
ASNU	Acta seminarii neotestamentici upsaliensis
BASP	*Bulletin of the American Society of Papyrologists*
BBB	Bonner biblische Beiträge
BETL	Bibliotheca ephemeridum theologicarum Lovanensium
BEvT	Beiträge zur evangelischen Theologie
BG	Berlin Gnostic Papyrus 8502
BIFAO	*Bulletin de l'institut français d'archéologie orientale*
BLE	*Bulletin de littérature ecclésiastique*
BU	Biblische Untersuchungen
BZ	*Biblische Zeitschrift*
BZNW	Beiheft zur Zeitschrift für die alttestamentliche Wissenschaft
CE	Common Era
CG	Cairensis Gnosticus
CH	Corpus Hermeticum
ConBNT	Coniectanea biblica, NT series
CRINT	Compendia rerum iudaicarum ad Novum Testamentum
EKKNT	Evangelisch-katholischer Kommentar zum Neuen Testament
EPRO	Études préliminaires aux religious orientales dans l'empire Romain
ET	English translation
ETL	*Ephemerides theologicae lovenienses*

ETR	*Études Théologiques et Religieuses*
EvT	*Evangelische Theologie*
FRLANT	Forschungen zur Religion und Literatur des Alten und Neuen Testaments
FS	Festschrift
HDR	Harvard Dissertations in Religion
HeyJ	*Heythrop Journal*
HR	*History of Religions*
HThKNT	Herders theologischer Kommentar zum Neuen Testament
HTR	*Harvard Theological Review*
HTS	Harvard Theological Studies
ICC	International Critical Commentary
JAAR	*Journal of American Academy of Religion*
JAC	*Jahrbuch für Antike und Christentum*
JBL	*Journal of Biblical Literature*
JSNT	*Journal for the Study of the New Testament*
JTS	*Journal of Theological Studies*
KEK	Kritisch-exegetischer Kommentar über das NT
LCC	Library of Christian Classics
LD	Lectio divina
LXX	Septuagint
Neot	*Neotestamentica*
n.F.	neue Folge (new series)
NHC	Nag Hammadi Codex/Codices
NHMS	Nag Hammadi and Manichaean Studies
NHS	Nag Hammadi Studies
NovT	*Novum Testamentum*
NTAbh	Neutestamentliche Abhandlungen
NTD	Das Neue Testament Deutsch
NTS	*New Testament Studies*
NTTS	New Testament Tools and Studies
OrChrA	Orientalia Christiana Analecta
PTMS	Pittsburgh Theological Monograph Studies
SAC	Studies in Antiquity and Christianity
SBB	Stuttgarter Biblische Beiträge
SBL	Society of Biblical Literature
SBLDS	SBL Dissertation Series
SBLSCS	SBL Septuagint and Cognate Studies

SBLSP	*SBL Seminar Papers*
SBS	Stuttgarter Bibelstudien
SBT	Studies in Biblical Theology
SD	Studies and Documents
SecCent	*Second Century*
SJLA	Studies in Judaism in Late Antiquity
SNTSMS	Society for NT Studies Monograph Series
StPatr	*Studia Patristica*
SUNT	Studien zur Umwelt des Neuen Testaments
Sup	Supplement
TDNT	*Theological Dictionary of the New Testament*, ed. G. Kittel and G. Friedrich (ET, Grand Rapids: 1964–76)
ThHKNT	Theologischer Handkommentar zum NT
TRu	*Theologische Rundschau*
TU	Texte und Untersuchungen zur Geschichte der altchristlichen Literatur
VC	*Vigiliae Christianae*
WMANT	Wissenschaftliche Monographien zum Alten und Neuen Testament
WUNT	Wissenschaftliche Untersuchungen zum NT
ZKG	*Zeitschrift für Kirchengeschichte*
ZNW	*Zeitschrift für die Neutestamentliche Wissenschaft*

Introduction

Thomas *at the crossroads*
New perspectives on a debated gospel

When the complete Coptic version of the *Gospel of Thomas*, found among the Nag Hammadi codices, was first made available to a larger audience four decades ago, it raised strong expectations among many scholars (and laypersons as well) for being a possible new source for tracing the authentic teaching of Jesus. Assessments of the value of the gospel, however, divided the scholarly community soon after its publication, and this great chasm has continued to exist in the field of Thomasine studies to the present day. The heated debates about the date of the gospel are one example of this basic issue. The estimates of the scholars range mostly from the middle of the first to the middle of the second century CE. Many ancient Christian documents cannot be dated as accurately as one would wish, among them many of the Nag Hammadi writings, but none of them has created such a divisive controversy. There is clearly more at stake in dating the *Gospel of Thomas* than in the dating of most other sources for Christian origins.

The same is true for another large issue of Thomasine research, i.e. whether *Thomas* is dependent upon the canonical gospels. The question has dominated many studies over the four decades of Thomasine scholarship, and its crucial role was still emphasized by Stephen J. Patterson at the beginning of his recent extensive monograph.

> For the present study it [the issue of *Thomas'* relationship to the Synoptic Gospels] is a point of no small significance, for if, as many have argued, the *Gospel of Thomas* is dependent upon the Synoptic texts for its traditions, it might be possible to think of *Thomas* Christianity as a small and relatively insignificant spur, diverging from the main stream of the Jesus movement – a 'perversion' of the Jesus tradition, whose more original, and hence more authentic voice is to be heard in the Synoptic texts themselves. On the other hand, if the *Gospel of Thomas* is not dependent upon the Synoptic Gospels, but rather has its own

1

roots, which reach deeply into the fertile soil of early Christian tradition . . . then *Thomas* presents those who wish to think critically about the problem of Christian origins with something much more important: another point of view from which to peer down into the murk of earliest Christianity.[1]

Thomas' relationship to the canonical gospels is, of course, a significant and intriguing issue.[2] But the high expectations that the new gospel would provide an alternative and reliable channel to early 'authentic' teaching of Jesus has raised the stakes of the issue much higher than they are in the case of some other early Christian gospels. For example, the literary relationship between the Gospel of John and the Synoptics continues to be an issue among scholars, but without a sense of gain and loss as strong as the one that has often been felt in the case of the *Gospel of Thomas*.

An obvious reason for this difference is that John is a canonical gospel while *Thomas* is extracanonical or, to use a more theologically loaded term, 'apocryphal.' Whereas the latter term has traditionally been connected with such overtones as 'obscure,' 'late imitation' or 'heretical,' Thomasine scholarship has played a significant role in the process by which the Christian canon is gradually losing its meaning as a category for evaluating the historical value of the traditions included in it. Even though some scholars still speak of the New Testament Gospels as the 'four rivers flowing out of Eden,'[3] the evidence of such documents as the *Gospel of Thomas* has made an increasing number of scholars interested in extracanonical sources as being of fundamental importance for understanding Christian origins. There is no *a priori* reason to assume that early Christian texts that were canonized at a certain time in the history of Christianity have more historical value than others that were lost or fell out of favor.[4]

The demand that the boundaries of the canon must not control

---

[1] *The Gospel of Thomas and Jesus* (Foundations and Facets: Reference Series; Sonoma: Polebridge Press, 1993) 9. Idem, 'The Gospel of Thomas and the Synoptic Tradition: A Forschungsbericht and Critique,' *Forum* 8.1–2 (1992) 45.

[2] See also e.g. C. Tuckett, 'Thomas and the Synoptics,' *NovT 30* (1988) 132–57. Tuckett argues that 'the problem is probably ultimately insoluble' (p. 133).

[3] R. Schnackenburg, *Die Person Jesu Christi im Spiegel der vier Evangelien* (HThKNTSup 4; Freiburg; Herder, 1993) 355–7, esp. 356 (Schnackenburg refers to Gen 2.10).

[4] E. A. Castelli and H. Taussig, 'Introduction: Drawing Large and Startling Figures: Reimagining Christian Origins by Painting like Picasso,' in E. A. Castelli and H. Taussig, eds., *Reimagining Christian Origins: A Colloquium Honoring Burton L. Mack* (Valley Forge: Trinity Press International, 1996) 11.

the study of early Christianity was, of course, made long before the Nag Hammadi documents were available to scholars.[5] But the principle is easier in theory than it is in practice. One could even ask whether the present-day zeal for extracanonical sources paradoxically is conditioned by the very theological presupposition it is attacking, i.e. the *a priori* value of the canonical texts. From such a point of view, the debates about the date and sources of *Thomas* are perhaps not completely uninfluenced by what Elisabeth A. Castelli and Hal Taussig, with some poignancy, describe as a romantic periodization of Christian origins:

> It has been a commonplace of New Testament scholarship to posit or presume an unparalleled pristine or ingenious quality on the part of the 'early churches' of the first century, a quality that gradually waned or was eventually corrupted very soon after the writing of the New Testament. From this point of view, the key to understanding early Christianity was to reveal the essence of the first-century dynamism and brilliance. Often, this romanticism has underwritten both scholarly reconstructions and practical 'back-to-the-origins' reform movements.[6]

It would be unfair to claim that earlier research on *Thomas* has been preoccupied by this biased and romantic understanding of early Christian history as a development from its 'authentic' beginning to its decline into 'early catholicism.' But it is important to raise the issue. Virtually all scholars who work in the field of early Christian history come from a Christian culture, and this means that they are in some way engaged with the Christian canon. Critical study of Christian origins, on the other hand, means a constant effort toward decanonization, that is, toward breaking down the wall of the 'sacred' history presented both in the canonical and in the extracanonical writings, and reconstructing fragments of profane history. It is, therefore, always necessary to ask self-critically what kinds of presuppositions lie behind our approaches to *Thomas*. What is ultimately at stake when we trace its roots into the 'fertile soil of early Christian tradition' or characterize the gospel as a second century 'Gnostic' writing?

---

[5] Already J. P. Gabler (1787) had made the point that the study of the apocrypha should be included in 'true biblical theology.' See H. Räisänen, *Beyond New Testament Theology: A Story and a Programme* (London: SCM Press; Philadelphia: Trinity Press International, 1990) 3–5, 13.

[6] Castelli and Taussig, 'Introduction,' 9.

The contributors to this volume are deeply indebted to earlier studies on the *Gospel of Thomas* and in particular to those which emphasize the value of the document in the reconstruction of the diverse ideologies and movements related to Jesus during the first one hundred years after Jesus' death. At the same, there are factors that seem to justify the contention that Thomasine scholarship is shifting toward new issues and approaches, and this book is part of such a development.

New interdisciplinary methods and approaches have fertilized the study of Christian origins long enough to have an impact on Thomasine scholarship. The influence of the new approaches is explicit in some of the articles included in this book. Folkloristic studies and studies on oral traditions (Uro in chapter 1) and feminist/women's studies (Marjanen in chapter 4) play a prominent role in these essays. Dunderberg's analyses of the literary and cultural relationship between the Gospel of John and *Thomas* (chapters 2 and 3) can be seen against the background of recent literary approaches, e.g. those dealing with the concept of 'authorial fiction' (chapter 3).

Furthermore, intensive studies on new sources and areas of interest have produced results that contribute to Thomasine scholarship in a significant way. Most importantly, the study of the Nag Hammadi codices has begun to change the old stereotypical views of 'Gnosticism,' and this has a bearing on the issue of *Thomas* as a Gnostic gospel (cf. Marjanen in chapter 5). The growing interest in the study of asceticism in different religious traditions and cultures has similarly provided a reason for reconsidering the issue of the encratite nature of *Thomas* (cf. Uro in chapter 6).

These new methods and areas of interest have made the range of issues in Thomasine scholarship wider. They have not removed the 'old' issues from the agenda of scholars, but they have supplemented and, to some degree, relativized the dominance of the controversies in the earlier studies on the *Gospel of Thomas*. Previously, the issue of *Thomas'* relationship to the canonical gospels was mostly dealt with in accordance with the traditional source-critical method, which focused on linear and directional influence of one writing upon another. Some of the essays in this volume, however, suggest more complex and nuanced ways of delineating connections between ancient documents. In chapter 1, Uro suggests indirect influence ('secondary orality') as a plausible explanation for selected parallels between the Synoptic gospels and Thomasine sayings. This conclusion emerges from Uro's discussion about the traditional form critical model of 'growing' tradition, which has been challenged by recent studies on orality. Instead of the rather solid view of oral gospel tradition represented by the form critics, one should strive for a model that allows much more interaction between oral and literary traditions than is usually presumed.

In his analysis of the 'I-Sayings' in the Gospel of John and *Thomas* (chapter 2), Dunderberg argues that while one cannot find evidence for a direct literary (or social) relationship between these writings (or their communities), there are important conceptual affinities which point to a shared theological and socio-historical context among early Christian groups. The analogy between John's Beloved Disciple and the apostle Thomas in the *Gospel of Thomas* (chapter 3), furthermore, demonstrates how early Christians at the turn of the second century attempted to give a ring of authenticity to the documents they produced or transmitted. Dunderberg's focus on the relationship between John and *Thomas* also brings him to a largely unexplored area, since until quite recently the discussion has centered on the more explicit parallels between *Thomas* and the Synoptics. These analyses also provide important clues to the date of the gospel.

The religious perspectives dominant in the *Gospel of Thomas* have often been defined by using such categories as 'Gnostic' and 'encratite' or 'ascetic.' Yet such labeling has proved to be inadequate without further definitions, since scholars often mean very different things when they use these terms.[7] Marjanen's essay (chapter 5) does not start with a stereotypical definition of 'Gnosticism,' but rather seeks to compare *Thomas'* use of the term 'world' and the gospel's cosmology in general to various Jewish and Christian writings representing different responses to the phenomenal world and its values. In contrast to many earlier studies, later Gnostic views are not 'read into' *Thomas*, but rather the Thomasine view of the world is put into a wider perspective of Jewish and Christian cosmologies. Under certain conditions this view can be called 'Gnostic,' but in that case the Gospel of John should also be categorized as such.

Similarly, there is no simple 'yes' or 'no' answer to the question

---

[7] The problems inherent in the category of 'Gnosticism' have been illustrated by M. A. Williams, *Rethinking 'Gnosticism': An Argument for Dismantling a Dubious Category* (Princeton: Princeton University Press, 1996).

whether *Thomas* should be understood as advocating an 'encratite' lifestyle, i.e. as representing a strict form of asceticism, particularly with regard to sexual activity. Even though *Thomas* is often understood to advocate uncompromising sexual asceticism, Uro (chapter 6) sees the gospel as much more ambiguous in this respect. The ambivalence of the gospel may reflect an ongoing discussion on the matter in *Thomas'* community. Marjanen's analysis of the role of the women disciples (chapter 4) adds to this the suggestion that the much-debated logion 114 on Mary Magdalene reflects a development toward a more rigid lifestyle in some groups of Thomasine Christians. Even though this saying does not exclude women from the community, it nevertheless reveals a more controversial attitude toward women than the other sayings in the gospel in which female disciples appear.

Such analyses raise the issue of the socio-historical background of the gospel. The final essay of Marjanen (chapter 7) examines those sayings which deal with Jewish religious practices and thus give hints about *Thomas'* relationship to Judaism. Marjanen argues that the overall negative attitude towards Jewish obligations reflects a religious environment where the Jewish-Christian controversy is not yet a settled issue. The dominance of such themes, as well as the tribute paid to James in saying 12, however, may reveal a religious development within groups of Thomasine Christians in which the hierarchical under-standing of Christian leadership has been replaced by the idea of 'masterless' Christian identity. Such observations may provide criteria for the stratification of the *Gospel of Thomas*, a task we are just beginning.

The essays included in this book do not provide a unified picture of *Thomas'* composition, theology, or background. They do not aim at a consensus with regard to the debated issues of Thomasine scholarship. In many cases consensus is not even desirable. One should rather welcome a wide range of methods and approaches producing a series of perspectives, of which this volume can offer only a limited selection.[8] It

---

[8]   For example, rhetorical criticism provides a promising avenue for understanding the *Gospel of Thomas* in the context of contemporary literary conventions, especially those used in the Hellenistic chriae collections. For such an approach, see e.g. the papers by V. K. Robbins ('Rhetorical Composition and Sources in the *Gospel of Thomas*') and J. Ma. Asgeirsson ('Arguments and Audience(s) in the *Gospel of Thomas*') published in the *Society of Biblical Literature 1997 Seminar Papers*. Asgeirsson's paper shows how the author(s) of the gospel manipulated the chriae components of the gospel in accordance with the customary methods described in the Hellenistic manuals on rhetoric (*progymnasmata*).

is through such a process that the *Gospel of Thomas* will gain its proper place in the history of early Christian literature and as a source for Christian origins.

1

Thomas and oral gospel tradition

Risto Uro

1.1. *Oral and Written Sources in* Thomas

The sources of the *Gospel of Thomas* constitute one of the most controversial issues in current research on early Christian gospels. Suggestions vary from early pre-Synoptic collections of Jesus' sayings[1] to Tatian's *Diatessaron*.[2] Thus, the sources of the gospel have in fact been dated over a period of at least 120 years. The most debated issue, of course, is the relationship between the *Gospel of Thomas* and the canonical gospels. Those advocating a direct literary dependence on the New Testament gospels usually assume that the *Gospel of Thomas* represents a harmonizing redaction of all four canonical gospels or at least of the Synoptic gospels.[3] By contrast, those who contend for *Thomas'* independence consequently suggest noncanonical sources of

---

[1] See e.g. H. Koester, 'One Jesus and Four Primitive Gospels,' in J. M. Robinson and H. Koester, *Trajectories through Early Christianity* (Philadelphia: Fortress Press, 1971) 186–7; 'Gnostic Writings as Witnesses for the Development of the Sayings Tradition,' in *The Rediscovery of Gnosticism: Proceedings of the International Conference on Gnosticism at Yale, New Haven, Connecticut, March 28–31, 1978*, vol. 1: *The School of Valentinus* (Studies in the History of Religions 41; Leiden: E. J. Brill, 1980) 238–61, esp. 249; *Ancient Christian Gospels: Their History and Development* (London: SCM Press; Philadelphia: Trinity Press International, 1990) 95. For a more specific theory about early, pre-70 layers in *Thomas*, see J. D. Crossan, *The Historical Jesus: The Life of a Mediterreanean Jewish Peasant* (San Francisco: Harper, 1991) 427–8.

[2] H. J. W. Drijvers, 'Facts and Problems in Early Syriac-Speaking Christianity,' *SecCent* 2.3 (1982) 157–75, esp. 173.

[3] The work most often referred to is W. Schrage, *Das Verhältnis des Thomas-Evangeliums zur synoptischen Tradition und den koptischen Evangelienübersetzungen: Zugleich ein Beitrag zur gnostischen Synoptikerdeutung* (BZNW 29; Berlin: Töpelmann, 1964). For further representatives of the view that *Thomas* depends upon the canonical gospels, see S. J. Patterson, 'The Gospel of Thomas and the Synoptic Tradition: A Forschungsbericht and Critique,' *Forum* 8.1–2 (1992) 45–97, esp. 50–63.

the gospel, either pre-Synoptic, such as some version of Q, or later Jewish-Christian gospels.[4]

Despite the fact that most scholars assume *literary* sources behind the *Gospel of Thomas*, it is widely suggested that the author of the gospel received at least part of his materials in the mode of *oral* transmission. Helmut Koester has strongly argued that independent oral traditions of Jesus' sayings were transmitted in early Christianity well into the second century.[5] While Koester himself appears to prefer some kind of remote literary relationship in the form of early sapiential sayings collections as the common ancestor of Q and *Thomas*,[6] others have stressed more the role of oral tradition and suggested that 'living oral tradition' was an important or even the primary channel through which the Synoptic sayings entered into the *Gospel of Thomas*.[7] The idea of oral traditions is also presupposed when the 'rule of multiple attestation' is applied to *Thomas*' sayings and their parallels in the quest for the historical Jesus.[8] This criterion is not met if parallels, say, in Mark, Q, and *Thomas*, all ultimately derive from one written record, however early this document may have been. Only if one assumes an independent oral trajectory for the tradition history is the use of *Thomas* as an autonomous witness of Jesus' teaching reasonable.

The hypothesis of oral traditions in the *Gospel of Thomas* has also

[4] The latter view has been elaborated by Gilles Quispel in several works. See e.g. ' "The Gospel of Thomas" and the "Gospel of Hebrews" ' *NTS* (1965–6) 371–82; *Makarius, das Thomasevangelium und das Lied von der Perle* (NovTSup 15; Leiden: E. J. Brill, 1967); and 'The *Gospel of Thomas* Revisited,' in B. Barc, ed., *Colloque international sur les textes de Nag Hammadi* (Bibliothèque copte de Nag Hammadi, Section 'Études' 1; Québec: University of Laval; Louvain: Peeters, 1981) 218–66.

[5] See his *Synoptische Überlieferung bei den apostolischen Vätern* (Berlin: Akademie-Verlag, 1957) and several later works.

[6] See above, note 1.

[7] See J. M. Robinson, 'On Bridging the Gulf from Q to the Gospel of Thomas (or Vice Versa),' in C. W. Hedrick and R. Hodgson, Jr, eds., *Nag Hammadi, Gnosticism and Early Christianity* (Peabody: Hendrickson, 1986) 167; note also A. F. J. Klijn, *Edessa, die Stadt des Apostels Thomas: Das älteste Christentum in Syrien* (Neukirchener Studienbücher Band 4; Neukirchen-Vluyn: Neukirchener Verlag, 1965) 70; S. J. Patterson, in J. S. Kloppenborg, M. W. Meyer, S. J. Patterson, and M. G. Steinhauser, *Q-Thomas Reader* (Sonoma: Polebridge Press, 1990) 87; J. H. Sieber, 'The Gospel of Thomas and the New Testament,' in J. E. Goehring, C. W. Hedrick, J. T. Sanders, and H. D. Betz, eds., *Gospel Origins & Christian Beginnings in Honor of James M. Robinson*, Vol. 1 (Sonoma: Polebridge Press, 1990) 66; C. W. Hedrick, 'Thomas and the Synoptics: Aiming at a Consensus,' *SecCent* 7.1 (1989–90) 41.

[8] This rule constitutes an important methodological criterion in a magisterial study on the historical Jesus by J. D. Crossan (*The Historical Jesus*).

played an important role in a quite different source-critical solution. In 1961, Ernst Haenchen suggested that the Synoptic sayings in the Gospel are not easily explained on the basis of a direct utilization of the canonical texts, Thomas having randomly selected words from one gospel and then from another, and so on. Instead, according to Haenchen, one has to infer that the author of the *Gospel of Thomas* drew upon free oral memory and interpretation of the Synoptic gospels as used in Gnostic circles.[9] On this assumption, the *Gospel of Thomas* is indeed dependent upon the canonical gospels, but indirectly through a secondary oral transmission of the sayings. In the same vein, Klyne Snodgrass has in a provocative article asserted that 'any suggestion that *Thomas* was sitting with manuscripts of the four canonical gospels in hand while compiling his own document is naive.' Instead one is to assume that the material of the gospel 'is determined by oral tradition that is partly dependent on the canonical gospels.'[10] Thus, in Snodgrass' judgment, *Thomas* renders oral traditions of Jesus' sayings. They are not the pure and unmixed stream of the Jesus-tradition suggested by the keenest proponents of *Thomas'* independence but rather witness to a 'secondary orality.'[11]

The aim of this paper is to consider these different views about the oral traditions used in the *Gospel of Thomas*. To what degree one can identify 'independent' or 'secondary' oral traditions is of course a question that cannot be answered without a thorough analysis of all the

---

[9] 'Literatur zum Thomasevangelium,' *TRu* 27 (1961) 178. For a similar view, see H. Schürmann, 'Das Thomasevangelium und das lukanische Sondergut,' *BZ* 7 (1963) 255. Cf. also Schrage, *Verhältnis*, 9.

[10] K. R. Snodgrass, 'The Gospel of Thomas: A Secondary Gospel,' *SecCent* 7.1 (1989–90) 19–38 (citations are from p. 27).

[11] 'Gospel of Thomas,' 28. The term is borrowed from W. H. Kelber, who uses it in *The Oral and the Written Gospel: The Hermeneutics of Speaking and Writing in the Synoptic Tradition, Mark, Paul, and Q* (Philadelphia: Fortress Press, 1983) 197. A brief remark about the terminology is in order here. 'Secondary orality' and its contrasting term, 'primary orality,' have sometimes been used in the field of orality/literacy studies to compare cultures untouched by any knowledge of writing or print with the present-day high-technology culture, in which a new orality is sustained by various electronic devices; see e.g. W. J. Ong, *Orality and Literacy: The Technologizing of the Word* (London: Methuen, 1982) 11, 135–8; J. M. Foley, 'Introduction,' in J. M. Foley, ed., *Oral Tradition in Literature* (Columbia: University of Missouri Press, 1986) 1. Such a definition of 'secondary orality' is of course inappropriate for the Christian gospels or any literature of antiquity and differs from the meaning suggested above. Neither would it be proper to speak of 'primary orality' in the context of early Christianity, if such a term is restricted to cultures in which there is no literacy. Snodgrass' use of 'secondary orality,' which I have adopted, clearly differs from such terminology.

relevant material. That would go beyond the sphere of this article. An example from *Gos. Thom.* 14 will have to suffice here. But before we proceed with that, it is useful to consider some general questions concerning the study of oral traditions. In a closer examination, concepts like 'independent oral tradition' or 'oral source' used in the study of the *Gospel of Thomas* may prove to be more complex than scholars have usually assumed. It may be helpful, therefore, to take a brief look at some recent discussions about orality and literacy in general and about oral traditions of the early Christian gospels in particular, and to see what the insights achieved in such studies contribute to our understanding of the oral sources in the *Gospel of Thomas*.

1.2. Insights from studies on oral traditions

Various aspects of orality and oral traditions have attracted a considerable interest among contemporary folklorists, anthropologists, historians, and representatives of related fields.[12] This discussion has also been reflected in studies on the gospel traditions, even though such cross-fertilization has not yet been very penetrating.[13] In the following,

---

[12] The relationship between orality and literacy, in particular, has been the topic of several recent contributions. See e.g. J. Goody, ed., *Literacy in Traditional Societies* (Cambridge: Cambridge University Press, 1968); idem, *The Interface between the Written and the Oral* (Cambridge: Cambridge University Press, 1987). H. Bekker-Nielsen, P. Foote, A. Haarder and H. F. Nielsen, eds., *Oral Tradition, Literary Tradition: A Symposium* (Odense: Odense University Press, 1977). Ong, *Orality and Literacy*; Foley, ed., *Oral Tradition in Literature*; R. Finnegan, *Literacy and Orality: Studies in the Technology of Communication* (Oxford: Basil Blackwell, 1988); S. Niditch, *Oral World and Written Word: Ancient Israelite Literature* (Library of Ancient Israel; Louisville: Westminster Press/ John Knox, 1996).

[13] A significant ground-breaking work was done by Kelber (*The Oral and the Written Gospel*) in the United States; see also two *Semeia* volumes, 39 and 65, edited by L. H. Silberman and J. Dewey, respectively. For an earlier discussion, see the dialogue between Albert B. Lord and Charles H. Talbert in W. O. Walker, Jr., ed., *The Relationships among the Gospels: An Interdisciplinary Dialogue* (Monograph Series in Religion 5; San Antonio: Trinity University Press, 1978). In Europe, two symposia were arranged in 1989–90 around the theme of 'Jesus and the Oral Gospel Tradition.' The papers were published in H. Wansbrough, ed., *Jesus and the Oral Gospel Tradition* (JSNTSup 64; Sheffield: Sheffield Academic Press, 1991) 51. Note also the study by B. J. Henaut, *Oral Tradition and the Gospels: The Problem of Mark 4* (JSNTSup 82; Sheffield: Sheffield Academic Press, 1993), which draws attention to a number of important issues concerning the oral gospel traditions.

I shall summarize some points of the discussion which, in my judgment, are pertinent to our problem of oral traditions in the *Gospel of Thomas*. It is necessary to stress that I am not writing as one who has mastered the whole field of 'orality-literacy' studies. The view offered here is restricted to those issues which have been discussed in the context of New Testament research.

1.2.1. The fallacy of 'pure' oral traditions

The idea of an oral phase of Jesus traditions preceding the literary composition of the earliest Christian gospels has been commonplace in scholarship since the emergence of form criticism. The form-critics worked with a model which presupposed a view of a rather solid and homogeneous oral tradition. The written gospels were considered to be *Kleinliteratur,* works closer to oral folklore than real literature. This closeness to the preliterary stage allowed an optimistic search for oral forms in the literary compositions of the canonical gospels. Although the form critics presupposed the Two Document hypothesis and occasionally written presynoptic sources other than Q, the difference between written and oral transmission was not important to them. As Bultmann emphasized, there is no definable boundary between oral and written traditions.[14] The written gospels, therefore, only functioned as an extension of the oral tradition.

This view of an unbroken and homogeneous tradition process did not withstand later modifications. The results achieved in the redaction-critical analyses of the gospels showed that the evangelists were not passive receivers of the tradition but rather creative authors.[15] Others have challenged the form-critical presuppositions from the point of modern textlinguistics.[16] The proponents of the Scandinavian tradition-historical school, although suggesting a much more solid and fixed

---

[14] *The History of the Synoptic Tradition* (2nd ed.; translated by J. Marsh; Oxford: Blackwell, 1968) 321.

[15] Later form critics, however, were inclined to make a sharper distinction between oral and written modes of transmission than Bultmann had done. See e.g. K. Koch, *Was ist Formgeschichte?: Methoden und Bibelexegese* (3rd rev. ed.; Neukirchen-Vluyn: Neukirchener Verlag, 1974) 108–12, and K. Berger, *Formgeschichte des neuen Testaments* (Heidelberg: Quelle & Meyer, 1984) 13–16.

[16] E.g. E. Güttgemanns, *Offene Fragen zur Formgeschichte des Evangeliums* (BEvT 54; Munich: Chr. Kaiser, 1970). Trans. by W. G. Dotz, *Candid Questions Concerning Gospel Form Criticism: A Methodological Sketch of the Fundamental Problematics of Form and Redaction Criticism* (PTMS 26; Pittsburgh: Pickwick, 1979).

oral tradition, were able to point to some problems in the form critics' romantic understanding of the tradition as communal folklore.[17] Yet the common view of oral traditions in present-day New Testament scholarship depends by and large on the heritage of form criticism. Oral traditions are usually understood as a kind of 'storage' of materials, a clearly definable entity, which was utilized by the gospel writers. Or, to use another common image, the tradition is imagined as a 'stream' which originated from small springs that opened into gospel reservoirs,[18] but also continued its independent life until it finally dried out in the canonization process.

Werner Kelber is the scholar who has most vigorously attacked this kind of view of tradition, which is inherent in the form-critical model.[19] According to Kelber, the form-critical view is based on the modern tendency to think predominantly in linear, visual and literary terms.[20] Drawing upon contemporary theorists of orality, Kelber emphasizes the great chasm between the oral and literary media of communication. In his model, the gap between the fluidity of orality and the frozen and stable world of textuality is deep. In orality, Kelber argues, words have no existence apart from speaker and hearers, who cooperate in efforts to assure a direct and immediate hermeneutical transaction. In written gospels, by contrast, the cooperation between speaker and hearers is abolished.[21] While sayings collections like Q and the *Gospel of Thomas* still reveal a closeness to oral (prophetic) hermeneutics,[22] Mark's writing manifests 'a freezing of oral life into textual still life ... a transmutation more than mere transmission.'[23]

---

[17] B. Gerhardsson, *Memory and Manuscript: Oral Tradition and Written Transmission in Rabbinic Judaism and Early Christianity* (ASNU 22; Lund: C. W. K. Gleerup; Copenhagen: Munksgaard, 1961) esp. 12; H. Riesenfeld, *The Gospel Tradition* (Philadelphia: Fortress Press, 1970).

[18] Kelber, *Oral and Written Gospel*, 4.

[19] Ibid.; note also his 'The Authority of the Word in St. John's Gospel: Charismatic Speech, Narrative Text, Logocentric Metaphysics,' *Oral Tradition* 2 (1987) 108–31; 'Narrative as Interpretation and Interpretation of Narrative: Hermeneutical Reflections on the Gospels,' *Semeia* 39 (1987) 107–33; 'In the Beginning Were the Words: The Apotheosis and Narrative Displacement of the Logos,' *JAAR* 58 (1990) 69–98.

[20] *Oral and Written Gospel*, 2.

[21] Ibid., 92.

[22] Ibid., 23, 199–203. For the *Gospel of Thomas*, see Kelber's 'Authority of the Word,' 118, and 'In the Beginning Were the Words,' 78–80.

[23] *The Oral and the Written Gospel*, 91.

Kelber's emphasis on radical differences between orality and textuality may function as a necessary corrective to the form-critical assumption that the gospels were mere extensions of oral tradition. But his approach is also open to criticism. To begin with, we could ask whether the thesis on the 'oral hermeneutic of Q' (and of other sayings gospels) is tenable. Kelber sees indications of oral mentality in several theological characteristics of Q, for example in the lack of references to Jesus' suffering, the reluctance to draw a distinction between the pre-Easter and post-Easter voice of Jesus, and the 'prophetic self-consciousness' of the document. On the other hand, in Kelber's analysis the canonical gospels represent a counterform to the oral genre of Q; they deprived the latter of 'the prophetically living voice of Jesus,' since they were unable to tolerate the oral equation of Jesus with the living Lord.[24]

The combination of oral mentality and the genre of Q in this way is problematic. One can, for example, refer to several recent analyses in which this 'prophetic self-consciousness of Q' has been identified as a decisive factor in the document's literary history, or more accurately, in a specific moment of this history.[25] The impression given by these recent analyses is not that the 'prophetic' redaction of Q is a literary by-product of a process which was predominantly an oral and free transmission of Jesus' sayings. Rather the redaction seems to have been deeply involved in a literary process which according to many recent studies consisted of several subsequent editions or redactional stages. There is no compelling reason for the assumption that the theological tendencies at work in this literary process could only happen in the 'oral mind' in contrast to the 'scribal mentality.' This assumption is particularly unwarranted because some of these tendencies are genre-bound and connect the document with the *literary* phenomena of

---

[24] Ibid., 203.

[25] Most of the recent redaction-critical analyses agree in assuming a so-called 'deuteronomistic redaction' as a significant step in the formative history of Q; see J. S. Kloppenborg, *The Formation of Q: Trajectories in Ancient Wisdom Collections* (Studies in Antiquity and Christianity; Philadelphia: Fortress Press, 1987); R. Uro, *Sheep Among the Wolves: A Study on the Mission Instructions of Q* (AASF DHL 47; Helsinki: The Finnish Academy of Science and Letters, 1987); M. Sato, *Q und Prophetie: Studien zur Gattungs- und Traditionsgeschichte der Quelle Q* (WUNT 2.29; Tübingen: J.C.B. Mohr [Paul Siebeck], 1988); A. D. Jacobson, *The First Gospel: An Introduction to Q* (Sonoma: Polebridge Press, 1992).

various wisdom and chriae collections widely disseminated in antiquity.[26]

It is a precarious approach, therefore, to make a close connection between some *ideological* tendencies and a *technique* of communication. One should be cautious not to adopt too romantic a picture of a free 'savage mind' living in a state of sheer orality and threatened by the new technology of literacy.[27] This presumption of 'pure orality' is problematic in light of evidence presented both by some theorists of orality and by scholars of the gospels. Instead of the sharp dichotomy between orality and literacy, they suggest, we should strive for a model which would allow for an interaction between oral and written traditions in the New Testament world and antiquity in general. This is not to disregard the high residual orality that existed in the contemporary world of the New Testament gospels but simply to accept the fact that in that culture literary works were a significant means of communication.

1.2.2. Interplay between oral and written traditions

Kelber's ideas that writing a gospel meant 'silencing of sounded words' or 'the termination of the dialogical situation'[28] appear problematic not least in light of ancient reading practices.[29] In antiquity books were most often read aloud, not infrequently before audiences.[30] Silent

---

[26] See the seminal article by J. M. Robinson, 'LOGOI SOPHON: On the Gattung of Q,' in J. M. Robinson and H. Koester, *Trajectories*, 71–113. For further discussion see Kloppenborg, *Formation of Q*, 263–328.

[27] Kelber refers to the reluctance and anxiety expressed by some early Church Fathers with regard to writing, and to Plato's famous critique of literacy in *Phaedrus* 274e–277a (*The Oral and the Written Gospel*, 92–3). Cf., however, W. V. Harris' comment on this ancient critique: '... the notion that the spread of literacy might have negative effects on an individual or a community, or the lack of it was a matter of indifference, had only very slight circulation among writers who survive from antiquity. It apparently gained some strength with modern interest in and idealization of primitive cultures.' *Ancient Literacy* (Cambridge: Harvard University Press, 1989) 37.

[28] Cf. *The Oral and the Written Gospel*, 94.

[29] For a similar criticism of Kelber, see e.g. B. Gerhardsson, *The Gospel Tradition* (ConBNT 15; Lund: C. W. K. Gleerup, 1986); G. L. Bartholomew, 'Feed My Lambs: John 21.15–19 as Oral Gospel,' *Semeia* 39 (1987) 69–96; P. J. Achtemeier, 'Omne verbum sonat: The New Testament and the Oral Environment of Late Western Antiquity,' *JBL* 109 (1990) 27 n. 156.

[30] For public reading, see e.g. Harris, *Ancient Literacy*, 225–6.

reading was, if not exceptional, at least much more rare than in modern society.[31] Texts were not only read in public recitations, but even solitary readers would often vocalize the texts they were reading to themselves (the most familiar instance is the Ethiopian eunuch in Acts 8.30).[32] This oral-aural character of writing was not, however, restricted to reproducing written words in sounds. It was also an essential part of producing new texts, whether this happened by dictation or even by writing in one's own hand. This means that the word 'reader' should be put in quotation marks when used in the context of ancient literature. Written texts were much more involved in orality than modern books, which are read mostly in silence and privately. In certain respects, therefore, texts in the ancient world functioned rather more like our tape recorders than our books,[33] or to use another comparison, like musical notation.

It is clear that we must allow for a great deal of mutual influence of oral tradition and written texts as we seek to reconstruct the history of the gospel traditions. The oral–aural transmission of texts had an impact on the way in which the authors composed their writings. It has been observed, for example, that various stylistic devices like repetition, parallelism, chiasm etc. were used to provide aural clues to one who listened to the document rather than to provide a visual/textual structure.[34] On the other hand, public oral performances of the text certainly influenced the transmission of the gospel traditions among Christian groups who lived in the orbits of various gospels. It is important to remember that in the ancient world writing tended to be

[31] Scholars have often mentioned Augustine's reference to Ambrose in *Confessiones* 6.3 as one of the rare exceptions; but note also Cyril of Jerusalem, *Procatechesis* 14 (M. Slusser, 'Reading Silently in Antiquity,' *JBL* 111 [1992] 499) and further evidence provided recently by F. D. Gilliard ('More Silent Reading in Antiquity,' *JBL* 112 [1993] 689–94). Gilliard criticizes Achtemeier's generalization that in antiquity '*no* writing occurred that was not vocalized' ('Omne verbum sonat,' 15), but Gilliard also admits the predominance of orality in ancient reading and writing practices.

[32] For further examples, see J. Balogh, '"Voces Paginarum:" Beiträge zur Geschichte des lauten Lesens und Schreibens,' *Philologus* 82 (1927) 84–109, 202–42, and Achtemeier, 'Omne verbum sonat,' 16.

[33] I owe this comparison to Ø. Andersen, 'Oral Tradition,' in H. Wansbrough, ed., *Jesus and the Oral Gospel Tradition* (JSNTSup 64; Sheffield: Sheffield Academic Press, 1991) 51.

[34] Achtemeier, 'Omne verbum sonat,' 3–27. For an analysis on oral categories and techniques in the *Didache*, see I. Henderson, 'Didache and Orality in Synoptic Comparison,' *JBL* 111 (1992) 283–306.

used as an *aid to memory* rather than as an autonomous and independent mode of communication.[35] The publication of the Gospel of Mark, thus, hardly delivered a decisive blow to the 'living' oral transmission, as Kelber argues, but rather facilitated the latter wherever the gospel was recited, and certainly also contributed to it.

Kelber's theoretical framework was influenced by the so-called 'oral formulaic school,' which arose from the Homeric studies of Milman Parry in the 1920s and 30s, and was later developed by his assistant Albert B. Lord.[36] The results gained from the analyses of the oral composition of the Homeric poems were tested on the coffee-house bards in the area of the former Yugoslavia. They have proven very influential in the study of Homeric epics and orality research in general.[37] The 'composition-in-performance' technique of the singers, their situational improvisation, has now been largely accepted as a typical characteristic of all oral traditions, not just oral epic.[38] In such theories of orality, oral and literary forms of communication have often been considered as mutually exclusive.[39]

Yet universal claims based on the preliterary period of Greece and twentieth-century Balkan practice may also be misleading. Ruth Finnegan, perhaps more than anyone else, has warned against overly generalizing tendencies at work in some studies of orality.[40] Instead of

---

[35] Achtemeier, 'Omne verbum sonat,' 5. Socrates in Plato's *Phaedrus* (275c-d) spells out this idea well: 'So the man who thinks that he has left behind him a science in writing, and in his turn the man who receives it from him in the belief that anything clear or certain will result from what is written down, would be full of simplicity ... , in thinking that *the written words were anything more than a reminder to the man who knows the subjects to which the things written relate.*' Trans. by C. J. Rowe in *Phaedrus: Translation and Commentary on Plato* (Warminster: Aris & Phillis, 1987); emphasis added.

[36] For a concise introduction to the theory, see J. M. Foley, *The Theory of Oral Composition: History and Methodology* (Bloomington: Indiana University Press, 1988). For a recent analysis of Kelber's indebtedness to the oral formulaic theory, see Henaut, *Oral Tradition*, 75–119.

[37] For a classic work elaborating the theory, see A. B. Lord, *The Singer of Tales* (Harvard Studies in Comparative Literature 24; Cambridge: Harvard University Press, 1960). See also Foley, *Theory of Oral Composition*, 57–129.

[38] However, the limitations of the theory with respect to many genres of folklore have been stressed, e.g. by A. Dundes in his 'Foreword' to Foley's *Theory of Oral Composition* (p. xi).

[39] E. A. Havelock, *The Literate Revolution in Greece and Its Cultural Consequences* (Princeton: Princeton University Press, 1982) 9.

[40] See especially her *Oral Poetry: Its Nature, Significance and Social Context* (Bloomington: Indiana University Press, 1992 (orig. 1977) and *Literacy and Orality*.

what she calls the 'Great Divide' theories,[41] Finnegan wants to show that orality and literacy, rather than being contradictory poles, can interact and support each other.[42] She finds a considerable amount of such interaction, for example, in the contemporary context of the South Pacific, even though the Pacific traditions have often been thought to arise from 'pure orality.' Finnegan furthermore singles out three models of interaction:[43] First, 'there is a striking *overlap* between oral and written literature.'[44] In a number of instances forms originally composed in an oral context later become dependent on writing for their circulation and transmission. And vice versa, written material, like biblical stories, can easily find their way into oral traditions. Moreover, professional orators often use notebooks as an aid to oral performance. Secondly, sometimes traditions held to be oral and primitive both by performers and audience turn out on closer scrutiny to be of *written origin*.[45] The third model, especially interesting to us, is that of a *feedback* from written sources into an oral tradition. There have been numbers of literate people around in the Pacific since the nineteenth century, as well as many books, and 'many people had an opportunity to know, directly or indirectly, the contents of these works. One can never assume without question, therefore, that the accounts in "oral narratives" came purely from "oral tradition." '[46] Such a situation is certainly not too far from that of the New Testament gospels!

We should thus be cautious in using the results of Parry's and Lord's

---

[41] *Literacy and Orality*, 86.

[42] See also *Oral Poetry*, 160–8. For a similar emphasis, see e.g. B. A. Rosenberg, 'The Complexity of Oral Tradition,' *Oral Tradition* 2 (1987) 73–90; Andersen, 'Oral Tradition,' 45–7; Havelock, *Literate Revolution*, 166–84; note also W. J. Ong, 'Text as Interpretation: Mark and After,' *Semeia* 39 (1987) 23. Henaut (*Oral Tradition*) also passionately criticizes the chasm scholars have suggested between oral and literary traditions, but sometimes goes to the other extreme. For example, in his analysis of the Parable of the Sower he concludes that 'in the light of the extensive literary parallels, there is simply no guarantee that the story ever circulated orally in the Christian communities' (p. 242). It seems that for Henaut a *possibility* of literary sources behind a gospel text often changes to a *proof* against orality.

[43] *Literacy and Orality*, 110–22.

[44] Ibid., 111.

[45] The most famous instance of such artificial orality is the 'Kaunitoni myth' in Fiji, which turned out to be a creation of literate people of the late 19th century on the basis of contemporary historical speculation about Fiji origins. See Finnegan, *Literacy and Orality*, 113–15.

[46] Ibid., 117; cf. also *Oral Poetry*, 160–8, in which Finnegan provides examples e.g. from medieval popular songs.

investigations in the reconstruction of the oral phase of the gospel traditions.[47] The cultural context of the New Testament gospels was not a preliterate oral society, as the context of the Homeric traditions is assumed to have been. Neither were the tradents of the gospel material illiterate 'singers of tales.'[48] The evangelists and their predecessors were not transmitters of rhythmic epic poetry; rather they delivered aphoristic, parabolic and narrative traditions about Jesus. Especially in view of Finnegan's findings we should be open to a more complex solution than has usually been suggested in tracing the oral and written sources of the gospels.

1.3. Corollaries for Thomasine studies

The few selected issues of recent studies of orality do not, of course, give a ready answer to the specific question of the oral traditions used in the *Gospel of Thomas*. Yet they provide us with a useful perspective as we proceed to a more detailed evaluation of different source-critical solutions.

One thing seems to be clear enough in light of the discussion above. It is very difficult to make any absolute claims about the independence of the *Gospel of Thomas* traditions as compared to those preserved in the canonical gospels. Even if we could remove all later interpolations and harmonizations in the translation process, the suggestion that *Thomas* had access to some 'pure' oral traditions, uninfluenced by any written

---

[47] It would be unfair to claim that Kelber is not aware of the distinction (see *The Oral and the Written Gospel*, 78), but his approach belongs in any case, to use the language of Finnegan, to the 'Great Divide' theories rather than to those emphasizing interaction between orality and literacy. For a similar criticism, see Henaut, *Oral Tradition*, 115–17.

[48] The spread of literacy in first-century Palestine would require a special treatment. S. Safrai concludes that 'as early as the first century CE and perhaps even earlier, the majority of the children received education at school.' This education included reading. See 'Education and the Study of the Torah,' in S. Safrai and M. Stern, eds., *The Jewish People in the First Century* (CRINT: Section One: II; Assen: van Gorcum, 1976) 945–70 (esp. 946 and 949). Against this is Harris' assessment that the 'mirage of mass literacy in first-century Judaea ... would be very much at odds with what we know of Greek literacy' (*Ancient Literacy*, 281–2). Harris, however, does not discuss Jewish evidence. In view of the importance that the study of the Torah and the institution of the synagogue had in Jewish society one may suspect that a greater number than a small elite minority of the Jewish population could at least read in first-century Palestine. For a similar estimation, see H. Y. Gamble, *Books and Readers in Early Church: A History of Early Christian Texts* (New Haven: Yale University Press, 1995) 7. The ability to write, however, was less widespread (see Safrai, ibid., 952).

records of Jesus' sayings, is simply unrealistic. We have seen that, in the absolute sense, the concept of 'pure orality' is impossible in the literate culture in which the early Christian gospels were written. But even if we accept a less absolute view of oral tradition and argue for a relative independence of the *Thomas* tradition,[49] we still have to face a number of questions. To begin with, it is difficult to exclude the possibility of common sources (cf. Koester) and, as I have argued in the beginning of this paper, dependence on a common literary source, however remote, is not independence, to say nothing of independent *oral* traditions. Moreover, the great number of parallels between the *Gospel of Thomas* and the Synoptics poses a problem. According to Stephen J. Patterson, roughly half of *Thomas'* sayings can be categorized either as Synoptic 'twins' or 'siblings'; that is, they are more or less closely paralleled by sayings in the Synoptic gospels.[50] To argue that such an amount of common material entered into the *Gospel of Thomas* basically through an 'unmixed' oral transmission presupposes a view of a very solid tradition. As we have seen, this form-critical presumption has rightly been criticized in several recent works on the oral gospel tradition. It is worth noting that according to the usual source-critical theories the Synoptic gospels did not get their common materials from some oral Synoptic source; the great similarity is based on literary utilization. Although we cannot settle the question of the relationship between *Thomas* and the Synoptics on these general grounds, it is important to realize that the thesis of independent oral traditions behind the *Gospel of Thomas* presupposes an oral Synoptic source for *Thomas*, but not for the Synoptic gospels themselves.

We have not dealt with one important part of the 'oral source' hypothesis. Scholars have often referred to the preface of Papias of Hierapolis to his five-volume *Exegesis of the Sayings of the Lord* (recorded in Eusebius, *Hist. eccl.* 3.39) as a proof of a vital (independent) oral tradition in the first half of the second century.[51] In his famous

49   Cf. the 'autonomous tradition' suggested by Patterson in *The Gospel of Thomas and Jesus* (Foundations and Facets: Reference Series; Sonoma: Polebridge Press, 1993) 93.

50   Ibid., 95–7.

51   E.g. Hedrick, 'Thomas and the Synoptics,' 41 n. 11; but cf. also Gerhardsson, *Memory and Manuscript*, 205–27, and R. Cameron, *Sayings Traditions in the Apocryphon of James* (HTS 34; Philadelphia: Fortress Press, 1984) 93–112. Cameron argues that the term 'remembering' used by Papias was 'regularly employed in the early church to introduce collections of sayings of Jesus, *both oral and written*, that date from a time in which sayings traditions were not restricted to the written gospels of the NT' (112; emphasis added).

statement, Papias explains that he writes on the basis of what he has learned from personal hearing from those 'who had accompanied the "elders"' and that for him the 'living and abiding voice' is a much more profitable source than written books. It is important to notice, however, that Papias uses ancient rhetorical conventions in his preface.[52] The appeal to *viva vox* and the preference over written texts was commonplace in antiquity. It often simply meant that in education one should favor a personal presence of the teacher and fellowship with him to the impersonal study of books.[53] Papias' statement gives us an important piece of information from the period in which the four canonical Gospels were not yet established as the only legitimate sources of Jesus teaching.[54] But his highly idealized and apologetic picture of the chain of tradition through which he claims to have received (some of) his information can hardly be taken as an argument for the *solidity* of oral gospel traditions (and, as argued above, the hypothesis of an oral Synoptic source behind the *Gospel of Thomas* presupposes such a view). Papias' preface is simply a conventional rhetorical strategy for saying that his *own book* represents a primitive and truthful tradition as compared to some other books.[55]

The criticism against the hypothesis of an independent oral tradition in the *Gospel of Thomas* does not mean that we should make an *a priori* decision for the view of a direct or indirect use of the canonical gospels by *Thomas*. The above considerations anticipate that there is no simple 'yes or no' answer to the question. However, all that has been said about the interaction between written and oral communication makes 'secondary orality' a noteworthy alternative in the source-critical analyses of the sayings in the *Gospel of Thomas*. Of course, it does make a difference whether one assumes early pre-Synoptic collections or all four canonical gospels as sources of *Thomas*. But even if we concluded

---

[52] See e.g. Cameron, *Sayings Traditions*, 95.

[53] See e.g. E. F. Osborn, 'Teaching and Writing in the First Chapter of the *Stromateis* of Clement of Alexandria,' *JTS* 10 (1959) 335–43; H. Karpp, 'Viva vox,' in A. Stuiber and A. Hermann, eds., *Mullus: Festschrift Theodor Klauser* (JAC Ergänzungsband 1; Münster: Aschendorff, 1964) 190–8.

[54] U. H. J. Körtner, *Papias von Hierapolis: Ein Beitrag zur Geschichte des frühen Christentums* (FRLANT 133; Göttingen: Vandenhoeck & Ruprecht, 1983) 173.

[55] Cf. Cameron, who argues that 'despite Papias' defense of the Gospel of Mark, his comments about Mark (and, most likely, Matthew as well) are still disparaging' (*Sayings Traditions*, 112 n. 85). For a similar view, see B. H. Streeter, *The Four Gospels: A Study of Origins* (London: Macmillan, 1924) 19–20.

that the latter is more probable, such a conclusion does not devalue the *Gospel of Thomas* as a 'secondary gospel' (*pace* Snoddgrass) on the periphery of the Synoptic tradition. Matthew and Luke are 'secondary gospels' as well and I am not sure if there is any 'primary gospel' among our sources at all.[56]

1.4. A test case: Logion 14 and its Synoptic parallels

Jesus said to them: 'If you fast, you will give rise to sin for yourselves; [2]and if you pray, you will be condemned; [3]and if you give alms, you will do harm to your spirits. [4]When you go into any land and walk about in the districts, if they receive you, eat what they will set before you, and heal the sick among them. [5]For what goes into your mouth will not defile you, but that which issues from your mouth – it is that which will defile you.[57]

Gos. Thom. 14 is a cluster of injunctions which can be divided into three parts, viz., a rejection of fasting, prayer and almsgiving (14.1–3); an instruction on wandering, eating and healing (14.4); and a saying on defiling (14.5). The first part reminds one of Matt 6.1–8, 16–18, in which the same triad of observances occurs, although in a different order. Apart from the appearance of these Jewish practices (cf. also Tob 12.8 and *2 Clem.* 12.4), there is no close parallelism between Matt 6 and *Gos. Thom.* 14.1–3, and the assumption of a direct or indirect literary relationship is therefore not necessary. The sayings in *Gos. Thom.* 14.4–5, however, reveal close similarity to passages in Luke 10.8–9a and in Matt 15.11 (cf. also Mark 7.15), and scholars have often argued for literary dependence. For R. M. Grant and D. N. Freedman, to take but one example, this passage was a conclusive proof of the fact that '*Thomas* relies on our written Gospels, at least in some

---

[56] The question of the relationship between the Gospel of John and the Synoptics provides a good analogy to our problem. The old consensus that John is literally independent from the Synoptic gospels has recently been challenged by several scholars; see e.g. F. Neirynck, 'John and the Synoptics: 1975–1990,' in A. Denaux, ed., *John and the Synoptics* (BETL 101; Leuven: Leuven University Press/Peeters, 1992) 3–62; and especially I. Dunderberg, *Johannes und die Synoptiker: Studien zu Joh 1–9* (AASF DHL 69; Helsinki: The Finnish Academy of Science and Letters, 1994). Assuming that they are right, does such a result devalue the Gospel of John as a source for early Christian history and religion?

[57] Trans. by T. O. Lambdin in B. Layton, ed., *Nag Hammadi Codex II, 2–7 together with XIII,2*, Brit. Lib. Or.4926(1), and P.Oxy. 1, 654, 655*, Vol. 1 (NHS 20; Leiden: E. J. Brill, 1989) 60–1.

measure, rather than on oral traditions.'[58] By 'oral,' we are to assume, they mean *independent* oral traditions.

Two factors have been crucial in the discussion. First, apart from the different personal pronoun, *Gos. Thom.* 14.5 is almost identical with what seems to be Matthew's redactional reformulation of Mark 7.15. Mark's contrast of 'outside/out of a man' has in Matthew become a contrast of 'into the mouth/out of the mouth'; the awkward construction of the Markan saying is smoothed out to a better parallelism. Secondly, a command to heal the sick appears redundant in its present context in *Thomas*, but could be explained on the basis of an alleged source, namely the Mission of the Seventy(-two) in Luke 10.1–20.[59]

1.4.1. Gos. Thom. *14.5 and Matt 15.11 (cf. Mark 7.15)*

Although specific interpretations of Matthew's editorial activity in 15.1–20 vary, most scholars agree that the changes in Matt 15.11 with regard to Mark 7.15 are due to Matthew's conscious redactional work.[60] Granting Markan priority, we must conclude that Matthew was using Mark as his source and following Mark's sequence, not only in the present passage but without a considerable interruption from Matt 14.1 onwards (cf. Mark 6.14ff). In vv. 15.1–20, Matthew has omitted the Markan explanation in Mark 7.3–4, unnecessary to his Jewish-Christian audience, strengthened the criticism of the Pharisees by adding the accusation in Matt 15.14–15 (cf. Luke 6.39 and *Gos. Thom.* 34) and made several stylistic and structural improvements in Mark's pericope. Matthew has, for example, following his special

---

[58] *The Secret Sayings of Jesus* (London: Collins, 1960) 100.

[59] See e.g. ibid., 100, 128; H. Montefiore and H. E. W. Turner, *Thomas and the Evangelists* (SBT 35; London: SCM Press, 1962) 35–6; J.-É. Ménard, *L'Évangile selon Thomas* (NHS 5; Leiden: E. J. Brill, 1975) 99–101.

[60] For analyses, see e.g. G. Barth, 'Das Gesetzverständnis des Evangelisten Matthäus,' in G. Bornkamm, G. Barth and H. J. Held, eds., *Überlieferung und Auslegung im Matthäusevangelium* (WMANT 1; Neukirchen: Neukirchener Verlag, 1960) 80–6; R. Hummel, *Auseinandersetzung zwischen Kirche und Judentum im Matthäusevangelium* (Munich: Chr. Kaiser, 1963) 46–9; C. Carlston, 'The Things that Defile (Mark vii.14) and the Law in Matthew and Mark,' *NTS* 15 (1968–69) 75–96; H. Hübner, *Das Gesetz in der synoptischen Tradition: Studien zur These einer progressiven Qumranisierung und Judaisierung innerhalb der synoptischen Tradition* (Witten: Luther-Verlag, 1973) 176–82; W. G. Kümmel, 'Äussere und innere Reinheit des Menschen bei Jesus,' in H. Balz and S. Schulz, eds., *Das Wort und die Wörter: Festschrift für Gerhard Friedrich* (Stuttgart: Kohlhammer, 1973) 35–46; U. Luz, *Das Evangelium nach Matthäus (Mt 8–17)* (EKKNT 1.2; Zürich: Benzinger Verlag; Neukirchen-Vluyn: Neukirchener Verlag, 1985–90) 416–19, 424–5.

interest, enhanced the parallelism between several sentences (cf. v. 2a with v. 3; v. 4 with 6a; and v. 11b with v. 18) and narrowed the focus of the text by modifying the end of the pericope (v. 20b makes it clear what the initial issue of the discussion was).

Matthew's changes in v. 11, therefore, are consistent with the specifying redaction and style elsewhere in the pericope. It seems that Matthew's redaction both advances the emphasis that was already present in Mark's own interpretation, namely in the editorial comment that Jesus was 'cleansing all foods' (Mark 7.19), and mitigates the sharpness of Mark's formulations that '*nothing* outside a man ... defiles a man' (Mark 7.15). Matthew may have wanted to ensure that Jesus' saying would not be understood as abolishing all kinds of purity rules.[61] Moreover, Matthew's redaction creates a contrast between keeping dietary rules and speaking evil. The importance of the right words is also emphasized by Matthew in 12.34–37. The ethical interpretation of the food laws, which is not foreign to Mark either (cf. Mark 7.20–23), can well be read together with Matthew's general concept of the Law (cf. e.g. Matt 5.17–48).

A standard redaction-critical procedure, therefore, would result in the suggestion that Matt 15.11 has been reformulated by Matthew to match his editorial purposes. Of course, it can be argued that Matthew's redaction *vis-à-vis* Mark 7.15 was not really an *ad hoc* creation and that he was using another extant version of the saying from the 'special material'[62] or from Q.[63] So John Dominic Crossan argues, who thinks that Mark 7.15, Matt 15.11 and *Gos. Thom.* 14.5 all represent 'independent' versions of the saying.[64] Crossan presents two main arguments to support his view. First, Acts 11.8 shows that Luke knew a saying about pure and impure *going into the mouth*. In this passage the evangelist makes Peter resist God's command to eat by saying: 'nothing common or unclean has ever *entered my mouth*.'[65]

---

[61] Luz, *Matthäus*, 424.

[62] See J. H. Sieber, 'A Redactional Analysis of the Synoptic Gospels with regard to the Question of the Sources of the Gospel According to Thomas' (Ph.D. Diss., Claremont Graduate School, 1965) 192.

[63] A case for Matt 15.11 deriving from Q has been made by J. D. G. Dunn in 'Jesus and Ritual Purity: A Study on the Tradition-History of Mark 7,15,' in F. Refoulé, ed., *A cause de l'Évangile: études sur les synoptiques et les Actes offerts au P. Jacques Dupont* (LD 123; Paris: Cerf, 1985) 251–76.

[64] See *In Fragments: The Aphorisms of Jesus* (San Francisco: Harper & Row, 1983) 250–5.

[65] Ibid., 252–3.

Secondly, according to Crossan, a dependence on Matthew 'does not explain why the Synoptic texts are in the third person while the Thomistic version is in the second person.'[66]

However, the force of these two arguments is not particularly strong. Luke's diction in Acts 11.8 (diff. 10.14) has a close parallel in Ezek 4.14 LXX (οὐδὲ εἰσελήλυθεν εἰς τὸ στόμα μου πᾶν κρέας ἕωλον), which shows that the idea of impure food going into the mouth need not be dependent on a saying similar to Matt 15.11 or *Gos. Thom.* 14.5. Moreover, nothing in the story of Peter and Cornelius reveals awareness of the dichotomy of going 'into the mouth/out of the mouth' that is characteristic of Matthew's and *Thomas'* version. As to the choice of personal pronouns, the second person in the *Gospel of Thomas* can readily be understood as an adaptation to the second person of the preceding parts (14.1–4).

Could Matthew then have used a saying from Q? This suggestion is not so far-fetched since Matthew has probably used another Q saying in Matt 15.14 (cf. Luke 6.39; note also Q 11.39–40).[67] However, there is no Q context for such a saying. If Acts 11.8 cannot be used as a parallel, as argued above, practically the only reason for suggesting a Q version of the saying is its appearance in the *Gospel of Thomas*, and such an argument would be circular when used in the present study.

The tradition history of Mark 7.1–20 and especially the authenticity of Mark 7.15 has been a subject of energetic discussion and cannot be dealt with here in detail.[68] Two considerations should be mentioned, however. First, although there is a long scholarly tradition of regarding Mark 7.15 as an authentic saying of the historical Jesus,[69] scholars have also raised serious doubts about the early date of the Markan saying.

---

[66] Ibid., 254, citing Sieber, 'A Redactional Analysis,' 193. See also Dunn, 'Jesus and Ritual Purity,' 263.

[67] Dunn, 'Jesus and Ritual Purity,' 263.

[68] See e.g. Bultmann, *History of Synoptic Tradition*, 17–18; Carlston, 'Things that Defile,' 75–96; Kümmel, 'Reinheit,' 35–46; J. Lambrecht, 'Jesus and the Law: An Investigation of Mk 7,1–23,' *ETL* 53 (1977) 24–79; H. Räisänen, 'Jesus and the Food Laws: Reflections on Mark 7.15,' *JSNT* 16 (1982) 79–100; 'Zur Herkunft von Markus 7,15,' in J. Delobel, ed., *Logia. Les paroles de Jésus – The Sayings of Jesus* (BETL 59; Leuven: Leuven University Press/Peeters, 1982) 477–84 (both articles reprinted in idem, *Jesus, Paul, and Torah: Collected Essays* [JSNTSup 43; Sheffield: Sheffield Academic Press, 1992] 127–48); Crossan, *In Fragments*, 250–5; Dunn, 'Jesus and Ritual Purity'; R. P. Booth, *Jesus and the Laws of Purity: Tradition History and Legal History in Mark 7* (JSNTSup 13; Sheffield: Sheffield Academic Press, 1986).

[69] E.g. Bultmann, *History of Synoptic Tradition*, 105.

Heikki Räisänen, for example, has taken notice of the missing *Wirkungsgeschichte* of the saying in early Christianity.[70] If a saying like Mark 7.15 was widely circulated, how can one explain the many disputes about food laws in early Christianity and especially the fact that Jesus' teaching played no role in these debates?[71] Moreover, one can ask, why did the opponents of Jesus in the canonical gospels, while accusing him of blasphemy, sabbath-breaking and so on, never accuse him of speaking against cultic purity and food laws?[72] One would expect that Jesus' rejection of the food laws, if an old and well-known tradition, would have left at least some traces in the Synoptic narratives. Such considerations may indicate that the provenance of Mark 7.15 is much closer to Mark's own milieu and time than has usually been thought.

A second consideration about the tradition-history of this saying is based on very simple reasoning. It is difficult to argue that Mark would have known the saying in the form that is closer to Matt 15.11 and *Gos. Thom.* 14.5, and then modified it to its present awkward shape in the gospel. A much more natural explanation is that Mark 7.15 is a *lectio difficilior*, whose meaning has been narrowed and interpreted by a later redactor.

To summarize the discussion, Matt 15.11 is a Matthean reformulation based on Mark 7.15. The possibility that Matthew drew upon another version of the saying in his rewriting of Mark 7.1–20 can hardly be categorically ruled out, but there are serious doubts as to whether the saying circulated widely in early Christianity. In any case, such a suggestion begs the question why the alleged pre-Matthean saying is well matched to Matthew's redaction elsewhere.

1.4.2. Gos. Thom. *14.4 and Luke (Q?) 10.8–9a*

The resemblance between *Gos. Thom.* 14.4 and Luke 10.8–9a is close, except for the difference between Luke's 'entering a *town*' and 'any

---

[70] 'Jesus and the Food Laws,' 79–100; 'Zur Herkunft von Markus 7,15,' 477–84; see also his *Paul and the Law* (WUNT 29; Tübingen: J. C. B. Mohr [Paul Siebeck], 1983) 245–8.

[71] Rom 14.14 is hardly an allusion to Mark 7.15; see Räisänen, 'Zur Herkunft von Markus 7,15,' 480–2; against Dunn, 'Jesus and Ritual Purity,' 272–3.

[72] This has been noted by W. D. Davies and D. C. Allison, *The Gospel According to Saint Matthew*, vol. II: *Commentary on Matthew VIII–XVIII* (ICC. Edinburgh: T&T Clark, 1991) 528, although their final conclusion differs from that of Räisänen.

land' in *Thomas* and for the fact that the latter has an additional expression for wandering ('walk about in the districts'). Luke 10.8–9a occurs in the Q context as part of the Mission Charge (Q 10.2–16) and it has a partial parallel in Matt 10.8 (cf. also 10.11). However, the reconstruction of the Q section is an extremely arduous task and opinions about the nature of Lukan redaction in 10.8–9 diverge greatly.

I have dealt with the reconstruction of the mission instructions of Q more comprehensively in other contexts, so I shall give only a short summary of the discussion here.[73] There are three main solutions to the problem of Luke 10.8–9. (1) The whole verse 10.8 is a Lukan creation; only the commands to heal and to proclaim the kingdom (Luke 10.9; cf. Matt 10.7–8) derive from Q.[74] (2) The command to eat what is set before you (Luke 10.8b) is a Lukan insertion in Q, which included the coming into the 'town' (Luke 10.8a; cf. Matt 10.11a) and the instructions in Luke 10.9.[75] (3) The 'town' scene and the command to eat were both in Q.[76]

It is only the third option that makes it possible to argue that *Gos. Thom.* 14.4 does not echo Lukan redactional elements, but due to the controversial evidence and the lack of a clear parallel for Luke 10.8 in Matthew, the inclusion of the verse in Q will remain uncertain. It is important to notice, however, that even this solution does not require an independent oral tradition history for the saying in *Gos. Thom.* 14.4,

---

[73] See Uro, *Sheep Among the Wolves*, 67–9, 80–3, and the contributions to the International Q Project (the Society of Biblical Literature in conjunction with the Institute for Antiquity and Christianity, Claremont, CA) to be published in *Documenta Q* (Peeters 1996–).

[74] The most extensive argument for Luke having introduced the 'town' scene to the Q instructions has been presented by P. Hoffmann; see his *Studien zur Theologie der Logienquelle* (NTAbh 8; Münster: Aschendorff, 1972) 276–83. Hoffmann contends that the original context of the command to heal the sick (Q 10.9a) was the 'house mission' (Q 10.5–7a). He argues that Matt 10.11a should be taken as a parallel to Luke 10.5a rather than to Luke 10.8a and that the Matthean formulation can be explained without Q, on the basis of Mark 6.10 and Matthew's language in 9.35 ('And Jesus went about all the *cities and villages*'). Moreover, according to Hoffmann, Luke has an interest in creating 'town' scenes for the preaching of the gospel (cf. Acts 26.26). The latter argument can be objected to (see Uro, *Sheep Among the Wolves*, 67 n. 188), but the first still carries some weight.

[75] This has been suggested e.g. by D. Catchpole in 'The Mission Charge in Q,' *Semeia* 55 (1991) 147–73 (esp. 164–5); reprinted in *The Quest for Q* (Edinburgh: T&T Clark, 1993) 151–88 (esp. 176–8).

[76] E.g. R. Laufen *Die Doppelüberlieferung der Logienquelle und des Markusevangeliums* (BBB 54; Bonn: Hanstein, 1980) 219–20; Uro, *Sheep Among the Wolves*, 68–9, 82–3, 222.

since Luke 10.8–9 conveys signs of secondary literary composition. This is particularly clear in Luke 10.8b ('eat what is set before you'). Whether the saying is a Lukan addition or not, most commentators agree that it is awkward in its present position. The thought flows smoothly from the 'coming into a town' in 10.8a to the command to heal the sick 'in it' (10.9a), and the admonition to eat, turning back to the hospitality issues in Luke 10.5–7, interrupts the otherwise clear logic. If it was Luke who added the saying, then it is best to assume that this tension arose from his redaction. If the saying was in Q, the most probable explanation is that Luke 10.8b was a redactional addition there and did not derive from the same redactor as the preceding exhortation to eat and drink (Q 10.7b). Luke 10.8b would thus derive from the stage of the history of the Q people during which problems of the mission to the Gentiles had arisen.[77] In both analyses, therefore, Luke 10.8b represents a secondary intrusion in the text, although opinions about the stage at which this addition was made diverge.

To be sure, a case has also been made for Luke 10.8–9 being a pre-Q tradition, which has been used both in Q and in the *Gospel of Thomas*.[78] In such analyses the presupposition of the 'independence' of the *Gospel of Thomas* has usually played a role in the reasoning. However, Philip Sellew has also presented additional arguments for the view that Luke 10.8–9 represents an 'independent dominical tradition.' Two points emerge from his discussion. First, Sellew thinks that *Thomas'* 'rurally evocative "lands and regions"' reveals a trait which is older than Q's 'city.' Secondly, the assumption that the commands to eat and to heal were already together in the tradition would explain the clumsy repetition in Luke 10.8b (cf. 10.7b).[79]

However, it is not clear how explicitly the words ⲉⲧⲉⲧⲛ̄ϣⲁⲛⲃⲱⲕ ⲉϩⲟⲩⲛ ⲉⲕⲁϩ ⲛⲓⲙ ⲁⲩⲱ ⲛ̄ⲧⲉⲧⲙ̄ⲙⲟⲟϣⲉ ϩⲛ̄ ⲛ̄ⲭⲱⲣⲁ ('when you go into any land and walk about in the districts') emphasize the rural character of the mission. The wording in the *Gospel of Thomas* can also

---

[77] It has often been felt that the command has to do with kosher rules, as is clearly the case in *Gos. Thom.* 14 (cf. also 1 Cor 10.27), and I think that is a reasonable assumption. Otherwise we have to take it as an unmotivated repetition of the preceding instruction about eating and drinking (Q 10.7b). For the issue of the Gentile mission in Q, see Uro, *Sheep Among the Wolves*, 210–23; Kloppenborg, *Formation of Q*, 236.

[78] P. Sellew, 'Early Collections of Jesus' Words' (Ph.D. Diss., Harvard Divinity School, 1985) 131–3; see also Patterson, *Gospel of Thomas*, 88–9 and Jacobson, *The First Gospel*, 142.

[79] Sellew, 'Early Collections,' 132.

be considered rather neutral in that respect. It may simply describe, first, coming into some land (ⲕⲁ2, Greek γῆ?) and then a movement from place to place (ⲭⲱⲣⲁ does not necessarily mean 'countryside').

The point may well be wandering through different countries and places rather than a mission's rural milieu. In any case, the expression is too vague for drawing any certain conclusions about the primitiveness of *Thomas'* saying as compared to the Q instructions. One can even argue for the opposite, namely that Q presupposes a mission in a Palestinian context whereas *Thomas* reflects a mission that has a larger geographical area in view.

Sellew's second argument can also be questioned. Even though the suggestion that Luke 10.8–9 comes from a pre-Q tradition would seem to provide an explanation for the redundancy of the Q instructions, it creates another problem. The words 'and they receive you' in Luke 10.8, present also in *Thomas*, clearly contrast with the negative reception in Luke 10.10 ('they do not receive you'; cf. Mark 6.11 and Matt 10.14). This detail shows that the present formulation of Luke 10.8–9 depends on its larger context in the Mission Charge and cannot reflect *as such* an independent tradition.

In sum, Luke 10.8–9 cannot be easily be regarded as an old tradition which entered into the *Gospel of Thomas* independently from any written gospel. Apart from the question of who is responsible for its present shape, whether Q or Luke, it is a secondary composition, which has come into existence through a literary redaction of the mission instructions.

1.4.3. A secondary redaction?

It is difficult to escape the conclusion that *Gos. Thom.* 14 reveals elements that ultimately derive from the literary redaction of at least one canonical gospel. This is fairly obvious in the case of *Gos. Thom.* 14.5 which in all probability echoes Matthew's redaction in 15.11. The results of the analysis of *Gos. Thom.* 14.4 and Luke 10.8–9a are more complex, but the arguments for the view that the saying comes from a presynoptic 'free' tradition of Jesus' sayings are not convincing. It is possible that the saying derives from Q, but that does not necessarily mean an independent oral history.

It must be admitted that one logion is a very narrow basis for drawing general conclusions. One could argue that this saying reflects a secondary redaction or translation process in which the *Gospel of Thomas* was assimilated into the canonical gospels, while the original Greek gospel represented an essentially independent tradition. It is indeed quite probable that the *Gospel of Thomas* has a complex history of composition and may therefore contain traditions which are of different origin and derive from diverse sources. Although we still have to look forward to extensive analyses in the composition history of the gospel, a few remarks can be made about the position of *Gos. Thom.* 14.

It has been suggested that *Gos. Thom.* 14 was originally meant to be an answer to the disciples' questions in logion 6.1: 'Do you want us to fast (Gr. How [shall we] fast?)[80] How shall we pray? Shall we give alms? What diet shall we observe?'[81] Indeed, logion 14 would be a much more suitable answer to these questions than what actually follows in *Gos. Thom.* 6.2–6 (note also that 6.6 parallels 5.2 in Coptic). Gilles Quispel argues that logions 6.1 and 14 formed a unit in *Thomas'* encratite source.[82] A different solution is presented by Stevan Davies, who thinks that the separation of the question and the answer originated from careless copying of the text.[83] It is indeed striking that fasting, prayer, almsgiving and dietary rules appear in both sayings in the same order, and therefore suggestions about an original connection have some plausibility. However, none of these explanations helps to remove the Synoptic redactional elements from the sayings in *Gos. Thom.* 14.4–5, unless we suggest completely different forms of the sayings in *Thomas'* alleged source or in the original version of the gospel – but that is all pure speculation. One should also notice that the suggested separation of logia 6.1 and 14 must be older than the Greek version of P.Oxy. 654, which excludes the possibility of a later harmonization by a Coptic translator.

It is necessary to emphasize that these observations do not exclude the possibility that *Gos. Thom.* 14 represents a late redaction in the gospel. One has to consider, nevertheless, that the tone of logion 14

---

[80] See H. W. Attridge, 'The Greek Fragments' [of the *Gospel According to Thomas*], in B. Layton, ed., *Nag Hammadi Codex II, 2–7 together with XIII,2*, Brit. Lib. Or.4926(1), and P.Oxy. 1, 654, 655*, vol. 1 (NHS 20; Leiden: E. J. Brill, 1989) 116.

[81] Trans. T. O. Lambdin in B. Layton, ed., *Nag Hammadi Codex II, 2–7*, 55.

[82] *Makarius*, 35–6.

[83] S. L. Davies, *The Gospel of Thomas and Christian Wisdom* (New York: The Seabury Press, 1983) 153–4.

accords well with the unresponsive attitude toward Jewish observances that is present in many other sayings in the gospel (cf. *Gos. Thom.* 6; 27; 53; 104).[84] Therefore, if *Gos. Thom.* 14 conveys a late redaction, we are hardly dealing with minor interpolations or harmonizations.

1.4.4. Direct or indirect use?

The usual objection to the view that *Thomas* is dependent upon the canonical Gospels is based on the improbability of a *direct* use. If the author of the *Gospel of Thomas* had a copy of a canonical gospel in front of his/her eyes, how can it be explained that the order of the sayings in the gospel has left so few traces in his/her editorial work?[85] One should note that another saying from the Mission Discourse, Luke (Q) 10.2 (*Gos. Thom.* 73), appears in the *Gospel of Thomas* in a quite different context, as part of a cluster of three sayings in 73–75. Similarly, a saying from Matthew's passage on ritual cleanliness in Matt 15.1–20, viz.15.14b (the blind leading the blind), has its parallel in *Gos. Thom.* 34. Indeed, one can hardly imagine a redactional process comparable to what we can observe in Matthew's and Luke's use of Mark.

A suggestion of an *indirect* use cannot be ruled out as easily. In light of the above analysis, one can argue that the editor of *Gos. Thom.* 14 was either freely quoting Matthew and Q or Luke from memory, or using traditions which were influenced by the reading of these gospels. The border between these two alternatives is fluid, and it is perhaps impossible to make a firm decision between them on the basis of the present evidence. Nonetheless, the Matthean redaction of Mark 7.15 produced a neat antithetical proverb, and its circulation as a separate wisdom saying is quite probable. Even Luke 10.8–9a, although one can hardly avoid the impression that it is an extract, could be cited independently. Especially if one thinks of the heated debates about food laws in early Christianity, a dominical injunction directed to the missionaries and allowing liberal conduct might have been more than welcome in many circles. Once Luke 10.8–9a was detached from its original context as part of the mission instructions, this point became

---

[84] For a detailed analysis of these sayings, see Marjanen, '*Thomas* and Jewish Religious Practices' in this volume.

[85] For a comparison of the sequences of *Thomas* and the Synoptics, see B. de Solages, 'L'Évangile de Thomas et les évangiles canoniques: l'ordre des péricopes,' *BLE* 80 (1979) 102–8.

more explicit. The assumption of 'secondary orality' has therefore some plausibility with regard to *Gos. Thom.* 14 and its Synoptic parallels. One may furthermore conclude that *Gos. Thom.* 14 was written in a milieu in which at least the Gospel of Matthew and Q (or Luke) were known. This makes the composition of Matthew the *terminus a quo* of the logion. Whether this conclusion is appropriate for the earliest version of *Thomas* as a collection of Jesus' sayings cannot be decided here.[86]

[86] This article is based on a paper presented in the Q Section of the the the Annual Meeting of the Society of Biblical Literature, Washington DC, November, 1993, and published in *Forum* 9.3–4 (1993) 305–29 under the title ''Secondary Orality' in the Gospel of Thomas? Logion 14 as a Test Case.' I have slightly modified the text and corrected some confusing passages due to defective printing. Since the first publication of my paper, further studies about the interaction of orality and literacy in early Christianity have been published. The Bible in Ancient and Modern Media Group of the Society of Biblical Literature has produced another volume of articles focusing on orality–literacy studies; see e.g. J. Dewey, ed., *Orality and Textuality in Early Christian Literature* (Semeia 65; Atlanta: Scholars Press, 1994) including helpful contributions from T. E. Boomershine, J. Dewey, M. S. Jaffee, V. K. Robbins, R. F. Ward, A. J. Dewey, A. C. Wire, J. M. Foley, B. B. Scott, and W. H. Kelber. See also P. J. J. Botha, 'Greco-Roman Literacy as Setting for New Testament Writings,' *Neot* 26 (1992) 195–215; 'The Verbal Art of Pauline Letters: Rhetoric, Performance and Presence,' in S. E. Porter and H. O. Thomas, eds., *Rhetoric and the New Testament: Essays from the 1992 Heidelberg Conference* (JSNTSup 90; Sheffield: Sheffield Academic Press, 1993) 409–59; B. B. Scott and M. E. Dean, 'A Sound Map of the Sermon on the Mount,' *SBLSP* 32 (1993) 672–725; and F. G. Downing, 'Word-Processing in the Ancient World: The Social Production and Performance of Q,' *JSNT* 64 (1996) 29–48. It remains to be seen how this growing interest in orality–literacy studies among New Testament scholars will affect the study of the gospel traditions in general.

2

Thomas' I-sayings and the Gospel of John

Ismo Dunderberg

2.1. Introduction

2.1.1. Features common to John and *Thomas*

At first sight, the *Gospel of Thomas* appears to stand essentially closer to the Synoptic gospels than to the Gospel of John. This impression does not only emerge from numerous verbal parallels between the *Gospel of Thomas* and the Synoptics, but also from the literary forms employed in the *Gospel of Thomas*. Parables, chriae, and *Schulgespräche* occur frequently in the *Gospel of Thomas* as well as in the Synoptic sayings tradition. These forms are more or less absent in the Gospel of John, in which sayings materials are usually incorporated in Jesus' lengthy discourses.

Although the *Gospel of Thomas* and the Gospel of John are formally quite distinct from each other, their symbolic universes coincide in many respects. In both gospels Jesus is regarded as pre-existent and associated with the origin of all things (*Gos. Thom.* 77; John 1.3; 8.58). Both gospels include anti-cosmic traits (*Gos. Thom.* 21; 56; 80; John 14.30; 15.19; 17.16) and a dualism of light and darkness (*Gos. Thom.* 24; 61; John 1.5; 8.12; 9.4; 11.9–10; 12.35). In each gospel, Jesus' incarnation is contrasted to human ignorance (*Gos. Thom.* 28; John 1.9–11, 14), and his words are associated with a promise of immortality (*Gos. Thom.* 19; John 8.31, 52), resulting either from an understanding (*Gos. Thom.* 1; 19) or keeping of these words (John 8.31, 51–52).[1]

---

[1] The phrase 'taste death' occurs in John 8.51–52 only in a reply of Jews, whereas Jesus himself speaks of 'seeing death.' Stephen R. Johnson has recently argued that this feature is due to a Johannine reaction against the Thomasine version of the promise of immortality; cf. S. R. Johnson, 'The *Gospel of Thomas* 76.3 and Canonical Parallels: Three Segments in the Tradition History of the Saying,' in J. D. Turner and A. McGuire, eds., *The Nag Hammadi Library After Fifty Years: Proceedings of the 1995 Society of Biblical Literature Commemoration* (NHMS 44; Leiden: E. J. Brill, 1997) 308–26, esp. 322–4. Yet it seems more likely that what is misunderstood by the Jews in John 8.51–52 is not the *wording* of Jesus' promise but his *authority* to make this promise.

Discipleship is expressed in terms of election (*Gos. Thom.* 49–50; John 6.70; 13.18; 15.16, 19), and it involves a persecution of Jesus' followers, either spiritual or concrete (*Gos. Thom.* 68–69; John 16.1–4).

Both the *Gospel of Thomas* and the Gospel of John also display what, with some hesitation, can be called 'realized eschatology':[2] a future orientation toward salvation is outweighed by its present aspects, and concepts elsewhere connected with future events are used in a non-apocalyptic fashion in each gospel. This orientation is, however, expressed in different terms. In the *Gospel of Thomas* the present aspects are visible in the sayings concerning the 'kingdom' (*Gos. Thom.* 3; 113), the 'end' (*Gos. Thom.* 18), and 'the repose of the dead' (*Gos. Thom.* 51), which all are understood as present realities. In the Gospel of John aspects of 'realized eschatology' are linked with other topics, including the resurrection of the dead (John 5.24–26; 11.24–27) and the final judgement (John 3.18–19, 36; 5.27; 12.31).[3]

Attitudes towards the Jewish Scriptures and customs are also similar.[4] According to both gospels, a study of the Scriptures may distract one from recognizing Jesus (*Gos. Thom.* 52; John 5.39). Fleshly circumcision is ridiculed in *Gos. Thom.* 53, whereas the Johannine Jesus speaks as an outsider both of circumcision and of the Law (John 7.19–24; 10.34–36; 15.25); he in effect shares his distant view on the Law with Pilate who also speaks of 'your law' with regard to it (John 18.31).[5] Moreover, in the two gospels 'Jews' are characterized by their misunderstandings. This is a recurring feature in John (e.g. John 6.41, 52; 8.48, 52–53), but appears also in *Gos. Thom.* 43, where Jesus

---

[2]   Karen L. King notes that, with regard to the kingdom language of the *Gospel of Thomas*, it is not quite accurate to speak of 'realized eschatology,' since the gospel employs the term 'kingdom' in a non-apocalyptic way; 'Kingdom in the Gospel of Thomas,' *Forum* 3.1 (1987) 48–97, esp. 50–2; see also Uro, 'Is *Thomas* an Encratite Gospel?' in this volume.

[3]   Cf. G. Richter, 'Präsentische und futurische Eschatologie im 4. Evangelium,' in J. Hainz, ed., *Studien zum Johannesevangelium* (BU 13; Regensburg: Friedrich Pustet, 1977) 346–82, esp. 367–8.

[4]   For this issue, see Marjanen, '*Thomas* and Jewish Religious Practices,' in this volume.

[5]   Interestingly enough, in the Gospel of John this does not prevent a positive use of the Jewish Scriptures. Not only are they frequently quoted but they can be regarded as witnessing to Jesus or as finding their fulfillment in him (cf. John 1.45; 5.39; 15.25). For different aspects of the use of the Jewish Scriptures in John, cf. W. A. Meeks, *The Prophet-King: Moses Traditions and the Johannine Christology* (NovTSup 14; Leiden: E. J. Brill, 1967) 287–91, and M. Kotila, *Der umstrittene Zeuge: Studien zur Stellung des Gesetzes in der johanneischen Theologiegeschichte* (AASF DHL 48; Helsinki: The Finnish Academy of Science and Letters, 1988).

blames the disciples, who have misunderstood him, that they 'have become like Jews.'

These similarities between the *Gospel of Thomas* and the Gospel of John are substantial enough to raise a question about their mutual relationship. Previous examinations, as the following survey of research will show, have reached different conclusions on this issue. The state of research is not only due to different attitudes toward the *Gospel of Thomas*, but it also reflects methodological difficulties involved in comparing the two related yet formally distinct gospels.

2.1.2. Survey of research

In the early 1960s, Raymond Brown devoted a lengthy article to the relationship between the Johannine writings and the *Gospel of Thomas*, concluding that the *Gospel of Thomas* is 'ultimately (but still indirectly) dependent on John itself.'[6] Since verbatim quotations are lacking, Brown suggests that there existed a Gnostic or Gnostic-like source which functioned as an intermediary between the two gospels.[7] Methodologically, Brown first examined all possible agreements between the *Gospel of Thomas* and the Johannine writings, and then classified them into remote and close parallels, of which only the latter are regarded as really conclusive.[8] Brown notices that the close parallels accumulate in two Johannine passages (John 7.37 – 8.59; 13–17), and that they are dispersed in different parts of these passages.[9] These Johannine passages, on the other hand, are usually regarded as composite discourses.[10] These observations exclude, in Brown's judgment, the possibility that the parallels might stem from one particular strand of pre-Johannine traditions. So Brown's conclusion is that the *Gospel of Thomas* must have been influenced by the Gospel of John.

---

[6] R. E. Brown, 'The Gospel of Thomas and St John's Gospel,' *NTS* 9 (1962–3) 155–77, esp. 176.

[7] Brown, 'Gospel of Thomas and St John's Gospel,' 177.

[8] Brown defines the remote parallels as 'so tenuous that they would be of significance only after a clear relationship between John and GTh had already been established' ('The Gospel of Thomas and St John's Gospel,' 174). These parallels include *Gos. Thom.* 2; 4; 6; 11; 15; 21–22; 23; 29; 30; 40; 42; 49; 52; 55–56; 64; 76; 90; 101; 104; 105; 110 and 114.

[9] Brown, 'Gospel of Thomas and St John's Gospel,' 175: John 7.37 – 8.52/*Gos. Thom.* Prologue, 1; 18; 19; 24; 28; 38; 43; 59; 61; 69.1; 77; 78; 91; 108; 111; John 13–17/*Gos. Thom.* 12; 13; 24; 27; 37; 43; 50; 51; 61; 69.1; 92; 100.

[10] Brown, 'Gospel of Thomas and St John's Gospel,' 175–6.

This manner of argumentation raises some serious questions. First, Brown seems to presuppose that the *Gospel of Thomas* is in any case a later writing than the Gospel of John and essentially Gnostic in character.[11] These presuppositions can no longer be taken for granted. There is an ongoing debate about the date and the Gnostic character of the *Gospel of Thomas*, and also about the accurate definition of the term 'Gnosticism.'[12] Second, Brown does not give exact criteria by which he defines the 'close parallels.' Third, the way Brown deals with 'close parallels' is not convincing. Their dispersion within the two Johannine discourses speaks no more for a Johannine influence on the *Gospel of Thomas* than the fact that the same parallels are scattered in the *Gospel of Thomas* speaks for the opposite conclusion. (It could be maintained with a similar argument that the author of the Gospel of John must have known the *Gospel of Thomas* as a whole!) The decisive issue, to which Brown seems not to pay due attention, is whether the sayings of the *Gospel of Thomas* include traits which are *specifically* Johannine, i.e. due to the Johannine redaction of the respective passages. Fourth, the inclusion of Revelation in the same group of Johannine writings as the Gospel and Epistles of John weakens the cumulative force of Brown's argument, for this view is far from being certain (Brown himself has discarded it later).[13]

Jesse Sell builds largely upon Brown's arguments but parts company with him by insisting that the *Gospel of Thomas* is directly dependent on the Gospel of John.[14] According to Sell, at least eight sayings in the *Gospel of Thomas* 'display the sort of echoes of Johannine ideas and vocabulary which lay the burden of proof on one who would deny the probability of some direct influence of "John itself"' on GT.'[15] In these sayings Sell finds 'echoes of fifty-three verses, *from seventeen different chapters of John*.'[16] In Sell's opinion, this speaks against Brown's theory,

---

[11] Cf. S. L. Davies, *The Gospel of Thomas and Christian Wisdom* (New York: The Seabury Press, 1983) 106–7.

[12] Cf. Marjanen, 'Is *Thomas* a Gnostic Gospel?' in this volume.

[13] R. E. Brown, *The Community of the Beloved Disciple* (New York: Paulist Press, 1979) 6 n. 5. That Revelation could, nevertheless, stem from the Johannine circle has been argued most recently by J. Frey, 'Appendix: Erwägungen zum Verhältnis der Johannesapokalypse zu den übrigen Schriften des Corpus Johanneum,' in M. Hengel, *Die johanneische Frage: Ein Lösungsversuch* (WUNT 67; Tübingen: J. C. B. Mohr [Paul Siebeck], 1993) 326–429.

[14] J. Sell, 'Johannine Traditions in Logion 61 of the Gospel of Thomas,' *Perspectives in Religous Studies* 7 (1980) 24–37. The eight sayings, according to Sell, are *Gos.Thom.* Prologue; 8; 13; 28; 38; 43; 91; 92.

[15] Sell, 'Johannine Traditions,' 25.

[16] Ibid., 27.

for the alleged intermediary would 'have had to represent nearly the complete structure of the present Gospel [of John].'[17] Sell, even more clearly than Brown, confuses two separate issues with each other by taking the *number* of parallels as an indication of the *structure* of the Fourth Gospel.

In addition to Brown and Sell, Miroslav Marcovich has argued that the *Gospel of Thomas* is dependent on John. According to Marcovich, *Gos. Thom.* 11 is both in its Coptic and Greek version (Hippolytus, *Refutatio* 5.8.32) inspired by the Gospel of John. In the Coptic version the sentence 'whensoever you are in the light' (Marcovich's translation) allegedly refers to several Johannine passages (John 12.36; 1 John 1.7; 2.9), and the phrase ζῶντα φαγεῖν in the Greek version recalls the 'predominantly eucharistic homily [John] vi.31–58.'[18]

An alternative theory is that the similarities between the Gospel of John and the *Gospel of Thomas* are due to early traditions of Jesus' sayings. Gilles Quispel suggests, yet only very tentatively, that the parallels between the two gospels hint at a common source of Jesus' sayings. This indicates that the author of the Fourth Gospel might have been familiar with some distinctively Palestinian traditions represented by the *Gospel of Thomas*.[19] On the other hand, Helmut Koester thinks that Johannine sayings traditions are related to those attested by the *Gospel of Thomas* and two other Nag Hammadi writings, the *Dialogue of the Savior* and the *Apocryphon of James*.[20] Koester argues that these

---

[17] Ibid., 28.

[18] M. Marcovich, 'Textual Criticism on the Gospel of Thomas,' *JTS* 20 (1969) 53–74, esp. 72–4.

[19] G. Quispel, 'Qumran, John and Jewish Christianity,' in J. Charlesworth, ed., *John and the Dead Sea Scrolls* (New York: Crossroad, 1991) 137–55, esp. 139–40, 144–6. Quispel's view on the sayings source behind the Gospel of John is based on B. Noack, *Zur johanneischen Tradition: Beiträge zur Kritik an der literarkritischen Analyse des vierten Evangeliums* (Copenhagen: Rosenkilde og Bager, 1954).

[20] H. Koester, 'Dialog und Sprachüberlieferung in den gnostischen Texten von Nag Hammadi,' *EvT* 39 (1979) 532–56; 'Gnostic Writings as Witnesses for the Development of the Sayings Tradition,' in B. Layton, ed., *The Rediscovery of Gnosticism. Proceedings of the International Conference on Gnosticism at Yale, New Haven, Connecticut, March 28–31, 1978*, vol. 1: *The School of Valentinus* (Studies in the History of Religions 41; Leiden: E. J. Brill, 1980) 238–61; *Introduction to the New Testament*, vol. 2: *History and Literature of Early Christianity* (Philadelphia: Fortress Press; Berlin: Walter de Gruyter, 1982) 178–80; 'Gnostic Sayings and Controversy Traditions in John 8.12–59,' in C. W. Hedrick and R. Hodgson, eds., *Nag Hammadi, Gnosticism, and Early Christianity* (Peabody: Hendrickson, 1986) 97–110; *Ancient Christian Gospels: Their History and Development* (London: SCM Press; Philadelphia: Trinity Press International, 1990) 256–63.

writings enable us to trace the tradition history of Johannine discourses with more certainty than before.[21] In fact, Koester believes that the *Gospel of Thomas* and the *Dialogue of the Savior* testify to earlier stages in a trajectory of Jesus' sayings than the Gospel of John:

> The *Gospel of Thomas* exhibits the first stage of transition from sayings collection to dialogue. The *Dialogue of the Savior* shows the initial stages of larger compositions ... The Gospel of John contains fully developed dialogues and discourses.[22]

This conclusion is drawn by Koester with regard to the sayings material in John 14.2–12, but it applies equally well to his view on John 8.12–59.[23] In the latter section, moreover, Koester recognizes a tension between the pre-Johannine sayings tradition and the Johannine author: the tradition betrays a 'Gnostic understanding of salvation' which the Johannine author attempts to refute.[24]

Koester's theory locates both the *Gospel of Thomas* and the Gospel of John within an impressive overall view of the development of sayings traditions.[25] At the same time, this overall view seems to determine Koester's method and results as well: instead of being examined case by case, parallels are usually presented only in larger groups. Scholars who presuppose a different view have been led to opposite conclusions by using the same method.[26] Moreover, Koester's approach does not fully take into account the possibility of the secondary development of the *Gospel of Thomas*. Although the form of this gospel may be more archaic than that of the Johannine discourses, it does not necessarily

---

21 Koester, *Introduction*, 179–80 (cf. also idem, *Ancient Christian Gospels*, 257): 'The Johannine speeches frequently contain sentences that can be clearly identified, with the help of the new texts from Nag Hammadi, as sayings that were originally isolated sayings.'

22 Koester, 'Gnostic Writings,' 253.

23 Cf. Koester, 'Gnostic Sayings.'

24 Koester, *Ancient Christian Gospels*, 263.

25 Cf. Koester, 'Gnostic Writings,' 251.

26 This has been demonstrated recently by Charlesworth and Evans, who argue that 'the presence of M, L, and Johannine elements in *Thomas* indicate that the latter, at least in its extant Coptic form, has been influenced by the New Testament gospels.' Their conclusion is in part supported by a list similar to Koester's: John 1.9/*Gos. Thom.* 24; John 1.14/*Gos. Thom.* 28; John 4.13–15/*Gos. Thom.* 13; John 7.32–36/*Gos. Thom.* 38; John 8.12; 9.5/*Gos. Thom.* 77. Cf. J. H. Charlesworth and C. E. Evans, 'Jesus in the Agrapha and Apocryphal Gospels,' in B. Chilton and C. E. Evans, eds., *Studying the Historical Jesus: Evaluations of the State of Current Research* (NTTS 19; Leiden: E. J. Brill, 1994) 479–533, esp. 498–9.

follow that all the materials included in the extant *Gospel of Thomas* are archaic.

Stevan Davies has coined yet another version of the common sayings traditions theory. His solution is not only totally opposite to Brown's and Sell's, but it also differs from those of Quispel and Koester. Davies suggests that the *Gospel of Thomas* had its origins in the *Johannine community* before the Fourth Gospel was written. According to Davies, this hypothesis elucidates many details that would otherwise remain unexplained:

> Indeed, the hypothesis that the Gospel of Thomas is a sayings collection from an early stage of the Johannine communities accounts for the fact that Thomas contains no quotations from the as yet unwritten Gospel and Letters of John, accounts for the use of both Johannine vocabulary and Synoptic-style sayings, and to a certain extent accounts for the fact that the ideas of Thomas are less well conceptualized than the ideas in John.[27]

Davies builds his hypothesis in part upon similar adaptations of sapiental motifs in both gospels,[28] in part on theological similarities (such as the present eschatology or the double sense of the 'world'),[29] and, above all, on his view of the oral tradition behind the Fourth Gospel. Unfortunately, this last and most important argument is based on a plethora of conjectures. A critical section of Davies' argumentation reads:[30]

> If we assume that the sayings of Jesus in the Gospel of John were in part derived from sayings of Jesus such as are found in the Synoptics, then the oral preaching of the early Johannine community must have contained sayings of Jesus modified in a Johannine way, but less modified than the sayings now preserved in John. One would expect then that a document which remained from the period of the oral preaching of the Johannine communities and which Thomas used would have been a sayings collection, as Thomas is. It probably would have contained some sayings closer to synoptic sayings than are the discourses in John, and would show signs of early development of the Johannine tendencies . . . [I]f we try to imagine what a sayings collection underlying Thomas from an

---

[27] Davies, *Gospel of Thomas*, 116.

[28] These include the pre-existence of Jesus, a dualism of light and darkness, Jesus' descent to earth and his teaching activity, a return of believers to the original state of creation (an issue which, in my opinion, is not evident in John) and the division among human beings that is accomplished by Jesus; see Davies, *Gospel of Thomas*, 107–12.

[29] Davies, *Gospel of Thomas*, 112–13.

[30] Ibid., 115–16.

early stage of the Johannine community would look like, it would look very much like Thomas itself.

At this point, several questions are left entirely open. To raise only one of them, why should it be assumed that a sayings collection of the Johannine community was more closely related to Synoptic sayings traditions than the extant Johannine discourses are? Moreover, one implication of Davies's hypothesis would be that the Synoptic-like sayings tradition of the community went virtually unnoticed as the Gospel of John was written, yet he offers no explanation for such an eclipse of earlier Johannine traditions in the community. In short, Davies's theory suffers from too many unproven assumptions with regard to the earliest history of the Johannine community. Failure in this respect, however, should not distract us from his otherwise sensitive remarks on theological similarities between the Gospel of John and the *Gospel of Thomas*.

More recently a few scholars have recognized in the Johannine writings signs of a debate with the views which now are attested by the *Gospel of Thomas*. Takashi Onuki holds that the author of 1 John argues against opponents who made use of a saying similar to *Gos. Thom.* 17,[31] whereas Gregory J. Riley contends that Johannine and Thomas Christians were engaged in controversy concerning, among other theological issues, physical resurrection,[32] and April D. De Conick thinks that the Gospel of John criticizes the mystical ascent soteriology of Thomasine believers.[33] Although these attempts throw light upon some important differences between the *Gospel of Thomas* and the Johannine literature, they have, in my opinion, failed to demonstrate that there was any specific linkage between the groups behind these documents.[34]

---

[31] T. Onuki, 'Traditionsgeschichte von Thomasevangelium 17 und ihre christologische Relevanz,' in C. Breytenbach and H. Paulsen, eds., *Anfänge der Christologie: Festschrift für Ferdinand Hahn* (Göttingen: Vandenhoeck & Ruprecht, 1991) 399–415.

[32] G. J. Riley, *Resurrection Reconsidered: Thomas and John in Controversy* (Minneapolis: Fortress Press, 1995).

[33] A. D. De Conick, *Seek to See Him: Ascent and Vision Mysticism in the Gospel of Thomas* (VCSup 33; Leiden: E. J. Brill, 1996) 72–3.

[34] For a closer review of these theories, I refer to my article 'John and Thomas in Conflict?' in J. D. Turner and A. McGuire, eds., *The Nag Hammadi Library After Fifty Years: Proceedings of the 1995 Society of Biblical Literature Commemoration* (NHMS 44; Leiden: E. J. Brill, 1997) 361–80.

2.1.3. Methodological considerations

Although the affinities between the *Gospel of Thomas* and the Johannine writings, especially the Gospel of John, are abundant enough to raise a question about their mutual relationship, several methodological difficulties are involved in a closer examination of this issue. To begin with, there is no certain way of knowing which of the two gospels antedates the other.[35] Moreover, since neither gospel quotes directly from the other, conclusions about their relationship can be drawn only by comparing their contents to each other. This approach must face the obvious dilemma that in each gospel the principles of ordering Jesus' words are entirely different: in the Gospel of John, Jesus' sayings are arranged into thematic discourses, whereas in the *Gospel of Thomas* they are treated as individual, small units.[36]

The differences in genre must be taken into consideration in comparing the *Gospel of Thomas* with the Gospel of John. Koester's contention that the *Gospel of Thomas* represents sayings traditions which are more archaic than the Johannine discourses is only one possibility. Because the *Gospel of Thomas* is a sayings collection, it is in any case unlikely that it would contain numerous references to the Johannine *narrative* order; neither would lengthy Johannine discourses have been suitable in the *Gospel of Thomas*. So even if its author(s) had known the Gospel of John, passages from it could not have been adopted as such; it would be more likely that Johannine elements would have been adapted to a sayings gospel genre. On the other hand, the reverse process is equally possible: if short sayings were derived from the *Gospel of Thomas* (or from its predecessors) by the Johannine author(s), in John they would have most likely been integrated into lengthy discourses. In sum, the lack of similar order in the two gospels

---

[35] With regard to the dating of the Fourth Gospel, it is worth while noting that the traditional dating of P[52] (about 125 CE) has recently been questioned by A. Schmidt, according to whom this papyrus dates no earlier than 170 CE; see A. Schmidt, 'Zwei Anmerkungen zu P.Ryl III,' *Archiv für Papyrusforschung* 35 (1989) 11–12.

[36] Even though there are, without doubt, central themes in the *Gospel of Thomas* (such as the kingdom, solitariness and immortality), the sayings concerning these themes are usually dispersed in different parts of the gospel instead of being collected into larger thematical units. Cf. H. Koester, 'Introduction' [to the *Gospel According to Thomas*], in B. Layton, ed., *Nag Hammadi Codex II,2–7 together with XIII,2*, Brit. Lib. Or.4926(1), and P.Oxy. 1, 654, 655*, vol. 1 (NHS 20; Leiden: E. J. Brill, 1989) 38–49, esp. 41: 'Apart from the introduction (sayings 1–2), central section (sayings 49–61) and conclusion (sayings 113–114), there are no thematic arrangements.'

is basically inconclusive. It may indicate that the gospels are independent of each other, but it can also be due to the fact that they are representatives of different literary genres.

Another methodological problem is involved in redactional analyses of the two gospels. It is commonly acknowledged that the *Gospel of Thomas* can be considered to be dependent on the Synoptics only if clear redactional traces of them can be found in it.[37] It is more difficult to apply this rule in comparing the *Gospel of Thomas* to the Gospel of John, because the question of the redaction history of both gospels is by and large an unsettled issue. None of several theories concerning the Johannine sources has gained a dominant position comparable to that of the Synoptic Two-Source Theory.[38] It is even more difficult to reach conclusions on the redaction history in the *Gospel of Thomas*. Differences between its Greek fragments and the extant Coptic manuscript (such as the placement of *Gos. Thom.* 30 and 77.2–3), as well as quotations of this gospel made by church fathers, indicate that there was diversity in its transmission.[39] Yet these materials are fragmentary and admit of no firm conclusions with regard to the redaction history of the whole gospel. The great variety in the gospel's transmission is most likely due to its genre: it was not too difficult to add new sayings to a collection of aphoristic words, or to omit other sayings.[40] Since it is possible that each saying of the *Gospel of Thomas* has a tradition history

[37] To be sure, regardless of the wide acceptance of this principle as such, it has not yielded unanimous results. Schrage's view, followed recently by Fieger, is that a large number of Synoptic redactional traits or even traits of the Sahidic translations of the New Testament can be found in the extant *Gospel of Thomas;* cf. W. Schrage, *Das Verhältnis des Thomas-Evangeliums zur synoptischen Tradition und zu den koptischen Evangelienübersetzungen: Zugleich ein Beitrag zur gnostischen Synoptikerdeutung* (BZNW 29; Berlin: Alfred Töpelmann, 1964); M. Fieger, *Das Thomasevangelium: Einleitung, Kommentar und Systematik* (NTAbh, n.F. 22; Münster: Aschendorff, 1991). Opposite conclusions in most (but not in all) cases are reached e.g. by Sieber and Patterson; cf. J. H. Sieber, 'A Redactional Analysis of the Synoptic Gospels with Regard to the Question of the Sources of the Gospel According to Thomas' (Ph.D. Diss., Claremont Graduate School, 1965); S. J. Patterson, *The Gospel of Thomas and Jesus* (Foundations and Facets: Reference Series; Sonoma: Polebridge Press, 1993).

[38] John 21 is often regarded as a secondary appendix to the gospel, but even those who are in favor of this view disagree as to whether this chapter stands alone or whether it represents a larger redactional layer visible also elsewhere in the gospel.

[39] Cf. Marcovich, 'Textual Criticism,' 53–74.

[40] Cf. J. M. Robinson, 'Die Bedeutung der gnostischen Nag Hammadi Texte für die neutestamentliche Wissenschaft,' in L. Bormann, K. Del Tredici and A. Standhartinger, eds., *Religious Propaganda and Missionary Competition in the New Testament World: Essays Honoring Dieter Georgi* (NovTSup 74; Leiden: E. J. Brill, 1994) 23–41, esp. 30–1.

of its own, the extant *Gospel of Thomas* might show variation in its relationship to the canonical gospels.[41]

Keeping these methodological difficulties in mind, strict concentration on a *literary* relationship between the *Gospel of Thomas* and the Gospel of John does not suggest itself. This issue is, of course, important and deserves to be examined first in each individual case. Yet this approach needs to be complemented by an analysis of their *conceptual* relationship. This analysis involves a broader comparison with other early Christian literature. It is necessary to clarify whether the affinities between the two gospels imply some particular connection, or whether their similarities are only confined to ideas which are commonly attested by early Christian literature. If the latter be the case, this part of the analysis will help to locate the two gospels more generally within early Christianity.

Since such a broader approach seems advisable, I have felt it necessary, instead of giving a full account of all possible parallels, to focus more closely on the I-sayings of the *Gospel of Thomas*. This group of sayings suggests itself as a test case for two reasons. First, these sayings form a relatively cohesive group in lending expression to Jesus' self-definition; and second, there are significant Johannine parallels to some sayings of this group. Thus the I-sayings seem to provide a good starting point for further examinations of the relationship between the *Gospel of Thomas* and the Gospel of John.

2.2. Jesus' I-sayings in the Gospel of Thomas

Sayings in which Jesus refers to himself occur frequently in the *Gospel of Thomas*. To begin with, it is possible to separate from this material a small group of *identification sayings*. In this group there are two positive sayings which consist of a nominal sentence, including an identification (ⲀⲚⲞⲔ ⲡⲉ, 'It is I,' 'I am') and a subsequent predicate (*Gos. Thom.* 61.3; *Gos. Thom.* 77.1). A negative nominal sentence occurs in *Gos. Thom.* 13 ('I am not your master'), and a verbal expression has been employed in another negative identification saying, *Gos. Thom.* 72 ('I am not a divider, am I?').

---

[41] Cf. K. Neller, 'Diversity in the Gospel of Thomas: Clues for a New Direction?' *SecCent* 7.1 (1989–90) 1–18, esp. 15–18.

Formally, the two positive identification sayings of the *Gospel of Thomas* resemble Johannine 'I am' sayings with predicate nominatives (John 6.35, 51; 8.12; 9.5; 10.7, 9, 11, 14; 11.25; 14.6; 15.1, 5).[42] Among the canonical gospels, such identification sayings occur only in John, and elsewhere in the New Testament only in Revelation (1.8, 17; 2.23).[43] Despite the formal resemblance, only one 'I am' saying is common to both gospels (John 8.12; *Gos. Thom.* 77). There is no close parallel to *Gos. Thom.* 61 within the Johannine 'I am' sayings, but it is conceptually linked with another Johannine passage (John 5.18). As to the negative identification sayings of the *Gospel of Thomas*, Johannine parallels can be found to *Gos. Thom.* 13 but not to *Gos. Thom.* 72.

Another set of sayings of the *Gospel of Thomas* in which Jesus constantly refers to himself consists of a group of *imperatives* (*Gos. Thom.* 90; 100), *promises* (*Gos. Thom.* 30; 99) and sayings expressing *conditions of discipleship* (19; 55; 101). Strikingly enough, there are no close Johannine parallels to this group. These sayings are all characterized by a Synoptic-like terminology. This cannot be due to a lack of similar material in John, for it does employ similar forms in relation to Jesus' own person (e.g. John 4.14; 5.24; 6.35; 7.37–38; 8.31–32; 12.26, 44–48). The lack of similarity indicates rather that at this point the Thomasine and Johannine traditions are basically independent of each other.

There are also a number of I-sayings in the *Gospel of Thomas* in which Jesus speaks of his own *actions* or *emotions* (*Gos. Thom.* 10; 16; 17; 23; 28; 29; 71; 104; 108; 114). Few Johannine parallels can be found to this group of sayings. Within this group, there are Johannine parallels to *Gos. Thom.* 17 (1 John 1.1–3), *Gos. Thom.* 23 (election of

---

[42] In fact, these Johannine sayings are, with the exception of John 9.5, rendered in Sahidic versions with nominal sentences similar to *Gos. Thom.* 61 and 77.

[43] In his short survey of *Thomas'* I-sayings, Koester argues that *Gos. Thom.* 61 and 77 are 'examples of "I am" as an identification formula.' whereas 'the "I am" sayings in the Gospel of John are instances of the recognition formula'; 'One Jesus and Four Primitive Gospels,' in J. M. Robinson and H. Koester, *Trajectories through Early Christianity* (Philadelphia: Fortress Press, 1971) 158–204, esp. 178. Koester's distinction between 'identification' and 'recognition' formulae is derived from R. Bultmann's analysis of different uses of the 'I am' sayings; cf. R. Bultmann, *Das Evangelium des Johannes* (21st ed.; KEK 2; Göttingen: Vandenhoeck & Ruprecht 1986) 167 n. 2. However, a clear distinction between these categories is not self-evident; see e.g. R. E. Brown, *The Gospel according to John: Introduction, Translation, and Notes* (2 vols.; AB 29–29A; Garden City: Doubleday, 1966–1970) 1:534.

the disciples, cf. John 6.70; 15.16), *Gos. Thom.* 28 (Jesus' incarnation, above all John 1.1–18), and *Gos. Thom.* 71 (the temple saying, John 2.22).

Finally, in some I-sayings of the *Gospel of Thomas* Jesus emphasizes the importance of his own words (*Gos. Thom.* 38; 43; 46; 62). *Gos. Thom.* 92 also belongs to this group as a negative affirmation: Jesus did not answer the questions of his hearers in the past, and now he finds no hearers. The notion that Jesus himself underscores the significance of his own words is shared by the Gospel of John (cf. John 3.11; 5.24; 8.31–52; 12.48; 14.23–24: 15.3, 20). Moreover, both in John 16.4 and in *Gos. Thom.* 92 a division is made between past and present with regard to Jesus' words. Again, it is striking that in spite of these common emphases close verbal similarities are usually missing, except possibly for *Gos. Thom.* 43.

This survey of the I-sayings of the *Gospel of Thomas* already indicates that the way this gospel presents Jesus' self-definition is in essence independent from the Gospel of John. Yet there are parallels, including 'I am' sayings (*Gos. Thom.* 61; 77) as well as some other sayings (*Gos. Thom.* 23; 28; 43; 71; 104) which deserve to be reviewed more closely in the following. *Gos. Thom.* 13 can also be included in these parallels which need to be examined in detail. However, this saying is closely associated with the characterization of Thomas in the *Gospel of Thomas*. It will therefore be dealt with in another article devoted to the relationship between Thomas and the Beloved Disciple.[44]

Gos. Thom. 17 could also have been included in this list, for its content seems, at first sight, to be opposite to that of 1 John 1.1–3. It is, however, not necessary to repeat my earlier analysis of this saying, but only to reiterate my conclusion that it remains unproven that the author of 1 John 1.1–3 would have reacted against a saying similar to *Gos. Thom.* 17.[45] Suffice it to say that the two texts are not even mutually exclusive. The Johannine author who made a claim of having been an eyewitness of Jesus would not necessarily have denied the contention of *Gos. Thom.* 17 that Jesus gives his followers something that nobody has experienced before.

---

[44] Dunderberg, 'Thomas and the Beloved Disciple,' in this volume.
[45] Cf. Dunderberg, 'John and Thomas in Conflict?' 365–70.

2.3. Analyses of individual sayings

2.3.1. Jesus' incarnation (*Gos. Thom.* 28)

> Jesus said, 'I took my place in the midst of the world, and I appeared to them in flesh. ²I found all of them intoxicated; I found none of them thirsty. ³And my soul became afflicted for the sons of men, because they are blind in their hearts and do not have sight; for empty they came into the world, and empty too they seek to leave the world. ⁴But for the moment they are intoxicated. When they shake off their wine, then they will repent.'[46]

Gos. Thom. 28 is related to the Gospel of John not only with regard to Jesus' incarnation but also because it combines this issue with the theme of human ignorance. While expressions of the latter motif are different (intoxication in *Gos. Thom.* 28.2, 4; rejection in John 1.11), there are close Johannine parallels to *Gos. Thom.* 28.1. The sentence 'I took my place the midst of the world' is similar to the Baptist's statement about Jesus in John 1.26 ('but in the midst of you is standing one whom you do not know'), and the sentence 'I appeared to them in flesh' is similar to John 1.14 ('The Word became flesh').

A parallelism between John 1.26 and the beginning of *Gos. Thom.* 28.1 is even closer than it might initially seem. The verb ἵστημι and the expression ἐν μέσῳ occur in both John 1.26 and the Greek version of *Gos. Thom.* 28 (P. Oxy. 1.11–12). Moreover, as in *Gos. Thom.* 28.1, the phrase 'to stand in the midst of' in John 1.26 is used in connection with the notion of the hidden Messiah,[47] and it refers indirectly to Jesus' incarnation in the Johannine context also. In addition, in John 1.26 the sentence μέσος ὑμῶν ἕστηκεν ὃν ὑμεῖς οὐκ οἴδατε is most likely a Johannine expansion of a more traditional form of the Baptist's saying. It does not occur in parallel Synoptic traditions (Mark 1.7–8; Q 3.16) and is in accordance with the Johannine context of the saying (cf. John 1.10, 31).[48] If the sentence was created by a Johannine author, as it seems, there is a possibility that *Gos. Thom.* 28 could be dependent on John 1.26. Nevertheless, this possibility remains uncertain, since the phrase 'to stand in the midst of,' which connects *Gos.*

---

[46] Translation by T. O. Lambdin in Layton, ed., *Nag Hammadi Codex II,2–7*, 65.

[47] Cf. Quispel, 'Qumran, John and Jewish Christianity,' 145.

[48] Cf. I. Dunderberg, *Johannes und die Synoptiker: Studien zu Joh 1–9* (AASF DHL 69; Helsinki: The Finnish Academy of Science and Letters, 1994) 56; H. Fleddermann, 'John and the Coming One (Matt 3.11–12/Lk 3.16–17),' *SBLSP* 23 (1984) 377–84, esp. 384.

Thom. 28.1 and John 1.26 to each other, is not unique in early Christian literature (e.g. Luke 24.36; John 20.19).

Jesus' incarnation is expressed in different ways in John 1.14 and *Gos. Thom.* 28.1. John 1.14 speaks of the Word that *became* flesh (καὶ ὁ λόγος σὰρξ ἐγένετο), whereas according to *Gos. Thom.* 28.1 Jesus *appeared* in flesh (ⲁⲩⲱ ⲁⲉⲓⲟⲩⲱⲛ︥ ⲉⲃⲟⲗ ⲛⲁⲩ ⲍ︥ⲛ ⲥⲁⲣⲝ/καὶ ἐν σαρκ[ε]ὶ ὤφθην αὐτοῖς, P.Oxy. 1.13–14). Gärtner argues that the appearance terminology indicates that *Gos. Thom.* 28 speaks of the celestial Christ who inhabitated the earthly Jesus. In support of his view, Gärtner points out that in the New Testament ὤφθην is used of 'somebody or something that belongs to a sphere above the world' (Mark 9.4 pars; Luke 1.11; 22.43; 24.34; Acts 9.17; 13.31; 26.16; 1 Cor 15.5ff.). Thus, according to Gärtner, *Gos. Thom.* 28 expresses the view that Jesus assumed a human form which people were able to comprehend, but that this form was only an ostensible one.[49]

However, Gärtner's interpretation fails to account for the fact that in *Gos. Thom.* 28 Jesus' human form does *not* make him more under-standable for other human beings. The reasoning is rather that as Jesus took this form he noticed that all human beings were intoxicated. Neither the saying itself nor the *Gospel of Thomas* as a whole contains clear references to the distinction between the celestial Christ and the earthly Jesus. This distinction is, rather, adopted from other sources and read into the saying by Gärtner. The interpretation suggested by Gärtner is not an unlikely proposal with regard to such readers who otherwise presupposed such a distinction, but it does not prove that this understanding would correspond to the original intention of the saying. Finally, Gärtner's view that the expression ἐν σαρκ[ε]ὶ ὤφθην is 'impossible to the NT'[50] is problematic in light of 1 Tim 3.16 ('He was revealed in the flesh, vindicated in spirit, seen by angels,' NRSV). Admittedly, ὤφθη is in this verse used of Jesus' appearance to the angels, whereas ἐφανερώθη refers to his appearance in the flesh. However, there is hardly any clear difference between the meanings of the two verbs. Both of them denote Jesus' appearances, and they are

---

[49] B. Gärtner, *Ett nytt evangelium: Thomasevangeliets hemliga Jesusord* (Stockholm: Diakoni-styrelsens Bokförlag, 1960) 128–9; cf. J.-É. Ménard, *L'évangile selon Thomas* (NHS 5; Leiden: E. J. Brill, 1975) 123.

[50] Gärtner, *Ett nytt evangelium*, 128.

employed in a parallel manner in 1 Tim 3.16.[51] So it would be an exaggeration to maintain that the appearance terminology (ὤφθην) reflects a docetic Christology in Gos. Thom. 28.1, whereas ἐφανερώθη in 1 Tim 3.16 does not.

Within early Christian literature, there is a wide variety in expressing Jesus' incarnation.[52] Different expressions are used already in the Pauline writings. Paul himself affirms that God sent his Son 'in the likeness of sinful flesh' (ἐν ὁμοιώματι σαρκὸς ἁμαρτίας, Rom 8.3). In the deutero-Pauline epistles the flesh of Jesus is associated with his death on the cross (Col 1.22; Eph 2.14). This connection between Jesus' flesh and his suffering is held also by other early Christian authors (1 Pet 4.1,18; *Barn.* 5.1,12–13; 6.3; 7.5; Ignatius, *Smyrn.* 1.2). However, in a number of early Christian texts of later date Jesus' flesh denotes his earthly life in general (1 Tim 3.16; Heb 2.14; 5.7; *1 Clem.* 32.2; Ignatius, *Smyrn.* 1.1; *Eph.* 20.2; *Magn.* 13.2).[53]

John 1.14 and *Gos. Thom.* 28.1 apparently share the latter understanding of incarnation, for neither of them refers directly to Jesus' death. Still, there are significant differences in terminology between the two gospels which indicate that they are based on different traditions. *Gos. Thom.* 28.1 is related to those early Christian texts which speak of Jesus' appearance in the flesh (cf. 1 Tim 3.16; *Barn.* 5.6; 6.7–16). On the other hand, the closest terminological parallels for John 1.14 are found in Ignatius' writings (ἐν σαρκὶ γενόμενος θεός, *Eph.* 7.2), and in the *Second Epistle of Clement* (εἷς Χριστός ... ἐγένετο σάρξ, *2 Clem.* 9.5). In other Johannine writings the expression ἔρχεσθαι ἐν σαρκί can be used instead of the phrase σὰρξ γίνεσθαι (1 John 4.2; 2 John 7; cf. also Ignatius, *Pol.* 7.1; *Barn.* 5.10–11; *Gos. Truth* 31,4–5), but the appearance terminology is lacking in them.

Although there are traces of sapiental traditions both in John 1.14 and in *Gos. Thom.* 28, the details derived from these traditions are different in each gospel. John 1.14 is connected with the Jewish

[51] In the Sahidic New Testament, as Brown, 'Gospel of Thomas and St John's Gospel,' 165 n. 5, points out, both verbs are translated with the same verb ⲟⲩⲱⲛϩ̄ ⲉⲃⲟⲗ.

[52] To the following, cf. E. Schweizer, 'σάρξ κτλ. (E & F),' *TDNT* 7 (1978) 124–51. The term 'incarnation' is used in this context in a broad sense, meaning different ways of connecting 'flesh' and Jesus in early Christian writings.

[53] Schweizer, 'σάρξ', 137.

Wisdom myth by the remark that Jesus tabernacled (ἐσκήνωσεν) among human beings (cf. Sir 24.8; a similar adaptation of the Wisdom myth occurs also in *Barn.* 5.14). The appearance terminology employed in *Gos. Thom.* 28.1 (ὤφθην, **ΛΕΙΟΓⲰΝϨ**) hints at another Wisdom tradition, according to which Wisdom 'appeared upon earth and lived among men' (μετὰ τοῦτο ἐπὶ τῆς γῆς ὤφθη καὶ ἐν τοῖς ἀνθρώποις συνανεστράφη, 1 Bar 3.38).

In sum, neither *Gos. Thom.* 28.1 nor the traditions upon which it is based betray any direct contact with the Johannine literature. Davies's hypothesis that the *Gospel of Thomas* had its origins in the Johannine community, on the other hand, does not account for terminological variations and different uses of the Wisdom literature. Nevertheless, it can be argued that the views of Jesus' incarnation in *Gos. Thom.* 28.1 and John 1.14 hint at a similar, relatively late phase of early Christianity. This is indicated by the fact that the closest parallels to their understanding of the flesh of Jesus (as denoting his earthly life altogether) are found, not in the earliest writings of the New Testament, but in later writings such as the deutero-Pauline First Letter to Timothy, Hebrews, and the texts written by (or ascribed to) Clement of Rome and Ignatius of Antioch at the turn of the first century CE.

2.3.2. Equality with God (*Gos. Thom.* 61)

Jesus said, 'Two will rest on a bed: the one will die, and the other will live.'

[2]Salome said, 'Who are you, man, *as though you were from the One?* You have come up on my couch and eaten from my table.'

[3]Jesus said to her, 'I am the one who exists from the *one who is equal.* I was given some of the things of my father.'

[4]<...> 'I am your disciple.'

[5]<...> 'Therefore I say, if he is *equal* he will be filled with light, but if he is divided, he will be filled with darkness.'[54]

In *Gos. Thom.* 61.3 Jesus identifies himself as the one who exists from **ⲡⲉⲧϢⲎϢ**. The translation of this expression with 'the one who is equal' by Sell is preferable to 'the undivided' (Lambdin), or to 'what is

---

[54] Translation by Lambdin (with modifications in italics) in Layton, ed., *Nag Hammadi Codex II,2–7*, 75–7.

whole' (Meyer),[55] for the basic meaning of the verb ϣⲱϣ is 'to make equal, level, straight,'[56] and its stative form (ϣⲏϣ) is frequently used as a translation of a Greek expression ἴσος εἶναι, 'to be equal.'[57] Sell argues moreover that the term recalls the Johannine statement that Jesus made himself equal to God (John 5.18), and that the second part of Jesus' answer in *Gos. Thom.* 61.3 ('I was given some of the things of my father') reflects the subsequent discourse in John 5.19–23 in which Jesus depicts his relation to the Father.[58] These observations lead Sell to the conclusion that *Gos. Thom.* 61 reflects the composition of John 5.18 and 5.19–23, which with all likelihood should be ascribed to the Johannine author.

The credibility of this conclusion is, however, considerably weakened by other parallels to *Gos. Thom.* 61.3 which go unnoticed in Sell's analysis. Already in a pre-Pauline hymn 'equality with God' is connected with Christ (Phil 2.6–7). Moreover, John 5.19–23 does not provide any closer parallel to *Gos. Thom.* 61.3 than the 'Johannine Thunderbolt' in Q (Matt 11.27/Luke 10.22). The passive voice of *Gos. Thom.* 61.3, in fact, is similar to this passage[59] rather than to John 5.19–23, in which active forms are used in describing the Father's relationship to the Son (cf. also John 6.37; 17.24). All the specific Johannine features of John 5.19–23, such as apprentice imagery, the love relationship between Father and Son, and the promise of the raising of the dead, are missing in *Gos. Thom.* 61. Thus, literary dependence of this saying on John is unlikely.

Nevertheless, the common emphasis on 'equality' hints at a conceptual relationship between *Gos. Thom.* 61, John 5.18, and Phil 2.6. It is disputed whether Phil 2.6 should be understood in terms of Christ's pre-existence or of an 'Adam Christology.' In the former case 'equality with God' goes together with 'the form of God' and denotes Christ's divine status which he had earlier, whereas in the latter case the same

---

[55] Ibid., 75; M. Meyer, *The Gospel of Thomas: The Hidden Sayings of Jesus* (San Francisco: Harper, 1992) 47.

[56] Cf. W. E. Crum, *A Coptic Dictionary* (Oxford: Clarendon Press, 1939) 606; cf. A. Marjanen, *The Woman Jesus Loved: Mary Magdalene in the Nag Hammadi Library and Related Documents* (NHMS 40; Leiden: E. J. Brill, 1996) 41 n. 30, and his article 'Women Disciples in the *Gospel of Thomas*,' in this volume.

[57] Sell, 'Johannine Traditions,' 30.

[58] Ibid., 32.

[59] ⲁⲩϯ ⲛⲁⲉⲓ ⲉⲃⲟⲗ ϩⲛ ⲛⲁ ⲡⲁⲉⲓⲱⲧ (*Gos. Thom.* 61.3)/ πάντα μοι παρεδόθη ὑπὸ τοῦ πατρός μου (Q 10.22).

notion 'probably alludes to Adam's temptation'[60] (cf. Gen 3.5). Whichever is the right alternative here, in Phil 2.6 Christ as a *human being* did not possess equality with God: either he abandoned this equality before incarnation, or he did not have it to begin with. In each case Phil 2.6 is in contrast to John 5.18, which affirms Jesus' equality with God during his earthly life as well.[61]

It is more difficult to determine the position of *Gos. Thom.* 61 on this issue. Salome's question obviously raises the issue of Jesus' identity, but otherwise the expression ϩⲱⲥ ⲉⲃⲟⲗ ϩⲛ̄ ⲟⲩⲁ ('as though from one') is ambiguous. The sentence has called forth various emendations,[62] but the text is not necessarily corrupt. Harold W. Attridge has suggested that ⲟⲩⲁ is a translation of a Greek indefinite pronoun, which in this case would have been used for 'someone special.' Following this interpretation, the sentence should be translated 'as if you were from someone special.'[63] The possibility that ⲟⲩⲁ might refer to the primordial unity[64] is rejected by Attridge on grammatical grounds: 'If ⲟⲩⲁ is indeed a translation of a Greek ἑνός, used in this metaphysical sense, we would certainly not expect it to be anarthrous in either language.'[65]

---

[60] J. D. G. Dunn, *Christology in the Making: A New Testament Inquiry into the Origins of the Doctrine of Incarnation* (London: SCM Press, 1980) 115; for a similar view see e.g. C. H. Talbert, 'The Problem of Pre-existence in Philippians 2.6–11,' *JBL* 86 (1967) 141–53, esp. 151.

[61] Cf. W. A. Meeks, 'Equal to God,' in R. T. Fortna and B. R. Gaventa, eds., *The Conversation Continues: Studies in Paul and John in Honor of J. Louis Martyn* (Nashville: Abingdon Press, 1990) 309–21, esp. 309.

[62] In the *editio princeps* it is assumed that the Greek original was ὡς ἐκ τίνος ('as from whom') which was read by the translator as ὡς ἐκ τινός ('as from somebody'). This assumption results in a translation 'and (ὡς) whose (son)?' Cf. A. Guillaumont et al., eds., *The Gospel According to Thomas : The Coptic Text Established and Translated* (Leiden: E. J. Brill; New York: Harper & Row, 1959) 35. Bentley Layton's translation ('like a stranger [?]') follows Polotsky's suggestion that the original was ὡς ξένος, understood by the ancient translator as ὡς ἐξ ἑνός; cf. B. Layton, *The Gnostic Scriptures* (Garden City: Doubleday, 1987) 391.

[63] H. W. Attridge, 'Greek Equivalents of Two Coptic Phrases: CG I,1.65,9–10 and CG II,2.43.26,' *BASP* 18 (1981) 27–32, esp. 31–2. His suggestion is taken up by Meyer, *Gospel of Thomas*, 47.

[64] This understanding is reflected by Lambdin's translation 'as though from the One' in J. M. Robinson, ed., *The Nag Hammadi Library in English* (Leiden: E. J. Brill, 1977) 124–5. In the third edition of the same book Lambdin has abandoned this translation; cf. J. M. Robinson, ed., *The Nag Hammadi Library in English* (3rd ed.; Leiden: E. J. Brill, 1988) 133. In the apparatus of Lambdin's translation in *Nag Hammadi Codex II,2–7* the text of *Gos. Thom.* 61 is considered to be erroneous at this point.

[65] Attridge, 'Greek Equivalents', 31.

This argument is, however, not incontestable. For *Exc. Theod.* 36.1, which maintains that the *angels* were created in Unity and are one, 'as though they came forth from One,' also attests an anarthrous use of εἷς (ὡς ἀπὸ ἑνὸς προελθόντες). In addition, *Exc. Theod.* 36.1 provides a formal parallel for the ambiguous phrase ϩⲱⲥ ⲉⲃⲟⲗ ϩⲛ ⲟⲩⲁ in *Gos. Thom.* 61.2, and bears witness to the view that divine beings were regarded as originating from the One. It would be too daring to suggest on account of these similarities that Salome with her question in *Gos. Thom.* 61.2 identifies Jesus with an angel (as Peter does in *Gos. Thom.* 13). Nevertheless, it is perhaps not too far-fetched to assume that Salome's ambiguous question in any case refers to Jesus' *divine origin* ('as though you were from the One').

Moreover, it is significant that in the immediate context of *Exc. Theod.* 36.1 the primordial unity is played off against a division among human beings. In the same context, an expectation of becoming 'one' also comes to expression (ἵνα ἡμεῖς οἱ πολλοὶ ἓν γενόμενοι, *Exc. Theod.* 36.2). As for *Gos. Thom.* 61, a similar notion is provided by its wider context. For Salome's question whether Jesus stems 'from the One' associates this saying with those sayings which display an ideal of 'becoming one' as the ultimate goal (*Gos. Thom.* 4; 11; 22–23; 106). Hence, as regards the primordial unity, the views of those Valentinian Christians to whom Clement refers in *Exc. Theod.* 36 coincide with those expressed in the *Gospel of Thomas.*[66] The theme of unity is also an important aspect of the eschatological expectation elsewhere in the *Excerpta ex Theodoto.* A separate study would be necessary in order to clarify the relationship between the two documents with regard to this issue.[67] Suffice it to say that it is unlikely that the *Gospel of Thomas* derived its ideal of unity from Valentinian Christians. For all the characteristically Valentinian features of the *Excerpta*, such as a threefold division between 'earthly,' 'psychic,'

---

[66] For the motif of 'becoming one,' see Uro, 'Is *Thomas* an Encratite Gospel?' in this volume.

[67] This necessity emerges in part from the fact that the *Exc. Theod.* consists of disconnected teachings of various persons, so it is not always clear whose opinion Clement presents. In addition, scholars disagree with regard to the interpretation of the 'final unity' in the document: does *Exc. Theod.* 63.1–2 speak of an ultimate equalization of 'pneumatics' and 'psychics' (thus E. H. Pagels, 'Conflicting Versions of Valentinian Eschatology: Irenaeus' Treatise vs. the Excerpts from Theodotus,' *HTR* 67 [1974] 35–53, esp. 44–6, or is their unification only temporary before the pneumatics proceed to the ultimate stage? (thus J. F. McCue, 'Conflicting Versions of Valentinianism? Irenaeus and the *Excerpta ex Theodoto*,' in B. Layton, ed., *The Rediscovery of Gnosticism,* vol. 2: *Sethian Gnosticism* [Studies in the History of Religions 41; Leiden: E. J. Brill, 1981] 404–16).

and 'pneumatic' natures (e.g. *Exc. Theod.* 54–56) as well as the references to the Pleroma and the Ogdoad (e.g. *Exc. Theod.* 26; 34–35; 63.2), are absent in the *Gospel of Thomas*.

In *Gos. Thom.* 61, Jesus' answer to Salome (61.3) corresponds to her question. The answer begins with an identification (**ⲁⲛⲟⲕ ⲡⲉ**) and repeats the prepositional phrase employed in the question (**ⲉⲃⲟⲗ ϩⲛ̄**). Parallels from the Sahidic New Testament suggest that behind the phrase **ϣⲱⲡⲉ ⲉⲃⲟⲗ ϩⲛ̄** is a Greek expression εἶναι ἔκ τινος (cf. John 1.46; 3.31; 18.37). Sahidic translations of John 3.31 and 18.37 testify, moreover, that a substantivized sentence **ⲡⲉⲧϣⲟⲟⲡ ⲉⲃⲟⲗ ϩⲛ̄** is used for rendering a Greek participle sentence ὁ ὢν ἐκ κτλ.[68] Hence it is possible to conjecture that the Greek original of Jesus' answer to Salome began with the words ἐγώ εἰμι ὁ ὢν ἐκ κτλ. This reconstructed Greek form indicates that Jesus identifies himself in terms of his *origin*, for this is a common usage of the phrase εἶναι ἔκ τινος.[69]

In *Gos. Thom.* 61.3 the origin of Jesus is defined by an expression which, as was argued earlier, denotes 'the one who is equal' (**ⲡⲉⲧϣⲏϣ**). The absolute use of this expression is somewhat obscure. Equal to whom? Both Phil 2.6 and John 5.18 speak of equality with God, but, within the symbolic universe of the *Gospel of Thomas*, this possibility would render the logic of *Gos. Thom.* 61 unnecessarily complicated: Jesus would come from someone who is equal to God. Irenaeus' account of the Valentinian system certainly includes the notion of the equality of the aeons (*Adv. haer.* 1.2.6),[70] but this provides us only with a very remote parallel to *Gos. Thom.* 61, since the *Gospel of Thomas* does not elaborate any theory concerning the pleromatic aeons. A closer Valentinian parallel is therefore provided by *Tri. Trac.* 67.36–37, in which 'equality' appears as an aspect of the

68 John 3.31: ὁ ὢν ἐκ τῆς γῆς = **ⲡⲉⲧϣⲟⲟⲡ ⲉⲃⲟⲗ ϩⲙ̄ ⲡⲕⲁϩ**; John 18.37: πᾶς ὁ ὢν ἐκ τῆς ἀληθείας = **ⲟⲩⲟⲛ ⲛⲓⲙ ⲉⲧϣⲟⲟⲡ ⲉⲃⲟⲗ ϩⲛ̄ ⲧⲙⲉ**.

69 See H. G. Liddell and R. Scott, *A Greek-English Lexicon* (9th ed.; Oxford: Clarendon Press, 1940) 488; W. Bauer, *Griechisch-deutsches Wörterbuch* (6th, completely rev. edition, ed. by K. Aland and B. Aland; Berlin: Walter de Gruyter, 1988) 454.

70 Cf. Ménard, *L'Évangile selon Thomas*, 162. Menard also considers *Gos. Truth* 25.8 to be a parallel to *Gos. Thom.* 61, but the verb **ϣⲱϣ** is in this passage used with another meaning, that of 'scattering'; cf. H. Attridge and G. W. MacRae, 'The Gospel of Truth,' *Nag Hammadi Codex I (The Jung Codex)* (2 vols.; NHS 22–23; Leiden: E. J. Brill, 1985) 1.55–117; 2.39–135, esp. 1.95.

Father which he did not reveal 'to those who had come forth from him.'

The conviction that the divine realm is characterized by equality comes to expression also outside of Valentinian thought. The absolute expression 'the one who is equal' in *Gos. Thom.* 61 could be understood in terms of Philo's statement that God is equal and similar only to himself (*Aet. Mund.* 43; *Sacr. Ac.* 10). Moreover, Philo regards equality with God as impossible for human beings: the mind that considers itself equal to God is 'selfish and ungodly' (*Leg. all.* 1.49; cf. 2 Macc 2.9),[71] and even Abraham became equal only to the angels after his death (*Sacr. Ac.* 5).

Yet the absolute use of 'equality' in the *Gospel of Thomas* more likely hints at a later development in which equality has become more clearly an aspect of the divine realm in general. This view is evident not only in *Tri. Trac.* 67.36–37 but also in *Exc. Theod.* 10.3. In the latter passage, Clement expresses his own view of seven leading angels whose works express 'unity, equality (ἰσότητα) and similarity.'[72] Although the *Gospel of Thomas* hardly shares Clement's angelology, the absolute use of ⲡⲉⲧϣⲏϣ in *Gos. Thom.* 61 hints at a similar association of equality with the divine world. Thus it is arguable that the saying speaks of Jesus' divine origin and underscores his equality either with God or, in more general terms, with the divine realm. This sense granted, *Gos. Thom.* 61.3 is conceptually in full accordance with John 5.18.

As for the latter part of Jesus' second answer to Salome (61.5), it is conceivable that ⲉϥϣⲏϥ ('destroyed') should be emended to ⲉϥϣⲏϣ ('equal').[73] This part of the saying is contrasted with the sentence 'if he is divided,' and it is more likely that the contrast is

---

[71] Cf. G. Stählin, 'ἴσος κτλ.,' *TDNT* 3 (1977) 343–55, esp. 351–2; Meeks, 'Equal to God,' 312.

[72] For the attribution of this passage to Clement, see R. P. Casey, 'Introduction,' in R. P. Casey, ed., *The Excerpta ex Theodoto of Clement of Alexandria* (SD 1; London: Christophers, 1934) 3–38, esp. 30–3.

[73] This emendation is usually accepted; see e.g. Guillaumont et al., eds., *The Gospel According to Thomas*; Layton's text edition (and his own translation in idem, *Gnostic Scriptures*, 391), Meyer, *Gospel of Thomas*, and Marjanen, *The Woman Jesus Loved* 41 n. 30; 'Women Disciples in the *Gospel of Thomas* in this volume. To be sure, Lambdin prefers ⲉϥϣⲏϥ in his translation ('if he is *destroyed* ').

between equality and division than that it would be between destruction and division.[74] If this emendation is accepted, *Gos. Thom.* 61.5 presents two possibilities to the audience: either one is equal and will be filled with light, or one is divided and will be filled with darkness. There is a slight difference between this saying and *Gos. Thom.* 24 in the use of the concepts of light and darkness: while *Gos. Thom.* 61 connects both with *future* events, *Gos. Thom.* 24 maintains that 'a man of light' has light already but is in danger of being darkness unless he shines. Nevertheless, the function of the two sayings is most likely similar. The qualification made in *Gos. Thom.* 24 indicates that the saying should be understood as an admonition addressed to the audience of the gospel: those who have the light are obliged to shine; otherwise they might lose their light. A similar, parenetic function can be seen in *Gos. Thom.* 61.5, since the saying does not distinguish between two ontic categories of human beings, but speaks of an individual to whom both possibilities are open: he or she *can* be either 'equal' or 'divided.'

Neither 'equality' nor 'division' belong to the recurring themes of the *Gospel of Thomas*. 'Equality' is mentioned only in *Gos. Thom.* 61, and 'division' is mentioned, in addition to this saying, only in *Gos. Thom.* 72. Nevertheless, the pairing of equality with division can be associated with two more relevant issues. First, a state of being divided can be contrasted not only with 'equality' but also with an ideal of unity which is of crucial importance in the *Gospel of Thomas*. Second, since *Gos. Thom.* 61 applies 'equality' also to individuals other than Jesus, it seems that the saying expresses a view similar to *Gos. Thom.* 13 and 108: Jesus, coming from 'the one who is equal,' is related to an individual who has a possibility of being 'equal,' i.e. of participating in the divine realm.

In this second respect the *Gospel of Thomas* differs clearly from the Gospel of John, which speaks of equality with God only in connection with Jesus. John 10.34–36 certainly includes a quotation from Ps 22.27 ('you are gods'), but a definition follows at once that by 'gods' are meant those to whom the word of God was addressed. Moreover, John 10.34–36 consists of an argumentation *minore ad maiorem*, the

---

[74] In fact, *Paraph. Shem* 39.23–26 attests a similar contrast between equality and division by associating the division of the clouds (ⲡⲧⲱϣⲉ ⲛ̄ ⲕⲗⲟⲟⲗⲉ; cf. *Gos. Thom.* 61: ⲉϥⲡⲏϣ) with a notice that they are 'not equal' (ⲥⲉϣⲏϣ ⲁⲛ).

real aim of which is to show that Jesus as God's envoy is authorized to call himself the Son of God. The unity between Father and Son is presented as paradigmatic for believers in John 17.11, 23–24, but only as a model for their mutual unity. John 15.15 might betray a tendency similar to *Gos. Thom.* 61 by calling the disciples 'friends' instead of 'servants,' but even here Jesus' relationship to his followers is not defined in terms of equality but of revelation, just as in John 10.35: the disciples are Jesus' friends, for they are recipients of his message.

2.3.3. The temple saying (*Gos. Thom.* 71)

Jesus said, 'I shall [destroy this] house, and no one will be able to build it [...]'[75]

In both *Gos. Thom.* 71 and John 2.19 the temple saying is attributed to Jesus himself, whereas the Synoptic tradition ascribes it to false witnesses (Mark 14.57–58; Matt 26.60–61; Acts 6.13–14).[76] In the Gospel of John the saying is associated with the resurrection of Jesus' body (John 2.21–22). Many scholars hold that the same association is implied by *Gos. Thom.* 71. Gärtner assumes that the 'house' mentioned in the saying is a metaphor for Jesus' body, and concludes that the saying is a Gnostic polemic against the resurrection of Jesus' body.[77] Gärtner's view is adopted by Gaston as far as 'the Gnostic editor' of the text is concerned; for this editor, the saying 'is a polemic against the concept of bodily resurrection.'[78] Nevertheless, Gaston argues that originally the temple was intended by the reference to the 'house.' The saying then 'goes back to a tradition which knew the temple saying only in the sense of destruction.'[79] Gärtner's interpretation is a point of departure also for Riley, according to whom different views of Jesus' body are expressed in *Gos. Thom.* 71 and John 2.19–22, indicating that the communities behind these texts 'are here in debate, each employing the saying in similar, but opposing ways, distinct from the uses of the other gospel writers; they are responding to each other.'[80]

---

[75] Lambdin's translation in Layton, ed., *Nag Hammadi Codex II,2–7*, 81.

[76] For these versions of the saying and its original meaning, cf. Riley, *Resurrection Reconsidered*, 134–46.

[77] Gärtner, *Ett nytt evangelium*, 158.

[78] L. Gaston, *No Stone on Another: Studies in the Significance of the Fall of Jerusalem in the Synoptic Gospels* (NovTSup 23; Leiden: E. J. Brill, 1970) 152.

[79] Ibid.

[80] Riley, *Resurrection Reconsidered*, 156.

Gärtner's interpretation of the saying is based on the presupposition that the *Gospel of Thomas* is a distinctively Gnostic text. Gärtner's definition of Gnosticism, however, is vague, for it includes practically everything that was different from 'the main traditions of the Great Church.'[81] The second presupposition is that the author of *Gos. Thom.* 71 knew not only the temple saying in the Johannine form (John 2.19) but also its Johannine interpretation (John 2.21–22) which associates the saying with the resurrection of Jesus' body. Only this presupposition enables Gärtner to combine *Gos. Thom.* 71 with the question of the destruction of body, for the saying itself does not speak of Jesus' body at all. Riley's approach is certainly methodologically sounder than that of Gärtner, for he seeks evidence for a view that the 'house' denotes body elsewhere in *Gospel of Thomas*. However, the evidence based on *Gos. Thom.* 21, 48, and 98 is ambiguous, for the association of the 'house' with the body results in each case from allegorical interpretations of these sayings rather than from their exact wording.[82]

Since *Gos. Thom.* 71 speaks of the destruction of the 'house' as Jesus' own action, the saying is closer to the Synoptic tradition than to the Johannine, in which Jesus demands that the Jews destroy the temple (λύσατε τὸν ναὸν τοῦτον). The Johannine form of the saying is most likely due to a subsequent interpretation which connects the saying with Jesus' body.[83] The imperative λύσατε refers in this context to the role the Johannine Jews later assume in killing Jesus.

The fact that there are no traces of this distinctively Johannine feature of the temple saying in *Gos. Thom.* 71 speaks against Gärtner's contention that the saying should be interpreted in light of John 2.19–22. Moreover, as Gaston has noted, it is not entirely unlikely that *Gos. Thom.* 71 refers to the destruction of the temple. It goes without saying that the temple *can* be called a 'house' (e.g. Mark 11.17/Matt

---

81 Gärtner, *Ett nytt evangelium* 9; 'the Great Church' (*den stora kyrkan*) has been omitted in the English translation of Gärtner's book: *The Theology of the Gospel of Thomas* (trans. E. J. Sharpe; London: Collins, 1961) 12.

82 As for *Gos. Thom.* 98, Riley suggests that 'the sword is the (ascetic) will and power of the individual soul, which is tested against the "house" of body'; in *Gos. Thom.* 48 'the "house" is the body in which the soul and heavenly counterpart are to be united,' and 'to you' in *Gos. Thom.* 21 refers to 'individuals, pictured as souls indwelling their bodies' (Riley, *Resurrection Reconsidered*, 152–3). For a similar criticism of Riley's interpretation of *Gos. Thom.* 71, see now S. Davies's review of Riley's book in *JBL* 116 (1997) 147–8.

83 Cf. Gaston, *No Stone on Another*, 71; E. P. Sanders, *Jesus and Judaism* (2nd ed.; London: SCM Press, 1987) 73.

21.13/Luke 19.46 [= Isa 56.7]; John 2.16–17). The non-apocalyptic tone of the *Gospel of Thomas* does not exclude this possibility.[84] For if there were, as seems likely, Christians whose eschatological hopes were connected with the destruction of the temple,[85] the sentence 'no one will rebuild it' can be understood in terms of an anti-eschatological polemic that comes to expression also in *Gos. Thom.* 3 and 113. Moreover, if *Gos. Thom.* 71 refers to the temple and its destruction, it would be in accordance with the anti-Jewish bias of the gospel. Thomasine Christians might have had their reasons, either religious or political, to welcome the destruction of the temple, but it is also not surprising that they did not link any eschatological hopes with this event.[86]

In conclusion, it is by no means certain that *Gos. Thom.* 71 indicates a conflict between Thomasine and Johannine Christians concerning the resurrection of the body. It is possible that both *Gos. Thom.* 71 and John 2.19–22 reflect vanishing eschatological hopes in connection with the destruction of the temple, the former by its anti-eschatological interpretation ('no one will rebuild it'), the latter through an allegorizing understanding of the temple saying (the temple = Jesus' body). Such interpretations are best explicable in a post-Jewish War context. Therefore it is highly improbable that *Gos. Thom.* 71 represents the original form of the temple saying.[87]

2.3.4. 'I am the light' (*Gos. Thom.* 77)

Jesus said, 'It is I who am the light which is above them all. It is I who am the all. From me did the all come forth, and unto me did the all extend. [2]Split a piece of wood, and I am there. [3]Lift up the stone, and you will find me there.'[88]

Both in *Gos. Thom.* 77.1 and in John (8.12; 9.5) Jesus identifies himself

---

[84] Thus, however, Riley, *Resurrection Reconsidered*, 151.

[85] Matti Myllykoski argues convincingly that the temple saying was originally circulated by Christians who thought that Jesus would return immediately after the destruction of the temple, and that Mark reacts against this view by ascribing it to false witnesses; cf. *Die letzten Tage Jesu: Markus, Johannes, ihre Traditionen und die historische Frage* (2 vols.; AASF, Ser. B 256, 272; Helsinki: The Finnish Academy of Science and Letters, 1991, 1994) 1.53–7, 119–21; 2.183.

[86] Cf. Patterson, *Gospel of Thomas*, 149–50.

[87] Pace J. D. Crossan, *The Historical Jesus: The Life of a Mediterranean Jewish Peasant* (San Francisco: Harper & Row, 1991) 356.

[88] Translation by Lambdin in Layton, ed., *Nag Hammadi Codex II,2–7*, 83.

with 'light.' As noted already, each gospel also attests a light-darkness dualism (John 1.5; 3.19; *Gos. Thom.* 24; 61) and speaks of lighting up the world by the light (John 1.9; *Gos. Thom.* 24). Otherwise light imagery is used differently in the two gospels. In the Gospel of John light is closely connected with Jesus' earthly existence (1.9; 3.19; 9.5; 12.46) and with believing in him (12.36, 46). Moreover, light imagery is connected with a certain way of life, either with good or bad actions (3.20–21) or with walking in light or darkness (8.12; 11.9–10; 12.35). In the *Gospel of Thomas*, on the other hand, light denotes a sphere whence believers have come and to which they will return (*Gos. Thom.* 11; 50). In addition, light can be found inside of human beings, yet in this case there is also a possibility of being 'in' or 'filled with' darkness (*Gos. Thom.* 24; 61). The use of light imagery indicates, therefore, no particular relationship between the two gospels. As for their few coincidences, it is not exceptional that divine figures identify themselves with light (e.g. CH 1.6), nor is a light-darkness dualism shared only by these two gospels; it comes to expression also in writings of the Qumran community (e.g. 1QS 3.20–21) and in Pauline and deutero-Pauline letters (1 Thess 5.5; 2 Cor 6.14; Eph 5.8–14).

It is a controversial issue whether or not *Gos. Thom.* 77.1 attributes to Jesus an agency in the creation of the world. In this saying Jesus speaks of himself as the originator and goal of 'the all' (ⲡⲧⲏⲣϥ), but it is not clear whether 'the all' refers to believers (and thus to their divine origin, as in *Gos. Thom.* 50) or to the visible world.[89] The latter view is at least possible in light of 1 Cor 8.6, in which τὰ πάντα, translated in the Sahidic New Testament with a singular form ⲡⲧⲏⲣϥ (likewise in Rom 11.36), without doubt refers to the world. If *Gos. Thom.* 77.1 refers to the creation of the world, its content would coincide with John 1.3, 10, but even in this case a lack of close verbal parallels does not suggest a literary relationship between the gospels. If the two gospels indeed share a similar view on Jesus' role in the creation, this can be explained as due to independent Christian adaptations of Jewish Wisdom traditions that assigned Wisdom a similar task (Prov 3.19; Wisd 8.6; Philo, *Det. pot. ins.* 54; *Fug.* 109).[90]

Moreover, the closest New Testament parallels to *Gos. Thom.* 77.1

---

[89] On the interpretation of this part of *Gos. Thom.* 77, see Marjanen, 'Is *Thomas* a Gnostic Gospel?' in this volume.
[90] Cf. Dunn, *Christology in the Making*, 165.

are found not in John but in the Pauline corpus. Jesus' self-identification is reminiscent of hymnic statements in 1 Cor 8.6, Rom 11.36 and Col 1.16.[91] Within these statements there is some variation. In 1 Cor 8.6 *God* is regarded both as the originator and as the goal of the all, and Christ as the mediator, whereas all three aspects are associated with God in Rom 11.36, and Col 1.16 presents Christ both as the mediator and as the goal. Differently from all these passages, *Gos. Thom.* 77.1 identifies Jesus as the originator and does not mention the mediator at all. Hence its Wisdom Christology is hardly derived directly from Paul or his successors. Nevertheless, only this saying and Col 1.16 portray Jesus (or Christ) as the *goal* of the all. This might indicate that *Gos. Thom.* 77 is related to a deutero-Pauline development of Wisdom Christology. To be sure, this possibility cannot be proposed with certainty. Although Colossians is most likely a post-Pauline letter, the hymnic section to which Col 1.16 belongs might harbor traditions that are significantly older than the letter itself. It is suggestive, however, that in the letters that are certainly Pauline, an identification of Jesus as the goal of everything is absent.

In sum, the similarities between *Gos. Thom.* 77.1 and John are more likely due to their common background in Wisdom Christology than to a literary relationship. There is, moreover, a significant conceptual difference with regard to Jesus' role. For by using the preposition διά John identifies Jesus as the mediator of creation, as do also 1 Cor 8.6 and Col 1.16. This nuance does not appear in *Gos. Thom.* 77.1.

2.3.5. Other parallels (*Gos. Thom.* 23, 43, and 104)

The theme of election links *Gos. Thom.* 23 with the Gospel of John.[92] Yet this theme alone is not sufficient for further conclusions, for the view that the disciples are elected by Jesus occurs also elsewhere (e.g. Luke 6.13; *Barn.* 5.9), and Eph 1.4 attests to the view that the Christian community was elected already before the foundation of the world. Again, nothing suggests a closer mutual relationship between *Gos. Thom.* 23 and John. In John, election is accompanied by two other

---

[91] A Stoic parallel to these statements is provided by Marcus Aurelius Antoninus, *Meditations*, 4.23 (ἐκ σοῦ τὰ πάντα, ἐν σοὶ τὰ πάντα, εἰς σὲ πάντα); cf. C. H. Dodd, *The Interpretation of the Fourth Gospel* (Cambridge: Cambridge University Press, 1960) 188; B. Reicke, 'πᾶς (B.3–4),' *TDNT* 5 (1967) 892–3.

[92] Cf. Brown, 'The Gospel of Thomas and St John's Gospel,' 164.

features that do not occur in *Gos. Thom.* 23. First, it is attached to the sections in which Jesus speaks of a traitor among the disciples (John 6.70; 13.18). Second, the election of the disciples is connected with the opposition of the world (John 15.16, 19).[93] In *Gos. Thom.* 23, on the other hand, election is understood as a future event ('I shall choose') and associated with the ideal of becoming one. Moreover, the saying affirms that the number of the elect will be restricted. With regard to this notion, the parallel provided by Matt 22.14 is significantly closer to *Gos. Thom.* 23 than anything in John.[94] In conclusion, *Gos. Thom.* 23 and the Gospel of John are representatives of different traditions.

The closest Johannine parallel to *Gos. Thom.* 43 is John 8.25, which not only contains the question of Jesus' identity (σὺ τίς εἶ) but also ascribes this question to the Jews. As the disciples pose a similar question to Jesus in *Gos. Thom.* 43, he answers that they 'have become like the Jews.' The fact that this association occurs in the *Gospel of Thomas* makes it difficult to accept Koester's view on the sayings traditions behind John 8.12–59. According to him, the author of this section compiled traditional sayings of Jesus, attested by parallels from the Nag Hammadi writings including the *Gospel of Thomas*, and another source which related Jesus' controversy with the Jews; this source is attested by *Papyrus Egerton 2*.[95] The real difficulty in Koester's theory is the position of *Gos. Thom.* 43. One would expect that 'the Jews' would not be mentioned in those pre-Johannine traditions which the *Gospel of Thomas* allegedly represents, but in the tradition including Jesus' controversy with the Jews. If Koester's theory were a starting

---

[93] Cf. G. Schrenk, 'ἐκλέγομαι (C–E),' *TDNT* 4 (1967) 168–76, esp. 172–4.

[94] Cf. Ménard, *L'évangile selon Thomas*, 116.

[95] Koester, 'Gnostic Sayings,' 106. To be sure, the value of *Papyrus Egerton 2* as a witness to the pre-Johannine tradition is debated. The possibility of a late dating of the papyrus (150–200 CE) is increased by a recent identification of P. Köln 255 as a part of it; cf. M. Gronewald, 'Unbekanntes Evangelium oder Evangelienharmonie (Fragment aus dem "Evangelium Egerton"),' *Kölner Papyri 6* (1987) 136–7; D. Lührmann, 'Das neue Fragment des PEgerton (PKöln 255),' in F. Van Segbroeck, C. M. Tuckett, G. Van Belle and J. Verheyden, eds., *The Four Gospels: Festschrift Frans Neirynck* (BETL 100; Leuven: Leuven University Press/Peeters, 1992) 2239–55, esp. 2246–7; F. Neirynck, 'The Apocryphal Gospels and the Gospel of Mark,' in F. Neirynck, ed., *Evangelica II: 1982–1991* (BETL 99; Leuven: Leuven University Press/Peeters, 1991) 715–22, esp. 754. Nevertheless, it may well be that the papyrus still incorporates earlier Jewish-Christian traditions which are independent of John; cf. K. Erlemann, 'Papyrus Egerton 2: "Missing Link" zwischen synoptischer und johanneischer Tradition,' *NTS* 42 (1996) 12–34.

point, it would be easy to argue that the mention of the Jews in *Gos. Thom.* 43 reflects the *Johannine* composition of John 8.12–59.

Baarda's suggestion that *Gos. Thom.* 42 and 43 together provide a close parallel to the narrative sequence of John 8.30–48 could add strength to the hypothesis that the *Gospel of Thomas* is at this point dependent on John. Baarda's view, however, presupposes his particular interpretation of *Gos. Thom.* 42 that the 'passers-by' mentioned in this saying should be understood as 'Hebrews,' and that the saying should be read together with the subsequent saying. In *Gos. Thom.* 42, in Baarda's opinion, Jesus calls his audience to be 'Hebrews,' which, in turn, raises among the audience the question of Jesus' authority to make such a demand, and leads finally to Jesus' comment that his listeners have become like the Jews.[96]

Baarda insists correctly that *Gos. Thom.* 43 refers to something that has been said previously, yet it is not quite certain that reference is made to the previous saying. The plural form employed in *Gos. Thom.* 43 (ⲉⲕϫⲱ ⲛ̄ⲛⲁⲓ ... ⲛⲁⲛ, 'to say *these things* to us') indicates that the saying refers not only, nor even primarily, to *Gos. Thom.* 42; rather, the reference is made to Jesus' sayings in general. Moreover, the linkage to the Johannine context remains vague, for *Gos. Thom.* 43 implies an audience that does not consist of 'Jews,' as in John 8.30–48, but of those who are in danger of becoming like them.

At face value, the affinities between John 8.25 and *Gos. Thom.* 43 hardly admit of any firm conclusions. The polemical association of the Jews with misunderstandings does not indicate a literary relationship between the two gospels, for this feature is in accordance with the negative view on Judaism which is evident in both gospels. As for the question of Jesus' identity ('Who are you?'), it can also be used in the *Gospel of Thomas* independently from the Gospel of John (*Gos. Thom.* 61).

Both *Gos. Thom.* 104 and John 8.46 assert that Jesus is sinless. Yet here, also, the narrative contexts are too different to suggest a literary relationship. *Gos. Thom.* 104 contains Jesus' reply to those who ask him to pray and fast: 'What is the sin I have committed, or wherein have I been defeated?' John 8.46, on the other hand, belongs to a section in

---

[96] T. Baarda, ' "Jesus said: Be Passers-by": On the Meaning and Origin of Logion 42 of the Gospel of Thomas,' in T. Baarda, *Early Transmission of Words of Jesus: Thomas, Tatian and the Text of the New Testament* (Amsterdam: VU, 1983) 179–205, esp. 196–7.

which Jesus blames his Jewish opponents for not having believed in him.

Jesus' sinlessness is by no means a theme that is restricted to these writings. It comes to expression explicitly in Hebrews 4.15,[97] and it is most likely reflected also in Matthew's account of Jesus' baptism, in which John the Baptist first refuses to baptize Jesus with the baptism of repentance, and finally consents only in order to 'fulfill all righteousness' (Matt 3.14–15). A fragment of the *Gospel of the Nazoreans* is apparently involved in the same 'apologetic process'[98] as Matt 3.14–15, but it takes it one step further by maintaining that, as his mother and brothers were going to be baptized by John the Baptist, Jesus refused to join them because he was not in need of a baptism 'unto the remission of sins' (*Gos. Naz.* 2).[99] In consequence, there is no certain indication of a literary relationship between *Gos. Thom.* 104 and John 8.46, but it seems, again, that their conceptual affinity hints at a later development within early Christian thought.

2.4. Conclusion

The analyses of the I-sayings of the *Gospel of Thomas* and their relationship to John yield a twofold result. First, no certain indicators of a literary dependence between the two gospels could be found, and neither did these materials suggest that the communities behind these texts had dealings with each other. The latter possibility is unlikely, above all, on account of the distinct ways of using similar Christian traditions and adapting Jewish Wisdom traditions in each document. Differences in this respect do not favor any of the views presupposing a closer contact between the *Gospel of Thomas* and the Johannine writings, be the presupposition either that the former was used in the Johannine community at an early stage, or that the communities behind these texts were engaged in a reciprocal controversy.

Second, regardless of the fact that there were no certain signs of a

---

[97] Cf. Brown, *The Gospel According to John:* 1.358.

[98] Crossan, *The Historical Jesus*, 233.

[99] This fragment provides, in fact, the closest parallel to *Gos. Thom.* 104. Each passage is an apophthegm in which Jesus is required by someone to partake in an action of cultic relevance, and Jesus declines to do so by posing a rhetorical question that affirms his sinlessness.

mutual relationship between these documents, a number of conceptual affinities indicated that the *Gospel of Thomas* and the Gospel of John are to be located within a similar context of early Christianity. In this direction point, above all, the following three observations: (1) Both John and the *Gospel of Thomas* share an emphasis found also in 1 Timothy, Hebrews, and the Apostolic Fathers that Jesus' *flesh* denotes not only his suffering and death but his earthly life generally. (2) Although the versions of the *Temple saying* are different in the two gospels, the interpretations of the saying hint in each case at a post-Jewish War setting. (3) That *Jesus was sinless* is affirmed explicitly, not only by *Gos. Thom.* 104 and John 8.46, but also by Heb 4.15 and *Gos. Naz.* 2, and the same tendency is most likely also reflected in Matthew's redaction of the story of Jesus' baptism (Matt 3.14–15).

In the cases of *Gos. Thom.* 61 and 77 the same conclusion could not be drawn with a certitude similar to that in the examples mentioned above. As regards the former saying, 'equality with God' is mentioned already in Phil 2.6. If this latter verse is to be understood in terms of Adam Christology, its content is different from *Gos. Thom.* 61, which associates the phrase 'the one who is equal' with Jesus' origin. If Phil 2.6, nevertheless, speaks of Christ's pre-existence, the difference between the two passages is no longer significant. In any case, the absolute use of the phrase 'the one who is equal,' which makes *Gos. Thom.* 61 different both from Phil 2.6 and from John 5.18, possibly refers to a later development within early Christian thought, for this feature remains unparalleled until the latter half of the second century CE. As for *Gos. Thom.* 77, it is not entirely clear whether the saying speaks of Jesus' agency in the creation. In any case, the notion that Jesus is the *goal* of all connects the saying with a possibly deutero-Pauline view visible in Col 1.16.

In conclusion, the coincidences between the Gospel of John and the I-sayings of the *Gospel of Thomas* do not betray any especially intimate relationship between these writings or the communities behind them, and neither do their similarities go back to the oldest traditions of Jesus' sayings. The evidence points, rather, to a common setting in early Christianity from 70 CE to the turn of the first century.

3

Thomas and the Beloved Disciple

Ismo Dunderberg

Recent studies have not only raised the question about the relationship between the Johannine and the Thomasine writings in general, but at least two prominent scholars have suggested that there is a close relationship between the anonymous Beloved Disciple of the Gospel of John and the apostle Thomas. Hans-Martin Schenke has entertained the possibility that the Syrian Judas Thomas tradition provided a historical model for the Beloved Disciple.[1] More recently, James Charlesworth has published a lengthy monograph in which he argues that the Beloved Disciple should be identified with Thomas. Charlesworth suggests that 'the author [of John 1–20] not only knew the identity of the Beloved Disciple, but intentionally in extremely subtle ways allowed his perceptive readers to discern that identity.'[2]

These two suggestions differ from each other with regard to the question of the historicity of the Beloved Disciple. Schenke considers the Beloved Disciple to be 'a redactional fiction who functions to give the Fourth Gospel the appearance of being authenticated and written by an eyewitness,'[3] whereas Charlesworth insists that the Beloved Disciple was a historical person.[4] Moreover, it seems that Schenke, unlike Charlesworth, is not necessarily suggesting that the Beloved

---

[1] H.-M. Schenke, 'The Function and Background of the Beloved Disciple in the Gospel of John,' in C. W. Hedrick and R. Hodgson, eds., *Nag Hammadi, Gnosticism, and Early Christianity* (Peabody: Hendrickson, 1986) 111–25.

[2] J. H. Charlesworth, *The Beloved Disciple: Whose Witness Validates the Gospel of John?* (Valley Forge: Trinity Press International, 1995) 21. In addition to Schenke and Charlesworth, P. de Suarez also identifies Thomas with the Beloved Disciple (see Charlesworth, *The Beloved Disciple*, 414–17).

[3] Schenke, 'Function and Background,' 116.

[4] Charlesworth, *The Beloved Disciple*, 418–19. The main reason for this conviction is John 21, which according to Charlesworth (and many other scholars) 'indicates that the Beloved Disciple has died' (ibid. 419).

Disciple should be *identified* with Thomas, for he presents Thomas as 'the historical model (in terms of history of traditions) for the Beloved Disciple figure of the Fourth Gospel.'[5] However, Schenke's opinion is not entirely clear at this point; his other comments may imply that he also is inclined to identify the two figures.[6]

Neither of these suggestions is entirely convincing. It will be argued later that there is no sufficient proof even for regarding Thomas as *the* historical model for the Beloved Disciple, not to speak of their complete identification. This is not to deny, however, that there are obvious similarities between the roles ascribed to Thomas in the *Gospel of Thomas* and to the Beloved Disciple in the Gospel of John. To begin with, both figures are presented as the authors of the respective writings. A claim for authorship by the Beloved Disciple has been seen in the concluding remarks of the Gospel of John (John 21.24), whereas the *Gospel of Thomas* begins with an incipit which says: 'These are the secret sayings [or 'words,' ⲚϢⲀϪⲈ] which the living Jesus spoke and which Didymus Judas Thomas wrote down.'[7]

Moreover, both Thomas and the Beloved Disciple are portrayed as possessing a unique relationship to Jesus in comparison to the other disciples. The Gospel of John depicts the Beloved Disciple as the one who at the Last Supper was reclining on Jesus' bosom (ἐν τῷ κόλπῳ τοῦ Ἰησοῦ, John 13.23). It lends special emphasis to this expression, which already as such denotes a place of honor at a meal,[8] that a similar phrase has been employed in John 1.18 for describing Jesus' close relationship to his Father (ὁ ὢν εἰς τὸν κόλπον τοῦ πατρός). The Beloved Disciple is also the only disciple present at Jesus' cross and the one to whom Jesus entrusts the guardianship of his mother (John 19.25–27). In the *Gospel of Thomas*, Thomas has a close relationship to

---

[5] Schenke, 'Function and Background,' 123.

[6] In the conclusion of his article, Schenke notes with regard to his theory: 'If this suggestion be correct, the redactor of the Fourth Gospel would in fact have doubled the figure of Thomas. For Thomas appears in the Gospel of John also under his own name, especially in the part of the Gospel written by the Evangelist, and then *reappears* in the part of the gospel added by the editor as the anonymous Beloved Disciple' ('Function and Background,' 124, emphasis added).

[7] Unless otherwise noted, the English translation of the *Gospel of Thomas* used in this article is that of T. O. Lambdin in B. Layton, ed., *Nag Hammadi Codex II,2–7 together with XIII,2*, Brit. Lib. Or.4926(1), and P.Oxy. 1, 654, 655*, vol. 1 (NHS 20; Leiden: E.J. Brill, 1989) 53–93.

[8] Cf. R. Meyer, 'κόλπος,' *TDNT* 3 (1966) 824–6, esp. 824 (with reference to Pliny, *Epistles* 4.22.4).

Jesus, though this relationship is expressed in terms different from those in the Gospel of John. According to *Gos. Thom.* 13, Jesus acknowledges the special understanding demonstrated by Thomas' words, takes him by himself, and tells him in privacy 'three secret words,' which Thomas refuses to tell to the other disciples.

Several questions emerge from these similarities between Thomas and the Beloved Disciple. 'Authorial fiction,' with which both figures are associated, is of great importance for the way writings are *intended* to be read. The fact that both figures appear not only as authors, but also as narrative figures in the respective writings, leads to the question of how the claims for authorship are related to the way these figures otherwise are portrayed in each text. Finally, it must be asked how the claims for authorship made in the *Gospel of Thomas* and the Gospel of John are related to other early Christian writings which also claim to have been written by Jesus' disciples, and in what context such claims became necessary.

Gos. Thom. 13 provides a good starting point for at least two reasons. First, only here does Thomas appear as a narrative figure in the *Gospel of Thomas*. Hence it is only this saying that sheds light on the manner in which the relationship of the alleged author to Jesus was understood in this writing. Second, modern interpretations of the saying reflect different views on the relationship between the *Gospel of Thomas* and the Gospel of John in general. The analysis of *Gos. Thom.* 13 has led Brown to maintain that 'there are some strong Johannine parallels for parts of this saying in *GTh*,'[9] whereas Schenke regards this saying as providing crucial evidence for his view that the Beloved Disciple was created on the basis of Judas Thomas traditions.

3.1. *Is* Gos. Thom. *13 dependent on John?*

> Jesus said to his disciples, 'Compare me to someone and tell me whom I am like.'
> [2]Simon Peter said to him, 'You are like a righteous angel.'
> [3]Matthew said to him, 'You are like a wise philosopher.'

---

[9]   R. E. Brown, 'The Gospel of Thomas and St John's Gospel,' *NTS* 9 (1962–3) 155–77, esp. 162.

⁴Thomas said to him, 'Master, my mouth is wholly incapable of saying whom you are like.'

⁵Jesus said, 'I am not your (sg.) master. Because you (sg.) have drunk, you (sg.) have become intoxicated from the bubbling spring which I have measured out.'

⁶And he took him and withdrew and told him three things. ⁷When Thomas returned to his companions, they asked him, 'What did Jesus say to you?'

⁸Thomas said to them, 'If I tell you one of the things which he told me, you will pick up stones and throw them at me; a fire will come out of the stones and burn you up.'

The narrative outline of *Gos. Thom.* 13 is similar to the Synoptic account of Peter's confession (Mark 8.27–33/Matt 16.13–23/Luke 9.18–22). The saying begins with a question Jesus addresses to his disciples concerning his identity and, in the scene which follows their answers, he is taken aside by Peter who begins to rebuke him in private (Mark 8.32).[10] The Johannine version of Peter's confession (John 6.66–71) is a more remote parallel to *Gos. Thom.* 13. In fact, those elements which link *Gos. Thom.* 13 with the Synoptic version of Peter's confession are entirely wanting in John 6.66–71. In this passage Peter's confession is not preceded by different identifications of Jesus, nor does a private discussion between Jesus and one of his disciples follow the confession. It is important to notice that, although both John 6.66–71 and *Gos. Thom.* 13 raise the question of their relationship to the Synoptic story, this question is called forth by different reasons in each text.[11] There is no agreement in structure that would link John 6.66–71 and *Gos. Thom.* 13 together.

Further indications which Brown has provided to suggest a literary dependence of *Gos. Thom.* 13 on the Gospel of John remain vague. First, Brown takes a notice of the 'ascending insight of the disciples' expressed both in *Gos. Thom.* 13 ('angel,' 'philosopher,' and unutterable) and in John 1.35–51 (rabbi, Messiah, a prophet-like-Moses, Son

---

[10] To be more exact, these features link *Gos. Thom.* 13 with the *Markan-Matthean* version of Peter's confession, for Luke 9.18–22 relates no instance of private discussion.

[11] *Gos. Thom.* 13 is connected to the Synoptic story by its outline in general (different opinions of Jesus, the correct answer, praise by Jesus, discussion in private), whereas John 6.66–71 is similar to the same story only in so far as Peter's confession is followed by the identification of the 'devil' among the disciples. Conclusions about the relationship of both texts to Mark 8.27–33 depend on the question whether the Marcan pericope is to be

of God).[12] However, as Brown himself admits, 'there is no similarity of the titles.'[13] Moreover, 'ascending insight' is a somewhat confusing description in connection with the respective texts,[14] and Brown's comment that 'only in John do individual disciples apply titles to Christ'[15] curiously ignores the Synoptic account of Peter's confession, the closest New Testament parallel to *Gos. Thom.* 13.

Second, Brown regards Jesus' words 'I am not your master,' which are addressed to Thomas in *Gos. Thom.* 13, as 'at least an ideological parallel to John xv. 15...: "No longer do I call you servants."'[16] However, since this parallel is indeed 'ideological,' it hardly justifies any conclusions with regard to the *literary* relationship between the two gospels. The wording of John 15.15 is too different from *Gos. Thom.* 13 to demonstrate specific Johannine influence on the *Gospel of Thomas.*

Third, Brown calls attention to Jesus' appraisal of Thomas in *Gos. Thom.* 13, in which the 'bubbling spring' and 'measuring' are mentioned. According to Brown, the Johannine parallels to these features include John 3.34; 4.14, and 7.38–39, in which the Spirit is identified with water. However, a closer comparison reveals again that no specific Johannine traits are visible in *Gos. Thom.* 13. Spring imagery can be derived independently from the sapiental tradition, in which God's Wisdom was identified with a spring (e.g. Prov 16.22; 18.4; 1 Bar 3.12;

---

regarded as a traditional unit or as a redactional composition by the second Evangelist. For this question, see I. Dunderberg, *Johannes und die Synoptiker: Studien zu Joh 1–9* (AASF DHL 69; Helsinki: The Finnish Academy of Science and Letters, 1994) 165–72. In this work I have argued for the latter possibility; if this view of Mark 8.27–33 is correct, it would imply that *Gos. Thom.* 13, in view of its compositional similarity to Mark 8.27–33, could also have been influenced by the extant Gospel of Mark. Admittedly, *Gos. Thom.* 13 has also been used as evidence for the opposite view that Mark 8.27–33 is a traditional unit; see e.g. U. Luz, 'Das Geheimnismotiv und die markinische Christologie,' *ZNW* 56 (1965) 9–30, esp. 21 n. 59.

[12] Brown, 'The Gospel of Thomas and St John's Gospel,' 162.

[13] Ibid., 162.

[14] It is not clear whether the 'wise man' mentioned in the second place in *Gos. Thom.* 13 would really be a more elevated title than the 'angel.' It seems more likely that both titles are *equally* contrasted with the more perceptive confession by Thomas. Likewise, it can be asked whether in John 1.35–51 the 'prophet' really is superior to 'Messiah' or to the 'Son of God.'

[15] Brown, 'The Gospel of Thomas and St John's Gospel,' 162; quoted in agreement by J. Sell, 'Johannine Traditions in Logion 61 of The Gospel of Thomas,' *Perspectives in Religious Studies* 7 (1980) 24–37, esp. 25.

[16] Brown, 'The Gospel of Thomas and St John's Gospel,' 162.

cf. Philo, *Poster. C.* 138),[17] for it has been used in different ways in each gospel. In addition, the vocabulary employed for the 'bubbling spring' in *Gos. Thom.* 13 suggests no close relationship to John 4.14.[18] The notice about 'measuring' suggests no closer affinity between the two writings either, for it would be difficult to explain how and why the Johannine saying that 'the Spirit is not given by measure' would have turned into the notion in *Gos. Thom.* 13 that it is Jesus who has measured out the bubbling spring.

In sum, it goes beyond the evidence to maintain that *Gos. Thom.* 13 has been influenced by the Gospel of John. The common elements are too vague to suggest any literary relationship between these writings. Hence, it is *not* the best explanation for the similar functions ascribed to Thomas and to the Beloved Disciple to assume that the *Gospel of Thomas* is dependent upon the Gospel of John (and its portrayal of the Beloved Disciple).

3.2. Is Thomas the (historical model for the) Beloved Disciple?

The fact that literary dependence between *Gos. Thom.* 13 and the Gospel of John could not be proven does not rule out Schenke's view of Thomas as the historical model for the Beloved Disciple. In this theory, it must be assumed that some Thomas traditions flourished already before the Gospel of John was written. This is not an unlikely hypothesis, for Thomas is mentioned in the Gospel of John (11.16; 20.24–29). It is perhaps more difficult to join Schenke in calling these traditions 'the entire Syrian Judas Thomas tradition,'[19] because the

---

[17] For spring imagery in connection with divine Wisdom, see B. Mack, *Logos und Sophia: Untersuchungen zur Weisheitstheologie im hellenistischen Judentum* (SUNT 10; Göttingen: Vandenhoeck & Ruprecht, 1973) 171–4; K.-G. Sandelin, *Wisdom as Nourisher: A Study of an Old Testament Theme. Its Development within Early Judaism and Its Impact on Early Christianity* (AAAbo, Ser. A, 64.3; Åbo: Åbo Akademi, 1986) 94–6.

[18] In *Gos. Thom.* 13 the verb used for 'bubbling' is ϥⲣⲃⲉ. The basic meaning of this verb is 'to boil.' Thus it would be an unexpected translation of the Greek verb ἅλλεσθαι used in John 4.14. In Coptic, ἅλλεσθαι is usually translated either with ϥⲱϭⲉ or ⲡⲏⲓ; ϥⲱϭⲉ is employed also in the Sahidic translations of John 4.14. On the contrary, no instance of translating ἅλλεσθαι with ϥⲣϥⲣ is mentioned in the standard Coptic dictionary. Cf. W. E. Crum, *A Coptic Dictionary* (Oxford: Clarendon, 1939) 42, 260, 625–7.

[19] Schenke, 'Function and Background,' 122.

dating of the emergence of this specific tradition of Thomas remains uncertain. In any case, the Gospel of John gives no direct hint at this tradition, for the double name 'Judas Thomas' does not appear in this Gospel.[20]

In Schenke's theory, however, it is more important to account for what makes Thomas the best candidate for being the historical model behind the Beloved Disciple. In his article Schenke notes in passing other figures, such as Mary Magdalene or James, who in various writings have also assumed a unique relationship to Jesus.[21] Why is it Thomas who is supposed to be the model for the Beloved Disciple, and not these other figures? There are, above all, three reasons which have lead Schenke to argue in favor of Thomas. First, in the *Book of Thomas* Jesus addresses Thomas as 'my twin and my true friend (ⲡⲁϣⲃⲣ̄ⲙ̄ⲙⲏⲉ)' (138.7–8). Schenke suggests that the Greek original behind ⲡⲁϣⲃⲣ̄ⲙ̄ⲙⲏⲉ could have read σὺ εἶ ... ὁ φίλος μου ὁ ἀληθινός. This conjecture is plausible, but it does not yet prove any connection between the Judas Thomas tradition and the Beloved Disciple. A more complicated argument is needed in order to establish this connection: 'Transposed into a form parallel with that of the Gospel of John, this would read "you are the one I truly love," or, in the third person singular, "he is the one whom Jesus truly loved." '[22] This part of Schenke's reasoning is speculative and remains unconvincing. Moreover, it blurs the difference between the *Book of Thomas,* which uses the *noun* 'friend' of Thomas, and the Gospel of John in which a *verbal phrase* 'the disciple whom Jesus loved' is employed for the Beloved Disciple. In the Gospel of John the noun 'friend' can be used of other figures (e.g. Lazarus, 11.11), but it is never used in connection with the Beloved Disciple.

Second, Schenke points out that both Thomas and the Beloved Disciple are affiliated with Jesus' family, the former as Jesus' twin

---

[20] For this issue, see I. Dunderberg, 'John and Thomas in Conflict?' in J. D. Turner and A. McGuire, eds., *The Nag Hammadi Library After Fifty Years: Proceedings of the 1995 Society of Biblical Literature Commemoration* (NHMS 44; Leiden: E. J. Brill, 1997), 361–80, esp. 371. The fact that the double name 'Judas Thomas' occurs in Syriac translations of John 14.22 cannot be taken as evidence for the view that 'the Syrian Judas Thomas tradition' was known to the author(s) of the Gospel of John.

[21] Cf. Schenke, 'Function and Background,' 122.

[22] Ibid., 123.

brother, the latter as the one to whom 'Jesus entrusts his mother.'[23] This, however, implies no specific linkage between Thomas and the Beloved Disciple, for their relationship to Jesus' family is expressed in entirely different ways (see below). In addition, in early Christian writings other prominent figures can also be associated with Jesus' family.[24] Hence, the way Thomas and the Beloved Disciple are presented in association with Jesus' kinship does not indicate any particular relationship between them.

Third, and most importantly, Schenke seeks evidence for the notion 'that Jesus promised Thomas that he would tarry till he comes, i.e. that he would not die before the return of Christ.'[25] There is no direct evidence for this notion; the conclusion is based on Schenke's guess of what the 'three secret words' in *Gos. Thom.* 13.6–8 might have been:

> It does not require much to imagine that one of these three 'words' could have been something like: 'You will remain until I come' or 'you will not experience death until I come.' At any rate a promise of this sort would lead understandably to the anticipated jealousy of the other disciples.[26]

There are, of course, a number of intriguing suggestions about the 'three secret words' of *Gos. Thom.* 13,[27] but none of them can be

---

[23] Ibid., 123.

[24] A prime example of them is James, whose kinship to Jesus is in *1 Apoc. Jas.* 24.12–15 and *2 Apoc. Jas.* 35.15–23 put in terms somewhat similar to Thomas as presented in the *Book of Thomas*; cf. J. D. Turner, *The Book of Thomas the Contender from Codex II of the Cairo Gnostic Library from Nag Hammadi (CG II,7): The Coptic Text with Translation, Introduction, and Commentary* (SBLDS 23; Missoula: Scholars Press, 1975) 125.

[25] Schenke, 'Function and Background,' 124. That this argument is of importance for Schenke is shown by the manner he introduces it: 'What is needed in order to make this theory *really plausible* ...' (emphasis added).

[26] Ibid.

[27] To take only a few recent suggestions, Gunther argues for 'Didymus Judas Thomas,' whereas Riley opts for the words derived from the Book of Thomas: ⲡⲁⲥⲟⲉⲓϣ, ⲡⲁϣⲃⲣ̄ ⲙ̄ⲙⲉ [sic! *Thom. Cont.* 138.8 reads ⲙ̄ⲙⲏⲉ], ⲡⲁⲥⲟⲛ ("my twin, my true companion, and my brother"),' and De Conick speaks in favor of 'God's secret divine name consisting of three words, אהיה אשר אהיה (Exod 3.14).' Cf. J. J. Gunther, 'The Meaning and Origin of the Name "Judas Thomas"' *Muséon* 93 (1980) 113–48, esp. 114, 125; G. J. Riley, *Resurrection Reconsidered: Thomas and John in Controversy* (Minneapolis: Fortress Press, 1995) 112–13; A. D. De Conick, *Seek to See Him: Ascent and Vision Mysticism in the Gospel of Thomas* (VCSup 33; Leiden: E.J. Brill, 1996) 112–13.

claimed to have absolute certainty.[28] The secret words were, according to *Gos. Thom.* 13.6, related only to Thomas and not to the audience of the *Gospel of Thomas*.[29] What is problematic for Schenke's suggestion in particular is that it leaves unexplained why the other disciples would try to *stone* Thomas, if he told these secret words to them. The anticipated stoning indicates that whatever the secret words might have been, their disclosure would be regarded as a serious offence against the Old Testament legislation by the other disciples.[30] Schenke's way of using *Gos. Thom.* 1 in support of his suggestion is not particularly helpful.[31] Although this saying associates the promise of immortality with 'the interpretation' of the following 'secret sayings,' it in no way indicates that the three secret words mentioned in *Gos. Thom.* 13 would have consisted of this promise.

The direct identification of Thomas with the Beloved Disciple suggested by Charlesworth is even more problematic than Schenke's theory. The fact that constitutes a major problem for this suggestion is that, in the Gospel of John, Thomas is not directly identified with the Beloved Disciple. If this identification were intended, why would the

---

[28] Thus Riley, for example, comments on his own suggestion concerning the three secret words: 'Confidence is impossible in such a case' (*Resurrection Reconsidered*, 113 n. 42).

[29] Cf. S. L. Davies, *The Gospel of Thomas and Christian Wisdom* (New York: The Seabury Press, 1983) 92: 'It is easy to make clever guesses about the identity of the three mysterious words, or logia, but it will be best to refrain from such guesswork. Thomas has been given "what no ear has heard" (17), but we have not.' In light of this comment, one is surprised to find that Davies also, in his more recent article, has a theory about the three secret words, arguing that they were, at least for 'the compiler of Thomas,' 'the first three commands of *Gos. Thom.* 14: Do not fast; do not pray; do not give alms.' S. L. Davies, 'The Christology and Protology of the *Gospel of Thomas*,' *JBL* 111 (1992) 663–82, esp. 676.

[30] Both Davies ('Christology and Protology,' 676), and De Conick (*Seek to See Him*, 112) think that stoning indicates that the three secret words would be regarded as *blasphemy* by the other disciples. This is perhaps the most likely interpretation. Nevertheless, stoning is presented in the Hebrew Bible as a common punishment for various severe crimes. Cf. R. Westbrook, 'Punishments and Crimes,' *ABD* 5 (1992) 546–56, esp. 555: 'Where the Bible specifies the method of execution, the most common is stoning: for apostasy (Lev 20.2; Deut 13.11; 17.5), blasphemy (Lev 24.14, 16, 23; 1 Sam 21.10), sorcery (Lev 20.27), sabbath violation (Num 15.35–36), disobedient son (Deut 21.21), and adultery by an inchoate wife (Deut 22.21, 24; cf. Ezek 16.40; 23.47).'

[31] 'Logion 1 of the *Gospel of Thomas* … could easily be taken to be a transformation (like John 21.23b) of "Jesus had said to Thomas: Since *you* have found the explanation of my sayings, *you* will not experience death"' (Schenke, 'Function and Background,' 124).

author of the Gospel have expressed this idea in such a cryptic (or 'subtle,' as Charlesworth puts it) manner?[32]

Nevertheless, the first of Charlesworth's twelve arguments merits closer attention. Charlesworth argues that the identification of Thomas with the Beloved Disciple is suggested by John 20.27 in which Thomas, asking for a more concrete proof of Jesus' resurrection, betrays his knowledge of Jesus' pierced side. Since the Beloved Disciple is presented as the only witness to this detail earlier in the narrative (John 19.34–35), Thomas seems to know what only the Beloved Disciple could know. This common knowledge, according to Charlesworth, points in the direction that Thomas should be identified with the Beloved Disciple.

This is a point worth considering, but it does not make the identification of Thomas with the Beloved Disciple inevitable. There are other instances of gaps in the Johannine passion narrative similar to that between John 19.34–35 and John 20.24–29. According to John 19.38–42, only Joseph of Arimathea and Nicodemus were present as Jesus was buried; so only they could know the place of his tomb. In the following scene, nevertheless, Mary Magdalene knows her way to the tomb even though it is not related that Joseph and Nicodemus informed her about its place (John 20.1). Although she seems to share this knowledge with Joseph and Nicodemus, she certainly should not be identified with either of them. Instead, this example shows that the author of the gospel apparently was not meticulous with such details. Far-reaching conclusions based on such narrative gaps are therefore unwarranted.[33] As regards the narrative logic in John 20.24–29, it seems

---

[32] As regards the identification of the Beloved Disciple in general, I am inclined to the view that this question must remain unsolved. In his recent study, Joachim Kügler has aptly stated that the endless efforts of scholars to identify the Beloved Disciple rather suggest that the whole quest is misguided, for in these efforts 'the anonymity created by the text is always regarded as something negative that should be unraveled and destroyed'; *Der Jünger, den Jesus liebte: Literarische, theologische und historische Untersuchungen zu einer Schlüsselgestalt johanneischer Theologie und Geschichte, mit einem Exkurs über die Brotrede in Joh 6* (SBB 16; Stuttgart: Katholisches Bibelwerk, 1988) 439–48, esp. 448.

[33] Another brilliant but likewise unconvincing point in Charlesworth's argumentation is the claim that Thomas' absence during the first appearance of the resurrected Jesus to his disciples (John 20.19–23) was due to the ritual impurity caused by his visit in Jesus' tomb (as the Beloved Disciple, John 20.2–10); see Charlesworth, *The Beloved Disciple*, 283–5. If Thomas' absence should in fact be explained as due to Jewish purification practises, one would expect that this would have been indicated more clearly by the author. By way of comparison, in John 2.6 the author explicitly mentions that 'there were six stone water jars for the Jewish rites of purification' (NRSV). The latter remark shows that the author

more important that the *audience* of the gospel already knows of Jesus' pierced side and is now able to identify the resurrected Jesus with the one who was crucified. In any case, no secrecy motif is connected with Jesus' pierced side in John. Admittedly, it is not related that the Beloved Disciple told the other disciples about Jesus' pierced side, but it is not claimed either that he would have kept silent about it. The fact that this particular issue goes unnoticed in the narrative indicates that the author most likely did not consider it to be of any great importance.

In summation, neither Schenke's suggestion that Thomas was the historical model for the Beloved Disciple nor Charlesworth's theory that the two figures should be identified with each other offers a tenable solution to the problem of the relationship between these figures. Schenke's view is based on too many uncertain conjectures about what might have been said in the *Gospel of Thomas*,[34] whereas the way Charlesworth reads the Gospel of John in support of his hypothesis is quite peculiar. It seems, rather, that the relationship between these figures should be understood in more general terms. This notion is supported by the following comparison between Thomas and the Beloved Disciple, which will demonstrate that these figures are cast in entirely different manners except for their alleged close relationship to Jesus and the claims of authorship connected with them.

3.3. Different characterizations of Thomas and the Beloved Disciple

Although both the Gospel of John and the *Gospel of Thomas* make a claim of being written by an ideal figure, i.e. by a disciple whose

does *not* presuppose from the audience knowledge of Jewish purification rites. As for the 'implied reader' of the Gospel of John, Culpepper maintains correctly (in light of John 2.6; 4.9; 18.28 and 19.40): 'Some Jewish beliefs and practises do require explanation, however. *Matters pertaining to the practise of ritual purity are particularly obscure*'; R. A. Culpepper, *Anatomy of the Fourth Gospel: A Study in Literary Design* (Philadelphia: Fortress Press, 1987) 221 (emphasis added). Moreover, Charlesworth's theory leaves unexplained why only Thomas' absence is mentioned in John 20.24, for according to John 20.6 Peter also went into the tomb of Jesus. In fact, Charlesworth is aware of this difficulty, but does not suggest any solution to it; cf. Charlesworth, *The Beloved Disciple*, 283 n. 189.

[34] Marvin W. Meyer points out that Schenke's suggestion seems to be based on 'a forced reading and interpretation of texts on Thomas'; see M. W. Meyer, 'The Youth in Secret Mark and the Beloved Disciple in John,' in J. E. Goehring, C. W. Hedrick, J. T. Sanders, and H. D. Betz, eds., *Gospel Origins & Christian Beginnings, in Honor of James M. Robinson* (Sonoma: Polebridge Press, 1990) 94–105, esp. 103.

relationship to Jesus was especially close, their ways of presenting these figures are different. The most apparent difference is that Thomas' relationship to Jesus is not put in terms of a love relationship in the *Gospel of Thomas*; he is not called 'the disciple whom Jesus loved.'[35] Another obvious difference is the *secrecy motif* which is clearly associated with Thomas but not with the Beloved Disciple. The motif comes to expression in the incipit of the *Gospel of Thomas*, which characterizes Judas Thomas as the one who has written down Jesus' secret words. In *Gos. Thom.* 13 the same motif takes an even more exclusive form. While the incipit did not cast Thomas as the only recipient of Jesus' secret words, according to *Gos. Thom.* 13 Jesus addressed the 'three secret words' exclusively to Thomas who, in turn, refused to transmit them to the other disciples.

As for the Beloved Disciple, there is no clear evidence for a similar secrecy motif. Many scholars, to be sure, have interpreted John 13.21–30 in terms of this motif, supposing that in this passage Jesus related the identity of his betrayer only to the Beloved Disciple.[36] However, this interpretation remains uncertain. In fact, John 13.26 leaves it open whether Jesus addressed his words to the Beloved Disciple or to all the disciples, for the short narrative introduction to these words ('Jesus answered') does not define their addressees. Moreover, in this interpretation, it should be assumed that the Beloved Disciple kept silent about the betrayer and that he is not included in the author's comment that no one at the table knew why Jesus asked Judas to leave (John 13.28).[37] Since neither of these notions stands in the text itself, it is more likely that the Johannine author did not intend

---

[35] Admittedly, in the *Book of Thomas* Jesus addresses Thomas as 'my true friend,' but even this provides no linkage between Thomas and the Beloved Disciple (cf. above). In this light Charlesworth's claim that 'the School of Thomas perceived Thomas to be none other than the Beloved Disciple' (*The Beloved Disciple*, 328) remains dubious.

[36] E.g. T. Lorenzen, *Der Lieblingsjünger im Johannesevangelium: Eine redaktionsgeschichtliche Studie* (SBS 55; Stuttgart: Katholisches Bibelwerk, 1971) 17.

[37] Lorenzen's comment demonstrates well that the latter view is in fact not in harmony with the text itself: 'As "nobody" (οὐδείς) in verse 28 shows, the Beloved Disciples assumes, in the evangelist's thoughts, a special place outside the circle of the disciples, for formally *he too should be included in the "nobody"*' (*Lieblingsjünger*, 17; emphasis added). Charlesworth's opposite interpretation of John 13.28 is in my opinion more faithful to what the text says: 'The Beloved Disciple is included within the sweeping authorial comment that the disciples did not know the meaning of Jesus' words to Judas, the son of Simon Iscariot' (Charlesworth, *The Beloved Disciple*, 54). For a similar view, see also K. Quast, *Peter and the Beloved Disciple: Figures for a Community in Crisis* (JSNTSup 32; Sheffield: Sheffield Academic Press, 1989) 160–1.

to characterize the Beloved Disciple in terms of secrecy in this passage.

In *Gos. Thom.* 13 Thomas' special status is underlined by affirming his judicious understanding. This understanding, shown by his confession that his mouth is unable to compare Jesus to anyone else, is met with approval from Jesus and leads to a private transmission of the secret words to him. Therefore Thomas could with good reason be depicted as 'the confidant of Jesus, whom the Lord recognizes as understanding him well' and as 'having a special knowledge of Jesus.'[38]

In fact, these descriptions, by which D. J. Hawkin has characterized the Johannine Beloved Disciple, suit Thomas *better* than the Beloved Disciple. Nowhere in the Gospel of John is the Beloved Disciple directly praised by Jesus for his special understanding. In John 13.21–30 he does not necessarily appear as a more understanding figure than the other disciples, nor is it clear that he would be portrayed as Jesus' confidant. The notion of his belief at Jesus' tomb might indicate that he is understood to be more perceptive than Peter (John 20.8), but it remains open whether the author meant that he immediately believed in Jesus' resurrection[39] or, as the context seems to suggest, that he only became convinced about what Mary Magdalene had told him, i.e. that Jesus' tomb was empty.[40] Only in John 21.1–14 is the Beloved Disciple clearly presented as more perceptive than the other disciples, for in this passage he recognizes the risen Jesus before they do (John 21.7). Yet not even here is his perceptivity emphasised by the author. Hence the Gospel of John is in any case far less explicit about the Beloved Disciple's special insight than the *Gospel of Thomas* is with regard to Thomas.

Thomas is obviously presented as a *paradigmatic figure* to the audience of the *Gospel of Thomas*. As Stephen Patterson puts it, '*Thom*

---

[38]   D. J. Hawkin, 'The Function of the Beloved Disciple Motif in the Johannine Redaction,' *Laval théologique et philosophique* 33 (1977) 135–50, esp. 143, 150.

[39]   For such a view see e.g. R. A. Culpepper, *John, the Son of Zebedee: The Life of a Legend* (Studies on Personalities of the New Testament; Columbia: University of South Carolina Press, 1994) 69: 'The Beloved Disciple ... becomes the only figure in the New Testament of whom it is said that he believed in the resurrection because of what he saw at the empty tomb.'

[40]   Cf. the lengthy discussion about John 20.1–10 by Charlesworth, *The Beloved Disciple*, 68–118, including many noteworthy arguments in favor of the latter view.

13 makes Thomas, in a sense, the prototypical Thomas Christian.'[41] This interpretation is supported by the close linkage between *Gos. Thom.* 13 and *Gos. Thom.* 108.[42] The two sayings share with each other the metaphor of drinking and the motif of disclosing secrets. *Gos. Thom.* 108 associates with these features the notion of becoming equal to Jesus:

> Jesus said, 'He who will drink from my mouth will become like me. I myself will become he, and the things that are hidden will be revealed to him.'

In fact, the close relationship between *Gos. Thom.* 13 and 108 may have contributed to the emergence of the tradition in which Thomas was considered to be the twin brother of Jesus. This idea is not spelled out in the *Gospel of Thomas*, but it comes to expression in the *Book of Thomas* (138.10) and, as a more recurring feature, in the *Acts of Thomas*.[43] This idea could have resulted from a juxtaposition of *Gos. Thom.* 13 with 108, for if *Gos. Thom.* 13 is read in light of *Gos. Thom.* 108, the most obvious conclusion must be that Thomas has already become like Jesus. This idea is not stated in the *Gospel of Thomas*, but its ramifications might be seen in the *Book of Thomas* and the *Acts of Thomas*.[44]

---

[41] S. J. Patterson, *The Gospel of Thomas and Jesus* (Foundations and Facets: Reference Series; Sonoma: Polebridge Press, 1993) 206.

[42] The connection between *Gos. Thom.* 13 and 108 has often been noted; cf. e.g. Davies, *Gospel of Thomas*, 91–4; idem, 'Christology and Protology,' 675; A. Marjanen, *The Woman Jesus Loved: Mary Magdalene in the Nag Hammadi Library and Related Documents* (NHMS 40; Leiden: E. J. Brill, 1996) 42–3.

[43] For this notion and its corollaries in the *Acts of Thomas*, see P.-H. Poirier, '*Évangile de Thomas, Actes de Thomas, Livre de Thomas*: Une tradition et ses transformations,' *Apocrypha* 7 (1996) 9–26, esp. 20–2; cf. also Gunther who argues that 'a fully developed theory of how Thomas uniquely resembled Jesus appears in the *Acts of Thomas*, ch. 11–12, 31, 34, 39, 45, 47–48, 57, 147–53' ('The Meaning and Origin of the Name "Judas Thomas,"' 113).

[44] Poirier has recently made the interesting suggestion that only the *Gospel of Thomas* and the *Acts of Thomas* can be regarded as 'authentically Thomasine,' whereas the *Book of Thomas* 'presupposes knowledge and use of the elements of the literary Thomasine tradition.' Among other things, Poirier points out that the prologue of the *Book of Thomas* (138.4–21) speaks of Thomas in terms attested elsewhere only in the *Acts of Thomas* ('brother,' 'twin,' and 'companion'). The way these common elements are introduced in the *Book of Thomas* ('it has been said that you are my twin and my true companion,' 'since you are called my brother,' etc.) betrays, according to Poirier, that the redactor of this writing employs 'a known theme to authenticate the following dialogue' (Poirier, 'Une tradition et ses transformations,' 23–5).

Be that as it may, in light of *Gos. Thom.* 108 it is possible to argue that Thomas is in *Gos. Thom.* 13 cast as exemplary for the audience of the gospel. In the *Gospel of Thomas*, Thomas' experience and insight with regard to Jesus are not unique in the sense that others could not achieve them. On the contrary, the audience of this gospel is through *Gos. Thom.* 108 encouraged to seek a relationship to Jesus similar to that which Thomas had achieved.

The question of the paradigmatic role of the Beloved Disciple is more complicated. Admittedly, his intimate position 'on Jesus' bosom' (John 13.23) or his faithful presence at Jesus' cross (John 19.25–26, 34–35) can be understood as exemplifying true faith in Jesus, and as such they could be exemplary for the gospel's audience. Nevertheless, it seems that these features are not presented as such in the Gospel of John. Rather, the author of this gospel presents them in order to point out that the Beloved Disciple had a unique relationship with Jesus. The Beloved Disciple is the one who was present at the Last Supper, who took care of Jesus' mother, bore witness to Jesus' death, and assumed a crucial role in the resurrection narratives. None of these features admits of imitation on behalf of the audience.[45] In the Gospel of John, the unique status of the Beloved Disciple is expressed in more exclusive terms than that of Thomas in the *Gospel of Thomas*.

Finally, as Schenke has pointed out, both the Beloved Disciple and Thomas are associated with Jesus' family. In the Thomas traditions Thomas can be described as Jesus' twin, whereas the Beloved Disciple is described as the new guardian of Jesus' mother after Jesus' death (John 19.25–27); thus he is supposed to have taken over a task which otherwise would have been a legal responsibility of Jesus' brothers (who are cast as unbelievers in John 7.2–9).[46] Yet two differences qualify this coincidence. First, the Beloved Disciple is not called Jesus' 'brother,' not to mention his 'twin.'[47] Second, as was noted, the *Gospel of Thomas* does not associate Thomas with kinship with *Jesus* (as his twin); this

---

[45] Cf. R. Bauckham, 'The Beloved Disciple as Ideal Author,' *JSNT* 49 (1993) 21–44, esp. 33.

[46] Cf. A. Dauer, 'Das Wort des Gekreuzigten an seine Mutter und den "Jünger den er liebte"': Eine traditionsgeschichtliche und theologische Untersuchung zu Joh 19,25–27,' *BZ* 11 (1967) 222–39; *BZ* 12 (1968) 80–93, esp. 81–2; Lorenzen, *Lieblingsjünger*, 84.

[47] In John 20.17 Jesus calls all disciples his 'brothers,' but even here the term is not confined to the Beloved Disciple in particular.

view comes to expression only in the *Book of Thomas* and in the *Acts of Thomas*.[48]

The comparison between the Beloved Disciple and Thomas shows that they have been depicted in different ways and for different purposes in the respective gospels. Although both the Gospel of John and the *Gospel of Thomas* claim to have been written by an ideal disciple, this similarity does not suffice for assuming a specific relationship between these figures. Nevertheless, the fact that both writings are ascribed to disciples who are characterized by their close relationship to Jesus might reflect a similar situation within early Christianity in which it had became increasingly necessary to supply the addressees of new writings with such figures. This, in turn, leads us to the broader issue of 'authorial fiction' in early Christian writings.

3.4. Definition and functions of authorial fiction

In his seminal study on the genre of Q, John Kloppenborg pays attention to ancient saying collections, and regards 'authorial fiction' as an important part of their 'hermeneutic.'[49] Kloppenborg defines 'authorial fiction' in connection with the ancient instruction collections as 'the way in which the instruction *represents its mode of production or creation*'.[50] It goes without saying that this definition of 'authorial fiction' should not be restricted to the instruction genre. Although the Jewish-Christian collection of *Testaments of the Twelve Patriarchs* is a representative of another genre, i.e. testament literature, authorial

---

[48] Although the Aramaic name 'Thomas' as well as the Greek 'Didymos' mean 'twin,' the *Gospel of Thomas* does not make use of the notion that Thomas would have been *Jesus'* twin; cf. Dunderberg, 'John and Thomas in Conflict?' 373.

[49] J. S. Kloppenborg, *The Formation of Q: Trajectories in Ancient Wisdom Collections* (Studies in Antiquity and Christianity; Philadelphia: Fortress Press, 1987) 263–316.

[50] Kloppenborg, *Formation of Q*, 274 (emphasis added). I find the term 'authorial fiction' a more accurate description for the explicit claims of authorship than 'implied author,' for the former focuses on the question of what a writing itself says about its author. Admittedly, the term 'implied author' has been used at least in connection with the Beloved Disciple (cf. Culpepper, *Anatomy of the Fourth Gospel*, 47). Nevertheless, this usage is confusing in light of Culpepper's definition of the 'implied author' as 'a sum of choices visible in the text' (ibid. 14–15). Every text thus has an 'implied author,' whereas there are texts without an 'authorial fiction,' i.e. an explicit account of the text's mode of production.

fiction, including the notion of 'parental instruction,' which is the prevaling mode of presentation in ancient instruction collections,[51] is of great importance for it also.[52] In this document, a more technical side of authorial fiction also comes to expression, as each of the Twelve Testaments begins with the notice that it presents 'a copy of the Testament of ... .' Authorial fiction plays an important role also in Jewish and Christian apocalyptic writings. In addition to the identification of the authors, which is a very important feature within this genre,[53] some representatives of it focus on the *act* of writing. In the Book of Revelation, John is commanded to write down what he sees (Rev 1.11).[54] In the Jewish apocalypses ascribed to Enoch, it is not only affirmed that the visionary himself wrote something down (e.g. *1 Enoch* 92.1, in which the 'Book of Enoch's epistles' is ascribed to Enoch). It can also be recounted in detail how Enoch is provided with a pen and other writing instruments in order to write down what a divine figure discloses to him (*2 Enoch* 22–23).

Kloppenborg regards it as typical for the instruction collections that 'the teaching is never considered to be the *creation* of the sage. On the contrary, it is something which he transmits and which his own experience confirms.'[55] This notion can be applied equally well to Enoch, the Beloved Disciple, and Thomas. Each of these figures is associated with the *transmission* of teachings rather than with originating them. Enoch's teaching is derived from the heavenly figures, that of the Beloved Disciple and of Thomas from Jesus.

The most obvious function of authorial fiction in various genres of ancient literature is that of authentication. Kloppenborg speaks with regard to the Egyptian instruction collections of 'the requirement of the

---

[51]   See Kloppenborg, *The Formation of Q*, 274, 284.
[52]   Each writing of this collection begins with an account of an occasion in which a patriarch addresses his last words of instruction to his sons and grandsons.
[53]   Cf. e.g. P. Vielhauer and G. Strecker, 'Introduction [to Apocalypses and Related Subjects],' in W. Schneemelcher, ed., *New Testament Apocrypha 2: Writings Relating to the Apostles, Apocalypses and Related Subjects* (English trans. ed. by R. McL. Wilson; Cambridge: James Clarke; Louisville: Westminster Press/John Knox Press, 1992) 542–68, esp. 545.
[54]   Cf. also other instances in the Book of Revelation of the divine writing command (Rev 1.19; 2.1, 8, 12, 18; 3.1, 7, 14; 15.13; 19.9; 21.5) and the prohibitive command (Rev 10.4).
[55]   Kloppenborg, *Formation of Q*, 275.

genre for an authoritative guarantor of the sayings.'[56] Similarly, it has been noted that, in Jewish visionary literature, ideal figures are introduced in order 'to lend weight to and authenticate the content of the revelation.'[57] In Enoch literature, for example, the visionary can himself affirm the reliability of his writing activity (2 Enoch 23.4; 40), and the reliable transmission of the writing can even be certified by claiming that its original manuscript was divinely safeguarded from the flood (2 Enoch 33.8–12). There is no doubt that the Beloved Disciple serves the same purpose in the Gospel of John. Not only is he identified with one of Jesus' disciples; specific notes are made to add credence to his eyewitness testimony (John 19.35; 21.24). The Gospel of Thomas is less explicit on this point, but already the fact that Thomas is introduced as the one who wrote down Jesus' secret words in the incipit of this gospel indicates that his function is to validate their reliable transmission.[58]

3.5. Jesus' disciples as figures of authentication

The use of Jesus' disciples as figures of authentication is, of course, not confined to the Gospel of John and the Gospel of Thomas. On the contrary, this notion has been embraced by various early Christian writers. There are writings which give themselves out as narrated by Jesus' disciples (e.g. the Gospel of Peter, the Apocryphon of John, the Apocalypse of Peter) or as written by them (e.g. the Infancy Story of Thomas; the Protevangelium of James). It seems that authorial fiction gradually assumed increasingly concrete forms. In addition to the documents which are allegedly written by Jesus' disciples, some writings claim to have been written by Jesus himself, either entirely (Epistula apostolorum) or in part (Jesus' letter to Abgar included in the

---

[56] Ibid.

[57] J. J. Collins and G. W. E. Nickelsburg, 'Introduction,' in J. J. Collins and G. W. E. Nickelsburg, eds., Ideal Figures in Ancient Judaism: Profiles and Paradigms (SBLSCS 12; Chico: Scholars Press, 1980) 1–12, esp. 8.

[58] Although Thomas is not introduced in terms of discipleship in the incipit of the Gospel of Thomas, its implied audience is most likely supposed to have knowledge of Thomas, being one of Jesus' disciples, for in Gos. Thom. 13 Thomas is associated with two other disciples of Jesus (Peter and Matthew).

Abgar Legend).[59] The same development is reflected also by the increasingly detailed accounts of ways in which some early Christian writings depict their mode of production. The *Book of Thomas* and *Pistis Sophia* provide us with prime examples of this tendency.

The *Book of Thomas* does not only identify its author, Mathaias, but it also includes a brief account of an incident in which he happened to hear Jesus' discussion with Thomas and wrote it down:

> The secret words that the savior spoke to Judas Thomas which I, even I Mathaias, wrote down. I was walking, as I heard them speaking with one another. (138.1–4.)[60]

The *Book of Thomas* differs from the *Gospel of Thomas* in making a clear distinction between the recipient (Thomas) and the scribe (Mathaias). In fact, this distinction is obscured by the title given to the writing at its end ('The Book of *Thomas*,' ⲡϫⲱⲙⲉ ⲛ̄ⲑⲱⲙⲁⲥ, 145.17).[61] The double ascription of the writing, along with other factors, has led

---

[59]   Further evidence for circulation of writings allegedly written by Jesus is provided by W. Speyer, 'Religiöse Pseudepigraphie und literarische Fälschung im Altertum,' in N. Brox, ed., *Pseudepigraphie in der heidnischen und jüdisch-christlichen Antike* (Wege der Forschung 484; Darmstadt: Wissenschaftliche Buchgesellschaft, 1977) 195–271 [originally published in *JAC* 8–9 (1965–66) 88–125], 254 n. 202.

[60]   The translation I follow here with modification is that of J. D. Turner, 'The Book of Thomas the Contender,' in B. Layton, ed., *Nag Hammadi Codex II,2–7 together with XIII,2*, Brit. Lib. Or.4926(1), P. Oxy. 1, 654, 655*, vol. 2 (NHS 21; Leiden: E. J. Brill, 1989) 181.

[61]   As Schenke has pointed out, the writing defines itself as the 'Book of Thomas' rather than the 'Book of Thomas the Contender,' for the 'contender' is the subject of the following circumstantial sentence (145.18–19: ⲡⲁⲑⲗⲏⲧⲏⲥ ⲉϥϩⲣⲁⲓ̈ ⲛ̄ⲧⲉⲗⲉⲓⲟⲥ); cf. H.-M. Schenke, *Das Thomasbuch (Nag Hammadi-Codex II,7)* (TU 138; Berlin: Akademie-Verlag 1989) 193–5. Yet in the present closing of the writing 'the contender' must also refer to Thomas, so it is not utterly mistaken to speak of the 'Book of Thomas the Contender.' The strict distinction Schenke makes between the 'Book of Thomas' and the following circumstantial sentence ('The contender writing to the perfect') is connected with his view that the latter had its original place at the beginning of an epistle (ibid., 194). Moreover, Schenke argues that in Platonic-Jewish Wisdom literature there is only one contender, Jacob the patriarch (ibid., 196). Thus, Schenke identifies behind the present *Book of Thomas* a source which is defined as 'a (pseudepigraphic) epistle of (Jacob) the Contender to the perfect,' or as 'an apocryphal letter of Jacob,' which was originally a *non-Christian* document (ibid., 196–7). Schenke's suggestion remains very dubious, for, in the *Book of Thomas,* Jacob of the Hebrew Bible is not mentioned by name, neither are there any allusions to any part of the Jacob narrative of the Hebrew Bible.

scholars to assume multiple layers behind the *Book of Thomas*.[62] However, the 'tension' between its incipit and its title is more apparent than real, for the title indicates only that Thomas, the interlocutor, was regarded as a more prominent figure for its hermeneutic than its alleged author, Mathaias; the latter has obviously assumed the secondary role of being merely the scribe in this writing. For this reason it is in fact not at all surprising that the writing is entitled 'the Book of Thomas.'

An even more concrete example of authorial fiction is provided by *Pistis Sophia*, usually regarded as a Gnostic writing of a relatively late date.[63] In this document, the task of writing down Jesus' words is assigned by Jesus himself to several disciples, including Philip, Matthew, and Thomas (*PS* 71.18–72).[64] The most detailed account of authorship is given with regard to Philip, for he is the only disciple whose act of writing is described within the narrative itself:

> It happened now when Jesus heard these words which Philip said, he said to him: 'Excellent, Philip, thou beloved one. Come now at this time, sit and write thy part of every word which I shall say, and what shall I do, and everything which thou shalt see.' And immediately Philip sat down and wrote (*PS* 75.1–6).[65]

The way Philip is characterized in *Pistis Sophia* can be seen as uniting

---

[62] While Robinson regards the title of the *Book of Thomas* as secondary to its introduction, Turner has argued that the *Book of Thomas* comprises a collection of Jesus' sayings ascribed to Mathaias and a dialogue of Thomas with the Savior. In this case the beginning of the *Book of Thomas* (excluding the references to Thomas) would originally have been an introduction to the sayings collection, and the closing of the writing could have been the title of the dialogue. Cf. J. M. Robinson, 'LOGOI SOPHON: On the Gattung of Q,' in J. M. Robinson and H. Koester, *Trajectories through Early Christianity* (Philadelphia: Fortress Press, 1971) 71–113, esp. 81–3; Turner, *The Book of Thomas the Contender*, 108–9. Criticism with regard to Turner's theory has recently been voiced by Uro (referring to Perkins and Schenke): 'a less complicated hypothesis is that the form of homiletical discourse was in the beginning and the discourse was appended to the dialogue between Thomas and Jesus at some stage of the redaction'; R. Uro, 'The Secret Words to Judas Thomas: The *Gospel* and the *Book of Thomas*' (Paper Presented at the Annual Meeting of the Society of Biblical Literature, New Orleans, November, 1996).

[63] Cf. Marjanen, *The Woman Jesus Loved*, 171–2: 'There is general agreement that both works of *Pistis Sophia* [i.e. I–III and IV] date from the third century. ... There is no doubt that both parts of *Pistis Sophia* are Gnostic works. They seem to presuppose a myth resembling that of the *Apocryphon of John*.' A similar, or even later, dating (the third or fourth century CE) is suggested by P. Perkins, 'Pistis Sophia,' *ABD* 5 (1992) 375–6.

[64] Cf. W. A. Bienert, 'The Picture of the Apostle in Early Christian Tradition,' in *New Testament Apocrypha* 2.5–27, esp. 18.

[65] The edition and translation I follow here are those of C. Schmidt and V. MacDermot, eds., *Pistis Sophia* (NHS 9; Leiden: E.J. Brill, 1978).

the best features of the Beloved Disciple and of Thomas, for he is presented both as an understanding and as a beloved disciple of Jesus. However, in *Pistis Sophia* even these qualities do not make Philip unique. In fact, *Pistis Sophia* introduces a number of 'beloved disciples,'[66] most of whom seem to understand Jesus well.[67]

In comparison to the detailed accounts of authorship included in the *Book of Thomas* and *Pistis Sophia*, both the Gospel of John and the *Gospel of Thomas* represent a less concrete stage of authorial fiction, for they do not yet relate an account of the *circumstances* in which they were allegedly written. In these gospels, the mere claim that they were authored by Jesus' disciples was still a sufficient means of authentication.

Admittedly, authorial fiction provides us with no absolute indication for dating early Christian writings, for it had assumed very concrete forms already in the writings which are earlier than any of them. There were representatives of Jewish visionary literature, dating from the first century CE or earlier, in which modes of production were already pictured meticulously (e.g. *1* and *2 Enoch*). Nevertheless, it might be a helpful tool in locating the place of the Gospel of John and the *Gospel of Thomas* within early Christianity. It can be maintained with some confidence that early Christian writings indicate that authorial fiction gradually turned in an increasingly concrete direction. In addition to the examples mentioned above, it has been noted that while in the gospels of the New Testament 'I' or 'we' are not used by the narrator (this, of course, would apply to the *Gospel of Thomas* as well), this feature is frequently attested by the extracanonical gospels.[68] Similar

---

[66] In the *Pistis Sophia*, John (*PS* 129.9; 204.18), James (*PS* 149.7) and Matthew (*PS* 161.23) are also called 'beloved.' Moreover, John and Mary Magdalene are regarded as superior to the other disciples (*PS* 232.26–233.2). Despite Mary's distinguished status among the disciples (cf. also *PS* 26.17–20), she is, however, never called 'beloved' in the *Pistis Sophia*. For Mary's exceptional role in the *Pistis Sophia*, see Marjanen, *The Woman Jesus Loved*, 173–88. Among other things, Marjanen points out that in the latter part of *Pistis Sophia*, *PS* IV, Mary 'is not elevated above other disciples in the same way she is in *Pistis Sophia* I–III,' ibid., 185.

[67] Cf. Marjanen, *The Woman Jesus Loved*, 174–5.

[68] Cf. W. Speyer, *Die literarische Fälschung im heidnischen und christlichen Altertum: Ein Versuch ihrer Deutung* (Munich: C. H. Beck, 1971) 51 (with reference to von Harnack), 262. As Speyer denotes, this feature is also typical of the later representatives of Acts literature (ibid.).

signs of increasing concreteness are visible also in later representatives of the acts literature.[69]

Moreover, already the gospels included in the New Testament point to the growing necessity of authentication. The gospels which are usually considered to be earlier (Mark and Matthew) do not give any account of the way they were created, whereas the Gospel of Luke begins with a note emphazising its reliability (Luke 1.1–4), and the Gospel of John introduces the Beloved Disciple in order to authenticate its contents. Interestingly enough, those passages in which the Beloved Disciple occurs as a narrative figure have close Synoptic parallels (John 13.21–30; 19.25–27; 20.1–10; 21.1–14). If these passages betray knowledge of the Synoptic Gospels, as seems likely,[70] the Beloved Disciple's authenticating function becomes even more apparent. For in that case the Johannine author who composed these passages has *added* the figure of the Beloved Disciple to them in order to authenticate them more successfully.[71] This author has thus chosen a different approach to earlier source materials than the author of the Gospel of Luke, who refers to the existence and use of previous sources. Although authorial fiction in the Gospel of John is less concrete than in many later early Christian writings, this Gospel has taken a crucial step into a more concrete way of describing its mode of production by introducing a figure who was supposed to be present as the narrated events took place, and then wrote about them.

On the one hand, it seems that the authorial fiction in the *Gospel of Thomas* represents a less concrete stage than that in the Gospel of John. The latter is obviously more concerned with affirming its claim of authorship than the former. In the Gospel of John, the reliability of the alleged author is underscored through specific remarks (John 19.35; 21.24). The *Gospel of Thomas* is less sophisticated in this respect, for its

---

[69] Cf. Speyer, *Literarische Fälschung*, 51.

[70] Frans Neirynck has in several articles argued convincingly that many details which occur in the Johannine passages of the Beloved Disciple are obviously redactional in the Synoptic Gospels; cf. his *Evangelica: Gospel Studies – Études d'évangile: Collected Essays* (BETL 60, Leuven: Leuven University Press/Peeters, 1982), esp. 365–455; idem, *Evangelica II: 1982–1991: Collected Essays* (BETL 99; Leuven: Leuven University Press/Peeters, 1991), esp. 571–616. Neirynck's conclusion about the Synoptic influence on the Johannine Beloved Disciple passages is followed by Kügler, *Der Jünger den Jesus liebte*.

[71] Cf. also Culpepper's judgment: 'As a conclusion to this survey of the references to the Beloved Disciple in John, we may underscore the point that each of them seems to be a secondary addition to earlier tradition' (*John, the Son of Zebedee*, 72). Culpepper does not, however, maintain that the 'earlier tradition' is dependent on the Synoptic Gospels.

author is identified without similar affirmations of reliability. On the other hand, the emphasis the *Gospel of Thomas* lays on Jesus' *secret sayings* seems to presuppose that his more 'public' words already were in circulation and commonly known. This notion of disclosing secrets may reflect a situation similar to that reflected in the appearance of the Beloved Disciple in the Johannine passages. In their distinctive ways, both gospels indicate awareness of the existence of other Jesus traditions which, in turn, could have required that they use Jesus' disciples as authenticating figures.

Although the Gospel of John and the *Gospel of Thomas* cast their modes of production in somewhat similar terms, there are also substantial differences in their authorial fictions. It was argued above that the ways these gospels present their authenticating figures do not suggest any mutual dependency. Rather, their claims for apostolic authorship connect them with a more broadly attested phenomenon within early Christianity. Not only are several later writings ascribed to Jesus' disciples (or to Jesus himself) but, as is commonly acknowledged, secondary claims to apostolic authorship are made already in the New Testament:[72] later writings of the Pauline School are ascribed to Paul himself (e.g. the Pastoral Epistles), whereas other epistles introduce as their authors disciples or relatives of Jesus (Peter, Jude, James) and/or make a claim for being written by an eyewitness (1 John 1.1–4; 2 Pet 1.16–18).[73]

The second century CE provides us also with what might be called 'secondary authorial fiction,' for there emerges gradually a tradition concerning the identity of the authors of the Gospels included in the New Testament. In this tradition the authors of the New Testament Gospels were identified either as Jesus' disciples (Matthew, John) or their close associates (Mark, Peter's interpreter, and Luke, fellow worker to Paul). At the same time, the question of apostolic succession became increasingly important. There are numerous indications of this development. It is reflected, for example, in the Papias fragment, in which a distinction is made between the more profitable 'living and abiding voice' of Jesus, transmitted through Jesus' own disciples, and the less profitable written accounts (Eusebius, *Hist. eccl.* 3.39.3–4). A

---

[72] Cf. Lorenzen, *Lieblingsjünger*, 102.
[73] For later instances of using 'eyewitness testimonies' in authenticating Christian writings, see Speyer, *Literarische Fälschung,* 51–6.

few decades later, claims for apostolic succession were apparently of equal importance to Irenaeus (*Adv. haer.* 3.3.4) and his opponents such as Basilides and Valentinus (cf. Clement of Alexandria, *Strom.* 7.106.4).[74]

It is this broadly attested tendency of claiming apostolic authority, taking place above all during the later generations of early Christianity, that offers the most plausible context for creating and using authenticating figures such as the Beloved Disciple in the Gospel of John and Thomas in the *Gospel of Thomas*. The more aware early Christian writers became of the diversity within early Christian traditions, the more important it became to convince their audience that the specific branch of tradition they were representing was the most reliable. Ascriptions of their writings to Jesus' disciples were one, and in light of their popularity apparently an effective, means to authenticate these traditions.

As for the relationship between the Gospel of John and the *Gospel of Thomas*, this result lends support to the view that neither of these gospels, at least in their extant forms, can be dated very early in the first century CE. The way authenticating figures are presented in these gospels connects them with Christian writings that are later than the earliest gospels, in which such ascriptions are still lacking. However, in these gospels authorial fiction has assumed less concrete forms than in some other early Christian writings. This indicates that they still stand at the threshold of the development which gradually led to increasingly concrete ways of authenticating pseudepigraphical writings in early Christianity.

---

[74] Cf. C. Markschies, *Valentinus Gnosticus? Untersuchungen zur valentinianischen Gnosis mit einem Kommentar zu den Fragmenten Valentins* (WUNT 65; Tübingen: J. C. B. Mohr [Paul Siebeck], 1992) 298–302. According to Clement, Basilides relied on Glaucias, Peter's interpreter, whereas Valentinus claimed to have heard Theodas, Paul's disciple (γνώριμος, *Strom.* 7.106.3–4).

4

Women disciples in the *Gospel of Thomas*

Antti Marjanen

Interpretations of *Thomas'* view of women have varied greatly during the past few years. Some readers of the gospel have regarded it as one of the most male chauvinistic voices of early Christianity, while others have placed it among those writings which opened new, more positive possibilities for women to delineate their self-identity within the world of antiquity. In the face of these confusing circumstances, there is an obvious need to investigate once again the difficult issue of women's position in *Thomas*. The purpose of this article is to analyze all those logia in the *Gospel of Thomas* where women disciples appear, and to see what role they play in the context of the writing, and what kind of general understanding of Christian women *Thomas'* presentation of Jesus' women disciples reflects.[1]

Although several logia of the *Gospel of Thomas* are presented in the form of a dialogue between Jesus and his nearest followers, there are only a few sayings where any of Jesus' interlocutors is mentioned by name.[2] The only exceptions are the male disciples Simon Peter (13; 114), Matthew (13), Thomas (13; cf. also incipit) and the two women, Mary Magdalene (21; 114)[3] and Salome (61). Besides these, the only

---

[1] The essay is a slightly revised and expanded version of a section in A. Marjanen, *The Woman Jesus Loved: Mary Magdalene in the Nag Hammadi Library and Related Documents* (NHMS 40; Leiden: E. J. Brill, 1996) 39–55.

[2] There are sixteen logia in which an anonymous body of the disciples collectively appear as interlocutors of Jesus (6; 12; 14; 18; 20; 22; 24; 37; 43; 51; 52; 53; 60; 72; 99; 113).

[3] Logia 21 and 114 refer to a woman called ⲘⲀⲣⲓⲌⲀⲘ. There is no doubt that in both cases the same woman is meant. In neither instance is the identity of ⲘⲀⲣⲓⲌⲀⲘ more closely specified. Nevertheless, the situation described in logion 114 makes it most probable that it is Mary Magdalene about whom the texts speak. The tension between Peter and ⲘⲀⲣⲓⲌⲀⲘ in logion 114 has its parallel in the *Gospel of Mary* and in *Pistis Sophia* where the conflict between these two is a prominent if not a central theme (*Gos. Mary* 17.16 – 18.10; *PS* 58.11–21; 162.14–21; 377.14–17). Apart from Mary Magdalene, no other Mary turns up in such a polemic context. The form of the name (ⲘⲀⲣⲓⲌⲀⲘ), which in Coptic texts is used of Mary Magdalene but not of the mother of Jesus, also bolsters this conclusion; for the evidence, see Marjanen, *The Woman Jesus Loved*, 63–4.

other character of early Christianity who is mentioned in the writing is James the Just (12). In light of the fact that only six persons of Jesus' intimate circle are featured in *Thomas*, it is conspicuous that two of them are women. This suggests that their choice as Jesus' interlocutors has not been accidental and that the compilers of the *Gospel of Thomas* had something special in mind when placing them in logia 21, 61, and 114. As will be shown later, the characterization of Mary Magdalene varies in logia 21 and 114, since the latter seems to derive from a later stage within the development of Thomasine traditions.

Before we look more closely at logia 21, 61, and 114, it is useful to examine briefly how the author of the *Gospel of Thomas* portrays other members of Jesus' nearest followers whom he mentions by name. Clearly, James and Thomas have a special role in the *Gospel of Thomas*. James is known to have been appointed the first leader of the disciples after Jesus' departure (12). Thomas is seen, not only as the one through whom the secret teachings of Jesus can be handed on to later readers (incipit), but also as the one who (after James?) has a unique understanding of Jesus. He represents a disciple who has drunk from a special spring, i.e. from the mouth of Jesus, and no longer has need of any master since he himself has become like Jesus (13; 108).

Although James' position as an authority was recognized by the compiler of the *Gospel of Thomas*, he relativizes it by placing logion 13 immediately after logion 12. While logion 12 emphasizes a leader-centered organization among the disciples, logion 13 points out that the disciples, having come to a full realization of Jesus' (and their own) real character, become 'Jesus-like' (cf. also 108). It is tempting to see in logia 12 and 13 a development from the hierarchical understanding of Christian leadership, connected with James, to the notion of a 'masterless' Christian self-identity, linked with Thomas.[4]

Simon Peter and Matthew, on the other hand, are pictured as possessing a mistaken conception of Jesus (13). Their inability to understand is underlined by the fact that if they (and other disciples) were to hear one word of the secret revelation Jesus imparted to Thomas they would try to

---

[4] Whether the tension between logia 12 and 13 can be used to reconstruct two clearly datable historical phases within the life of Thomasine Christians, however, is more uncertain; this has been suggested by J. D. Crossan, *The Historical Jesus: The Life of a Mediterranean Jewish Peasant* (San Francisco: Harper, 1991) 427–8, and S. J. Patterson, *The Gospel of Thomas and Jesus* (Foundations and Facets: Reference Series; Sonoma: Polebridge Press, 1993) 117.

stone the disciple. In the case of Simon Peter, logion 114 still corrobor-
ates the negative picture the gospel wants to paint of him.

4.1. *Salome and Mary Magdalene in logia 61 and 21*

Jesus said, 'Two will rest on a bed: the one will die, and the other will live.'

Salome said, 'Who are you, man, as though from the one[5] you have come up
on my couch and eaten from my table?'

Jesus said to her, 'I am he who exists from the equal(?). I was given some of
the things of my father.'

<. . .> 'I am your disciple.'

<. . .> 'Therefore I say, if he is equal(?)[6] he will be filled with light, but if he is
divided, he will be filled with darkness.' (*Gos. Thom.* 61.)

---

[5]   The text is not easy to understand at this point. T. O. Lambdin overlooks the words after
'man' and provides no translation; see 'The Gospel according to Thomas' (English
translation) in B. Layton, ed., *Nag Hammadi Codex II,2–7 together with XIII,2*, Brit. Lib.
Or. 4926(1), and P.Oxy. 1, 654, 655*, vol. 1 (NHS 20; Leiden: E. J. Brill, 1989) 75
(however, cf. Lambdin in J. M. Robinson, ed., *The Nag Hammadi Library in English*
[Leiden: E. J. Brill, 1977] 124–5). My translation 'as though from the one' is based on an
analysis of the text by Ismo Dunderberg; see his '*Thomas*' I-sayings and the Gospel of
John' in this volume. For other interpretations of the passage, see the critical apparatus of
B. Layton, ed., *Nag Hammadi Codex II,2–7*, 74.

[6]   The translation presupposes an emendation of the Coptic text. Instead of ⲉϥϣⲏϥ
('destroyed') one should read ⲉϥϣⲏϣ, a form of the verb ϣⲱϣ which appears also in
line 43.29 and characterizes the Father or his realm. It is not fully clear how the stative
form of the verb should be translated in this logion. According to W. E. Crum, *A Coptic
Dictionary* (Oxford: Clarendon Press, 1939) 606, the stative of ϣⲱϣ means 'to be
equal, level, straight.' This meaning of the word is adopted, e.g. by the translators of the
editio princeps; see A. Guillaumont, H.-C. Puech, G. Quispel, W. Till, and Y. 'A. al
Masīḥ, eds., *The Gospel according to Thomas: Coptic Text Established and Translated*
(Leiden: E. J. Brill, 1959) 35; cf. also J.-E. Ménard, *L'Évangile selon Thomas* (NHS 5;
Leiden: E. J. Brill, 1975) 66; Dunderberg, '*Thomas*' I-Sayings and the Gospel of John,' in
this volume. However, this interpretation of the verb is somewhat surprising in its context
unless 'being equal' is seen as a mysterious characterization of the disciple (and of the
Father) in the same way that 'equality' is presented as a trait of the Father and the
pleromatic entities in *Tri. Trac.* 67.36; 94.40 (cf. Irenaeus, *Adv. haer.* 1.2.6). Especially in
more recent translations, ϣⲏϣ is interpreted in light of its present context and in light
of Thomasine theology. Since the obvious opposite of ϣⲏϣ in the text is to 'be divided'
and since the gospel emphasizes the ideal of oneness, B. Layton suggests the translation 'to
be integrated'; see *The Gnostic Scriptures* (Garden City: Doubleday, 1987) 391; similarly
B. Gärtner, *Ett nytt evangelium? Thomasevangeliets hemliga Jesusord* (Stockholm: Diakonistyrelsens bokförlag, 1960) 122. Lambdin translates 'to be undivided' in Layton, ed., *Nag
Hammadi Codex II,2–7*, 75. M. Meyer renders the phrase 'to be whole'; see *The Gospel of
Thomas: The Hidden Sayings of Jesus* (San Francisco: Harper, 1992) 47. The problem with
these translations is that, to my knowledge, no parallel for this kind of use of ϣⲏϣ has
been found.

Mary said to Jesus: 'Whom are your disciples like?'

He said: 'They are like little children who have settled in a field which is not theirs. When the owners of the field come, they will say: 'Let us have back our field.' The children undress in their presence in order to let them have back their field and to give it back to them.

'Therefore I say, if the owner of a house knows that the thief is coming, he will begin his vigil before he comes and will not let him dig through into his house of his kingdom to carry away his goods. You, then, be on your guard against the world. Arm yourselves with great strength lest the robbers find a way to come to you. For otherwise they shall find the profit you expect. Let there be among you a person who understands.

'When the grain ripened, he came quickly with his sickle in his hand and reaped it. Whoever has ears to hear let him hear.'[7] (*Gos. Thom.* 21.)

In logia 61 and 21 Salome and Mary Magdalene are involved in a discussion which elucidates the nature of discipleship. They are not depicted as ones who misunderstand, but as ones who do not quite understand enough. They do not seem to have attained a level of perception equal to that of Thomas. Although the discussion between Jesus and Salome (61) gives the latter a chance to avow that she is his disciple, Jesus' comment after her confession seems to suggest that she is not yet a 'masterless' disciple in the sense of Thomas (13; cf. also 108). She is challenged to reach the highest level of discipleship and become 'equal(?) ... filled with light.'[8] It looks as if one can be a disciple in one sense without being a disciple in the Thomasine sense. The same seems to be true in logion 21.

Logion 21 begins with Mary Magdalene's question about the

---

[7] The translation follows that of Lambdin in Layton, ed., *Nag Hammadi Codex II,2–7*, 63, with the exception of the words 'For otherwise they shall find the profit you expect.' Lambdin translates: 'for the difficulty which you expect will (surely) materialize'; reasons for a different translation are given in Marjanen, *The Woman Jesus Loved*, 35. In addition, Lambdin's 'man of understanding' is changed to 'person who understands.'

[8] With reference to log. 13, Pheme Perkins suggests that 'eating from a table with the savior implies that an individual is enlightened'; see 'The Gospel of Thomas,' in E. Schüssler Fiorenza, ed., *Searching the Scriptures*, vol. 2: *A Feminist Commentary* (London: SCM Press, 1995) 552. This interpretation is not very convincing. While log. 61 indeed speaks about table fellowship, the context of Thomas' drinking in log. 13 is quite different. It implies that Thomas has drunk from the bubbling spring of the mouth of Jesus, i.e. he has received a special understanding of Jesus and himself, and has thus become a 'masterless' and 'Jesus-like' disciple. In log. 61 the reference to table fellowship need not indicate more than that Salome is hospitable to Jesus.

characteristics of the disciples.[9] Clearly, the question implies that she wants and needs to get more information about this matter. Should this be understood to suggest that she in fact does not yet belong to the circle of disciples who collectively act as interlocutors, but that she only deliberates whether she should and could join it? To answer this question in the affirmative would be too hasty a conclusion. Rather, like Salome, Mary Magdalene is a disciple in the ordinary sense of the word. She still lacks understanding and needs to be exhorted to become ΟΥΡⲰΜЄ ⲚЄⲠⲒⲤΤΗΜⲰΝ ('a person who understands'; 21). In other words, she is urged to reach the higher stage of discipleship that could be characterized as 'masterless' (13) or 'Jesus-like' (108).[10]

Mary Magdalene's or Salome's lack of understanding should not be overemphasized. They are by no means the only ones who have to receive a word of exhortation or a special instruction. Jesus' response to Mary Magdalene in logion 21 shows that his conversation with her is no private affair. The parenetic section after the parable of the thief is not directed to Mary alone but obviously to all the interlocutors, i.e. to all the disciples. It is also worth noting that in logion 22, where all the disciples ask whether they enter the kingdom as children, i.e. as disciples (cf. 21), Jesus points out that belonging to the circle of disciples is no automatic guarantee of entering the kingdom.[11] A disciple must become a disciple of the highest level in the special Thomasine sense in order to obtain the kingdom and immortality. Therefore the disciples as well as the later readers of the text need a special ability to hear, to understand, and to interpret the words of

---

[9] In the *Sophia of Jesus Christ* Mary Magdalene also asks a question about the disciples (III/4 114.8–12). However, in *Gos. Thom.* 21 the focus of Mary's question is on the essence of discipleship, whereas in *Soph. Jes. Chr.* III/4 114.8–12 she seeks to know where the disciples come from, where they will go, and what their task on the earth is.

[10] Differently Perkins, who thinks logia 21 and 61 show that Mary Magdalene and Salome 'are clearly disciples whose insight is similar to that of Thomas'; see 'The Gospel of Thomas,' 558. In the case of Mary Magdalene, Perkins tries to prove her thesis by claiming that 'the introduction to log. 21 coordinates it with log. 13. In the latter, Jesus tested his disciples by asking them to provide a simile or comparison that expressed what he was like. In the former, Mary poses the same challenge in reverse.' Yet the parenetic part of Jesus' reply indicates that Mary Magdalene is not testing Jesus' understanding but seeking to be taught by him.

[11] As a matter of fact, in the *Gospel of Thomas* being a disciple in the ordinary sense of the word is almost the same as having a dearth of understanding. Out of the twelve questions they put to Jesus at least seven reveal an explicit lack of understanding or a full misunderstanding (6; 18; 43; 51; 52; 99; 113).

Jesus (1). Like Thomas, they have to drink from the bubbling spring of Jesus' mouth as well (13; 108).

Although in the *Gospel of Thomas* the prototype of a spiritually advanced disciple is clearly Thomas, and all the other disciples including Mary Magdalene and Salome are in need of deeper instruction, nonetheless it is significant that they are singled out as spokespersons for the entire group of disciples. What is the reason for this? Does it simply reveal the influence of a developing tradition reflected in Gnostic revelation dialogues, according to which especially Mary Magdalene but also Salome had an active role in the conversations during which Jesus gave special, esoteric teachings to his disciples?[12] This is possible, although in the *Gospel of Thomas,* according to its own priorities, Mary Magdalene, at least, has a more modest role, and the discussions do not seem to take place after but prior to the death and resurrection of Jesus. Yet one can ask whether the use of a tradition fully explains the writing's interest in Mary Magdalene and Salome. Do the references to them rather indicate that the redactor has a concrete need, arising from the situation of the readers, to include in the writing logia dealing with women? We shall return to this question again when analyzing logion 114 and ask what it reveals about the attitudes of the writer towards women, and the position of women among the audience of the gospel.

4.2. Mary Magdalene in logion 114

ΠΕϪΕ ⲤⲒⲘⲰⲚ ΠΕΤΡΟⲤ ⲚⲀⲨ ϪⲈ ⲘⲀⲢⲈ ⲘⲀⲢⲒϨⲀⲘ ⲈⲒ ⲈⲂⲞⲖ Ⲛ̄ϨⲎⲦⲚ̄ ϪⲈ
Ⲛ̄ⲤϨⲒⲞⲘⲈ Ⲙ̄ΠϢⲀ ⲀⲚ Ⲙ̄ΠⲰⲚϨ
ΠΕϪⲈ Ⲓ̄Ⲥ̄ ϪⲈ ⲈⲒⲤϨⲎⲎⲦⲈ ⲀⲚⲞⲔ †ⲚⲀⲤⲰⲔ Ⲙ̄ⲘⲞⲤ ϪⲈⲔⲀⲀⲤ ⲈⲈⲒⲚⲀⲀⲤ
Ⲛ̄ϨⲞⲞⲨⲦ ϢⲒⲚⲀ ⲈⲤⲚⲀϢⲰΠⲈ ϨⲰⲰⲤ Ⲛ̄ⲞⲨΠⲚ̄Ⲁ̄ ⲈϤⲞⲚϨ ⲈϤⲈⲒⲚⲈ
Ⲙ̄ⲘⲰⲦⲚ̄ Ⲛ̄ϨⲞⲞⲨⲦ ϪⲈ ⲤϨⲒⲘⲈ ⲚⲒⲘ ⲈⲤⲚⲀⲀⲤ Ⲛ̄ϨⲞⲞⲨⲦ ⲤⲚⲀⲂⲰⲔ ⲈϨⲞⲨⲚ
ⲈⲦⲘⲚ̄ⲦⲈⲢⲞ Ⲛ̄Ⲙ̄ΠⲎⲨⲈ

---

[12] For the role of Mary Magdalene in Gnostic revelation dialogues, see Marjanen, *The Woman Jesus Loved.* In addition to *Gos. Thom.* 61, Salome appears as an interlocutor of Jesus in *Pistis Sophia.* She is also mentioned in *1 Apoc. Jas.* 40.25–26 and *Man. Ps. II* 192.24; 194.21. Cf. also the tradition preserved in the Greek *Gospel of the Egyptians*; for an English translation of the texts, see W. Schneemelcher, ed., *New Testament Apocrypha*, vol. 1: *Gospels and Related Writings* (English trans. ed. by R. McL. Wilson; Cambridge: James Clarke; Louisville: Westminster Press/John Knox Press, 1992) 209–11.

Simon Peter said to them: 'Let Mary leave us, for women are not worthy of life.'

[2]Jesus said: 'I myself shall lead her in order to make her male, so that she too may become a living spirit resembling you males. [3]For every woman who will make herself male will enter the kingdom of heaven.'[13]

Logion 114 is one of the most studied and debated logia in the entire gospel.[14] With regard to the interpretation of Mary Magdalene there are three sets of important questions which need to be discussed. First, is the train of thought in the comment of Jesus internally consistent? In other words, how can Jesus speak at the same time about Mary whom he will 'make male' and about women who 'make themselves male?' Is this a contradiction and if it is, can it be reconciled? Or is this only seemingly a problem due to a mistaken understanding of the syntax of Jesus' statement, as Schüngel has suggested in a recent article?[15] This reasoning inevitably poses the question of how the structure of the comment is to be analyzed and what kind of translation can be based on this analysis.

Second, what is actually meant by 'being made/making oneself male,' and how is this event related to 'making the two one ... so that the male not be male nor the female female' in logion 22 (cf. also 106)? Again we encounter a contradiction. Is it real or only apparent? If it is real, how is it to be explained? In addition, the phrase 'being made/making oneself male' forces one to ask what kinds of views of women are reflected in the text and how they possibly mirror the situation of the Christians among whom the logion was narrated and read.

---

[13] The text and the translation are taken from Layton, ed., *Nag Hammadi Codex II,2–7*, 92–3.

[14] For recent studies on this logion, see e.g. K. H. Rengstorf, 'Urchristliches Kerygma und "gnostische" Interpretation in einigen Sprüchen des Thomasevangeliums,' in U. Bianchi, ed., *Le Origini dello Gnosticismo: Colloquio di Messina 13–18 Aprile 1966* (Leiden: E. J. Brill, 1967) 563–74; W. A. Meeks, 'The Image of Androgyne: Some Uses of the Symbol in Earliest Christianity,' *HR* 13 (1974) 193–7; J. Dart, 'The Two Shall Become One,' *Theology Today* (1978) 321–5; J. J. Buckley, 'An Interpretation of Logion 114 in the *Gospel of Thomas*,' *NovT* (1985) 245–72; M. Meyer, 'Making Mary Male: The Categories "Male" and "Female" in the Gospel of Thomas,' *NTS* 31 (1985) 554–70; M. Lelyveld, *Les logia de la vie dans l'Évangile selon Thomas: A la recherche d'une tradition et d'une rédaction* (NHS 30; Leiden: E. J. Brill, 1987) 138–43; S. Arai, ' "To Make Her Male": An Interpretation of Logion 114 in the Gospel of Thomas,' *StPatr* 24 (1993) 373–6; P. Schüngel, 'Ein Vorschlag, EvTho 114 neu zu übersetzen,' *NovT* 36 (1994) 394–401; A. D. De Conick, *Seek to See Him: Ascent and Vision Mysticism in the Gospel of Thomas* (VCSup 33; Leiden: E. J. Brill, 1996) 18–21.

[15] Schüngel, 'Vorschlag,' 394–401.

Unavoidably, this leads to a third set of questions about the conflict between Peter and Jesus over the position of Mary Magdalene among the disciples. Is the conflict only a narrative device which gives the author a chance to present his/her view on this matter, or does the text reflect a real debate? Finally, were Peter and Mary Magdalene randomly picked out to be the protagonists of the text, or does the fact that they were chosen say anything more concrete about the nature of the debate?

4.3. The syntax and translation of logion 114

In his article Schüngel called attention to the fact that, according to all existing translations of logion 114, Jesus appears to make a contradictory statement.[16] On the one hand, he promises to make Mary Magdalene male so that she may become a living spirit and enter the kingdom of heaven. On the other hand, he states that 'every woman who will make herself male will enter the kingdom of heaven.' In other words, what Jesus seems to be doing for Mary Magdalene, all the other women are supposed to do for themselves. Schüngel thinks that this inconsistency is not actually in the text but in the minds of the translators, because they have not understood correctly the syntax of logion 114. Schüngel's own analysis of the syntax differs from the consensus of opinion in three points:[17] First, he interprets the first sentence of Jesus' answer after ЄІСꙅНнтЄ as a rhetorical question to which a negative answer is expected (114.2a). Second, the following ϢΙΝΑ-clause (114.2b) should not be taken together with what precedes, but with what follows. Third, ЄϥЄΙΝЄ after the ϢΙΝΑ-clause is not what the Coptic grammarians call a 'circumstantial' modifying an indefinite antecedent (ΟΥΠΝЄΥΜΑ), but a 'second present' which begins the main clause ('her pneuma is equal to that of you'). To these syntactical observations Schüngel adds one more concerning the semantics of the text. He argues that the word ꙅΟΟΥТ ('male') in the comment of Jesus should not be understood as a gender-

---

[16] Ibid., 394.
[17] Ibid., 397–400.

related term, but that it has the connotation 'firm, in a manly manner' or 'capable of controlling one's own life.'[18] Based on his analysis, Schüngel makes the following English translation of the text:[19]

> Simon Peter said to them: Mary should leave us, for life is not for women!
>
> Jesus said: Watch this! Is it me, who shall drag her in order that I might make her male? In order that she, too, may become a *pneuma* that is alive, her *pneuma* is equal to that of you,[20] you who are male. For every woman who makes herself male[21] does enter the kingdom of heaven.

With his interpretation, Schüngel tries to remove not only the terminological contradiction within Jesus' saying, but also the offense which the phrase 'every woman who makes herself male' causes. If logion 114 is understood in this way, it matches well, in Schüngel's opinion, the main thrust of the *Gospel of Thomas*. He thinks *Thomas'* central emphasis is found in a challenge, directed equally to women and men, to search for human growth and ethical independence through a process of finding one's potentialities, capacities, and limits.[22]

There is no possibility, nor any need, to assess here whether Schüngel's thesis about *Thomas'* central message can be maintained. However, if his understanding of logion 114 could be accepted, both syntactically and semantically, this would have some significance for the interpretation of Mary Magdalene in this passage. According to Schüngel, Mary Magdalene herself becomes more clearly a symbol of the human possibility of reaching salvation. This notion is held by a religious minority, whereas Peter represents the male-chauvinistic view of the ecclesiastical majority.

None of Schüngel's arguments which support his translation, however, is really convincing. The first argument, that the beginning of Jesus' statement should be understood as a rhetorical question to which

---

[18] Ibid., 399.

[19] Ibid., 400.

[20] At this point Schüngel's English translation differs from his German version as well as from the Coptic original. The Coptic text cannot be read to emphasize the similarity of Mary Magdalene's *pneuma* to those of the male disciples. Rather the comparison points out that Mary's *pneuma* does become male.

[21] It is surprising that ϩⲟⲟⲩⲧ is translated by Schüngel ('Vorschlag,' 399) as 'male,' even if he insists that the word no longer has a gender-related connotation.

[22] Schüngel, 'Vorschlag,' 400.

a negative answer is expected, is not impossible, but less likely than an alternative interpretation according to which the sentence is a mere statement.[23] The second assertion is obviously the most important one in Schüngel's argumentation, but it is also the most vulnerable. As claimed by him, a sentence can begin with a final ϢΙΝΑ-clause, but only if the main clause, which is supposed to come before it, is left out through an ellipsis.[24] It is extremely unlikely that a main clause comes after a final ϢΙΝΑ-clause. Therefore, it is much more probable that the ϢΙΝΑ-clause must be joined to the preceding, not to that which follows. Schüngel's third argument stands or falls together with the second. If the ϢΙΝΑ-clause is read together with the preceding, ΕϤΕΙΝΕ cannot but be a 'circumstantial' which modifies the indefinite antecedent ΟΥΠΝΕΥΜΑ. With his fourth argument, according to which 2ΟΟΥΤ does not have a gender-related connotation in logion 114 but only implies that a person is capable of controlling his/her own life, Schüngel creates alternatives which exclude each other even though they need not do so. It is evident that the word has a symbolic connotation which goes beyond its concrete meaning, but this 'something more' is clearly connected with the gender-related character of the word. This 'something more' represents human values or characteristics which can be defined as 'male' but obviously not as 'female.' Therefore, it is difficult to find in logion 114 the egalitarian emphasis which Schüngel sees in it.

Based on these observations, it should be concluded that the translation presented by Schüngel is implausible. The earlier renderings, represented for example by Lambdin's,[25] convey more correctly the meaning of the Coptic text. If this be accepted, the contradiction in Jesus' comment observed by Schüngel seems to remain. Yet perhaps the disagreement between 'Jesus making Mary male' and 'every woman

---

[23] Usually a rhetorical question is introduced by ΜΗ; see W. C. Till, *Koptische Grammatik* (Leipzig: VEB, 1978) 213–14. A good example of this is provided by the last clause of *Gos. Thom.* 72. This begins with the negation ΜΗ, which is followed by a 'second present.'

[24] The two examples of a ϢΙΝΑ-clause beginning a sentence which Schüngel ('Vorschlag,' 398) finds in the *Gospel of Thomas* are no examples at all. In the first case ϢΙΝΑ is not final but temporal (22), and in the second the conjunction clearly follows the main clause (103).

[25] 'The Gospel According to Thomas,' 93.

making herself male' is not so great after all. Both of the texts emphasize the transformation of a woman. In the first case, as an answer to Peter's attack against Mary Magdalene, the role of Jesus in the process of transformation is stressed, whereas in the general application of Jesus' instruction the situation is seen more from the vantage point of a woman being made/making herself male.

4.4. The meaning of being made/making oneself male

There are basically three lines of interpretation as to the difficult question of the meaning of the phrase 'being made/making oneself male.' These solutions do not necessarily exclude each other.[26] First, 'being made/making oneself male' has been interpreted as a concrete impersonation of a male by a woman.[27] This took place by means of cutting one's hair short and accepting male dress. The act signified an extremely radical ascetic choice. A woman, transformed by appearance into a male, shut herself outside the ordinary female ways of life, such as marriage and child-bearing. Thus it clearly meant a denial of all sexual life. The apocryphal acts provide several examples of this kind of behavior. We read about it in connection with Thecla (*Acts of Paul and Thecla* 25; 40), Mygdonia (*Acts of Thomas* 114), Charitine (*Acts of Philip* 44),[28] and perhaps also Maximilla (*Acts of Andrew* 9).[29]

With regard to making Mary Magdalene male, one text is especially instructive. In the fourth-century *Acts of Philip*, from chapter VIII on, including the so-called *Martyrdom of Philip* (94–148),[30] there appears a

---

[26] For a similar classification of the solutions, see K. L. King, 'Kingdom in the Gospel of Thomas,' *Forum* 3.1 (1987) 66.

[27] E.g. Patterson, *Gospel of Thomas*, 154–5, although he also sees other factors involved in the use of the expression.

[28] For these names, see Patterson, *Gospel of Thomas*, 154; E. Castelli, 'Virginity and Its Meaning for Women's Sexuality in Early Christianity,' *Journal of Feminist Studies in Religion* 2 (1986) 75–6.

[29] Later the term 'male' was also used to express the excellence of women ascetics. John Chrysostom, for example, praised the ascetic Olympias thus: 'Don't say 'woman' but 'what a man!' because this is a man, despite her physical appearance' (*Life of Olympias* 3); see K. J. Torjesen, *When Women Were Priests* (San Francisco: Harper, 1993) 211.

[30] For the text, see R. A. Lipsius & M. Bonnet, *Acta Apostolorum Apocrypha* (2 vols.; Leipzig: H. Mendelsohn, 1891–1903) II/2:36–90.

woman called Mariamne. In the *Acts of Philip* 95 the Savior says to her: σὺ Μαριάμνη ἄλλαξον σου τὴν ἰδέαν καὶ ὅλον τὸ εἶδος τὸ γυναικεῖον ('Mariamne, change your outward look and your entire feminine appearance').[31] In the previous chapter Mariamne is introduced as a sister of Philip. It is worth noting that she is given the responsibility of keeping a register of all the countries where the apostles are doing mission work. This detail appears in an unedited version of the writing.[32] When Jesus divides various places among the apostles, her brother Philip becomes unhappy and cries because of the place allotted to him. Then Jesus turns to Mariamne and asks her to follow and to encourage him. The *Martyrdom of Philip* (107–148) narrates how the same Mariamne, together with Bartholomew, travels with Philip and proclaims the gospel with a strong ascetic emphasis. The prominent role which Mariamne assumes within the circle of disciples makes it probable that she is to be identified with Mary Magdalene, although she has gained new legendary features, and possibly Mary of Bethany has also been integrated into her person.[33] If this is so, the *Acts of Philip* may provide the first witness to the interpretation that making Mary male in logion 114 refers to a concrete male impersonation. Be that as it may, it is at least clear that sometime in the second century 'making oneself male' could have been understood very concretely. It is not impossible that logion 114 provides an early indication of this practice.

The second way to look at logion 114 is to interpret it in light of the Platonic myth of the androgyne (Plato, *Symposion* 189de), as it is reflected in the interpretations of the creation stories of Genesis. De Conick, for example, thinks that 'becoming male' in logion 114 means the restoration of the androgynous prelapsarian man. 'Since Eve was taken from Adam's side, so she must reenter him and become "male" in order to return to the prelapsarian state of Adam before the gender

---

[31] Ibid., II/2:37. There is another version of the text where the transformation of Mariamne into a man is described somewhat differently; see F. Bovon, 'Le privilège pascal de Marie-Madeleine,' *NTS* 30 (1984) 58. To my knowledge, the manuscript is still unedited. Bovon's French translation of the text runs as follows: 'Quant à toi, Mariamné, change de costume et d'apparance: dépouille tout ce qui, dans ton extérieur, rappelle la femme, la robe d'été que tu portes, ne laisse pas la frange de ton vêtement traîner par terre.'

[32] See Bovon, 'Le privilège pascal,' 58.

[33] In the *Acts of Philip* 94 Mariamne is linked together with Martha.

division.'[34] According to De Conick, 'becoming male' in logion 114 is not in contradiction to 'neither male nor female' in logion 22. Both of them speak about a return to the pristine state of the androgynous prelapsarian man. The only difference is that while in the case of logion 114 the prelapsarian androgynous state is understood in terms of the situation when woman was still concealed in man (Gen 2), in logion 22 it is seen in light of the time before the gender differentiation had taken place in Gen 1.27. In both logia 'salvation is based on returning to Adam's Pre-Fall state before the division of the sexes, and subsequently before the tasting of the forbidden fruit, sexual intercourse.'[35]

The third solution represented with great erudition by Meyer tries to see logion 114 within the conceptual framework of the contemporary culture where 'female' represented that which was earthly, sensual, imperfect, and passive, while 'male' symbolized that which was transcendent, chaste, perfect, and active.[36] The transformation of 'female' into 'male' is then to be understood as a movement from that which is physical and earthly to that which is spiritual and heavenly.

If the first explanation of the phrase 'being made/making oneself male' interprets it from the perspective of its concrete application, the second and the third attempt to give a theological and sociocultural motivation for it. In fact, all explanations seem to be plausible in their own way. Common to them all is the ascetic connotation of the phrase.

Yet there is one point in De Conick's and Meyer's interpretations which requires a critical comment. Their insistence that logia 114 and 22 say essentially the same thing[37] does not do justice to the clear

---

[34] De Conick, *Seek to See Him*, 18; see also Lelyveld, *Les logia de la vie*, 142. Buckley ('Interpretation of Logion 114,' 245–72) also thinks that 'becoming male' is to be seen as a restoration of the lost unity reflected in Gen 2, but she suggests that this is not the ultimate goal for a woman. It is only the first stage of a salvific process which is followed by the 'living spirit' stage which corresponds to the 'living soul' in Gen. 2 (a similar interpretation is advocated by Arai, 'To Make Her Male,' 373–6). It is difficult to find support in the text for Buckley's two-stage model. 'Making Mary male' and 'becoming a living spirit resembling you males' must be synonymous expressions describing in two different ways the same stage of development.

[35] De Conick, *Seek to See Him*, 18. Unlike De Conick, Buckley ('Interpretation of Logion 114,' 270) does not think that the return to the lost unity of Adam in Gen 2 should necessarily be interpreted as a reference to sexual abstinence. For her, the *Gospel of Thomas* is not an ascetic document.

[36] Meyer ('Making Mary Male,' 563–7) provides plentiful evidence for this kind of use of the categories 'male' and 'female' in antiquity.

[37] De Conick, *Seek to See Him*, 18–20; Meyer, 'Making Mary Male,' 567.

terminological difference between them. Even if the aim of both logia is to stress the importance of returning to a prelapsarian state or the necessity of reaching a state of asexuality, it must be emphasized that in logion 114 the goal is not achieved by the removal of gender differentiation but by the transformation of female into male.[38] Thus, in logion 114 salvation is defined by employing the patriarchal language patterns of the contemporary culture. It is important to realize that it is not only Peter's statement which displays this attitude but also Jesus' response. Although advocating Mary's and all women's right to attain salvation in terms equal to their male colleagues within the circle of disciples and the kingdom, Jesus does so by using language which devalues women. In the *Gospel of Mary* the same thing is expressed somewhat differently. There Jesus does not make women 'male,' but he makes both women and men 'human beings (ⲣⲱⲙⲉ)' (9.20; cf. 18.16). Admittedly, even here salvation is defined in terms of male-oriented language. Yet ⲣⲱⲙⲉ does not have the same exclusive character as ϩⲟⲟⲩⲧ in *Gos. Thom.* 114.

Gos. Thom. 114 comes terminologically close to those Valentinian and Naassene texts which view salvation as a transformation of 'female' into 'male' (*Exc. Theod.* 21.3; 79;[39] Heracleon, *Fr.* 5; Hippolytus, *Ref.* 5.8.44–45).[40] It is noteworthy that when the parallels speak about the transformation of 'female' into 'male' they mean everybody, both men and women. Men too are 'female,' if their life is controlled by cosmic

---

[38] This was emphasized by P. Vielhauer, 'ΑΝΑΠΑΥΣΙΣ: Zum gnostischen Hintergrund des Thomasevangeliums,' in *Apophoreta: Festschrift für Ernst Haenchen zu seinem siebzigsten Geburtstag* (Berlin: Töpelmann, 1964) 298, and by Rengstorf, 'Urchristliches Kerygma,' 565–6.

[39] As K. Vogt ("Männlichwerden' – Aspekte einer urchristlichen Anthropologie,' *Concilium* 21 [1985] 434–5) has pointed out, Clement of Alexandria, who has preserved the *Excerpta ex Theodoto*, can himself in his own text use a similar expression when he describes a woman who has been liberated from fleshly concerns. In *Strom.* 6.100.3 Clement speaks about this kind of woman as follows: καὶ μή τι οὕτως μετατίθεται εἰς τὸν ἄνδρα ἡ γυνή, ἀθήλυντος ἐπ' ἴσης καὶ ἀνδρικὴ καὶ τελεία γενομένη ('And is not woman transformed into man, when she has become equally unfeminine, manly, and perfect?').

[40] The phenomenon of 'making a woman male' is also known from other religious traditions. Arai ('To Make Her Male,' 376) refers to Mahâyâna-Buddhism which 'developed a theory of the transformation of the female into male, whereby a woman too can become a Buddha.' In the mystical Islamic tradition of Sufism it is also said that one can receive instruction from a woman, because a woman who has become male on the road of God is no longer a woman; for the reference, see F. al-Din Attar, *Muslim Saints and Mystics: Episodes from the Tadkhirat al-Auliya'* (trans. by A. J. Arberry; Persian Heritage Series; London: Routledge & Kegan Paul, 1979) 40.

powers. It is difficult to say whether or not this is also true in the symbolic world of logion 114. It is only the position of women which is at stake in this logion.

The peculiar language of logion 114 raises the question of its relationship to the rest of the gospel. The contradiction between 'being made/making oneself male' and 'neither male nor female' (logion 22) is not the only feature which gives logion 114 a special position among *Thomas'* sayings. Logion 114 begins with a disciple addressing other disciples. This is a literary device not found anywhere else in the entire writing. It is also noteworthy that logion 113 seems to form a thematic inclusion with logion 3 and could thus be a natural ending for the collection. Based on these arguments, Davies has suggested that logion 114 is a later expansion of the gospel.[41] If this theory is accepted, logion 114 may have been attached to the gospel fairly late in the second century. The fact that the phenomenon and the phrase 'making oneself male' has very close, almost verbal parallels, on the one hand, in the second- and third-century apocryphal acts, and on the other, among the late second-century Valentinian and Naassene texts, speaks for the fairly late origin of the logion itself.

If the secondary character of logion 114 is accepted, the discussion of the role of Mary Magdalene, and of women in general, is placed in a new context. While in logia 21 and 61 Mary Magdalene and Salome have a relatively visible role among the disciples as the ones who seek a deeper understanding of Jesus' teaching, in logion 114 Mary Magdalene becomes the object of an attempt to exclude her from the circle of Thomasine disciples altogether. This suggests that logion 114 has been added to the collection in a situation in which the role of women in the religious life of the community has for some reason become a matter of debate. The one responsible for adding the logion to the gospel is clearly speaking on behalf of women. He/she does so by creating a saying in which Jesus speaks for Mary Magdalene against Peter. Yet the editor of the text is either so bound by his tradition, or so alienated from the earlier terminology of the Thomasine traditions, that he/she no longer uses the 'neither male nor female' language of logion 22 but

---

[41]   S. L. Davies, *The Gospel of Thomas and Christian Wisdom* (New York: The Seabury Press, 1983) 152–3, 155 (cf. also Dart, 'The Two Shall Become One,' 324). Davies also presents some arguments with regard to the terminology used in logion 114, but these are not very convincing.

resorts to employing the new expression, 'making female male,' which inevitably devalues women.

4.5. Conflict over the position of Mary Magdalene

One question remains: does the fact that Peter has been chosen to be the antagonist of Mary Magdalene tell us anything about the nature of the debate reflected in the text? Before any attempt can be made to answer this question, Peter's view of Mary Magdalene and of women in general has to be more carefully analyzed. In the first part of his statement Peter expresses his wish that Mary Magdalene leave the group he himself represents. The second part gives the reason: 'Women are not worthy of life.' The second part of Peter's comment as well as the last sentence of Jesus' reply show that Peter does not want to exclude Mary Magdalene and other women just from a group of privileged persons such as apostles, leaders, and teachers. What is at stake is a much more basic decision. Peter maintains that neither Mary Magdalene nor any other woman should have any part in salvation and the kingdom of heaven. Where in the world can one find such a narrow, discriminatory view of women? For example, if Peter is seen as a representative of a Christian majority view, as has been suggested,[42] where can this kind of conception of women be documented?

Certainly, Clement of Rome can write to his colleagues in Corinth: 'Let us guide our women toward that which is good ... let them make manifest the moderation of their tongue through their silence' (1 Clem. 21.6–7).[43] Similarly, the author of the Pastorals writes his well-known words: 'Let a woman learn in silence with all submissiveness. I permit no woman to teach or to have authority over men; she is to keep silent ... Woman will be saved through bearing children, if she continues in faith and love and holiness, with modesty' (1 Tim 2.11–12, 15). Yet neither of these writers, who clearly belong to the most candid advocates of patriarchal tendencies, comes close to the total exclusion of women from a Christian context recommended by Peter in Gos. Thom. 114. Nowhere in early Christian literature does one find an equally negative view of women.

[42]   Schüngel, 'Vorschlag,' 400; cf. also Lelyveld, Les logia de la vie, 141.
[43]   The translation is taken from J. B. Lightfoot, The Apostolic Fathers (edited and completed by J. R. Harmer; Grand Rapids: Baker, 1976) 23.

In light of these observations, one wonders whether Peter's comment was meant to be an exact documentation of any contemporary Christian view of women. Is it simply an exaggeration which underlines once again the greatness of the disciples' misunderstanding and correspondingly the importance of Jesus' correction, as is often the case in the *Gospel of Thomas* (cf. e.g. 51; 52; 89; 99; 104)? Or if it was meant to reflect a contemporary conception of women, was it presented in such a way – either unintentionally or polemically – that the particular people holding this view would not necessarily have recognized themselves in it? If that is the case, and Peter's comment somehow does mirror a contemporary view of women, there are at least two possibilities for understanding Peter. Either he can function as a caricature of a major ecclesiastical view with a clear subordination of women, or he can be seen as a mischaracterized representative of a developing ascetic perspective in which male celibates view the presence of women as threatening.

Since the first alternative appears to be quite modern, especially when the language used in the answer of Jesus, despite its non-subordinationist implication, does devalue women, the second is more probable. That is, Peter could be regarded as an archetype, although somewhat misrepresented and exaggerated, of those early Christian ascetics who stated: 'Pray in the place where there is no woman' (*Dial. Sav.* 144.16).[44] It is worth noting that one version of the *Acts of Philip* portrays Peter as a man who 'fled from all places where there was a woman' (142).[45] Some other, strictly ascetic writings link Peter with traditions according to which he eliminates the sexual threat of the female presence by causing a young woman to die[46] or to become paralyzed.[47] In light of these observations, logion 114 could perhaps reflect a conflict between two different encratic positions, one emphasizing that an ascetic group should not include people of both sexes, thus implying that women should be excluded because of their spiritual inferiority, the other, favored by the writer of the logion, insisting that

---

[44] For the interpretation of this text, see Marjanen, *The Woman Jesus Loved*, 88–91.

[45] See Lipsius & Bonnet, *Acta Apostolorum Apocrypha*, II/2.81.

[46] So in the *Pseudo-Titus Epistle*; for an English translation of the text, see W. Schnee-melcher, ed., *New Testament Apocrypha*, vol. 2: *Writings Relating to the Apostles, Apocalypses, and Related Subjects* (English trans. ed. by R. McL. Wilson; Cambridge: James Clarke & Co., 1992) 53–74, esp. 57.

[47] So in the *Act of Peter*; for the translation of the text, see J. M. Robinson, ed., *The Nag Hammadi Library in English* (Leiden: E. J. Brill, 1988) 529–31.

both male and female ascetics should have equal rights to fulfill their ascetic ideals within the same community.

Regardless of whether the conflict in logion 114 was a mere literary device or whether it mirrored a real although somewhat misrepresented debate over the position of women, either between those representing a mainstream view of the subordination of women and those opposing it, or between those holding two different ascetic conceptions, it is clear, at least, how the position of women is seen in the text-world of the saying. It is unequivocally the answer of Jesus which reveals this. Although patriarchal in its language, it gives Mary Magdalene and other women an equal position *vis-à-vis* salvation compared to their male companions. Yet with regard to terminology, the transition from the 'neither male nor female'-language to the 'being made/making oneself male'-language cannot be seen as a positive development from the vantage point of the female audience.

5

Is *Thomas* a Gnostic gospel?

Antti Marjanen

One of the most difficult questions in attempting to discover the religious landscape from which the *Gospel of Thomas* emerges is its relationship to Gnosticism.[1] This has been recognized by scholars since the first edition of the Coptic text was published in 1959.[2] In fact, an interest in this problem even precedes the discovery of the Nag Hammadi Library. When the Greek fragments of the *Gospel of Thomas* were found in Oxyrhynchus,[3] much before they were known to be part of that writing, the editors of the papyri addressed themselves, among other things, to the question of the possibly 'heretical' character of the texts.

Being well aware of the fact that they only had access to a portion of a gospel text or texts, they tried to exercise great caution in making their judgment. They thought that the fragments represented, at most, a very primitive kind of Gnosticism, if they were Gnostic at all. Not everybody agreed with their assessment, and scholars were divided as to the possible Gnostic character of these gospel texts.[4] When the Coptic version of the *Gospel of Thomas* was made available to scholars, the

---

[1] For major issues in the study of the *Gospel of Thomas*, see the surveys of literature by E. Haenchen, 'Literatur zum Thomasevangelium,' *TRu* 27 (1961–2) 147–78, 306–38; F. T. Fallon and R. Cameron, 'The Gospel of Thomas: A Forschungsbericht and Analysis,' *ANRW* II 25.6 (1988) 4195–251; G. J. Riley, 'The *Gospel of Thomas* in Recent Scholarship,' *Currents in Research: Biblical Studies* 2 (1994) 227–52.

[2] A. Guillaumont, H.-C. Puech, G. Quispel, W. Till, and Y. 'A. al Masīḥ, eds., *The Gospel according to Thomas: Coptic Text Established and Translated* (Leiden: E. J. Brill; New York: Harper, 1959). The book was published simultaneously in Dutch, French, and German translations.

[3] The editions of all the papyri are found in B. P. Grenfell and A. S. Hunt, *New Sayings of Jesus and Fragment of a Lost Gospel from Oxyrhynchus* (Egypt Explorations Fund: Graeco-Roman Branch; New York: Oxford University Press, American Branch, 1904).

[4] For the discussion, see Grenfell and Hunt, *New Sayings of Jesus*, 22–4.

quantity of material by which the matter could be evaluated grew remarkably. One might imagine that this would lead to a greater degree of consensus, but this is not the case.

After more than three decades of intensive study, during which much progress has been made, one nevertheless has to admit that the question of *Thomas'* relationship to Gnosticism has not found a generally accepted solution. There are still those who regard it in its present form as Gnostic[5] or at least gnosticizing,[6] and those who think that there is no reason at all to call it Gnostic.[7] Most scholars who think that the *Gospel of Thomas* is Gnostic do not try to determine more closely what kind of Gnosticism it represents, but those who have

---

[5] E.g. R. M. Grant, 'Notes on the Gospel of Thomas,' *VC* 13 (1959) 170–80; R. M. Grant and D. N. Freedman, *The Secret Sayings of Jesus* (London: Collins, 1960) 60–70; W. R. Schoedel, 'Naassene Themes in the Coptic Gospel of Thomas,' *VC* 14 (1960) 225–34; R. McL. Wilson, *Studies in the Gospel of Thomas*. London: A. R. Mowbray, 1960, 14–44; B. Gärtner, *The Theology of the Gospel of Thomas* (trans. E. J. Sharpe; London: Collins, 1961); E. Haenchen, *Die Botschaft des Thomasevangeliums* (Berlin: Töpelmann, 1961) 9–11, 34–74; H. E. W. Turner, 'The Gospel of Thomas: Its History, Transmission and Sources,' in H. E. W. Turner and H. Montefiore, *Thomas and the Evangelists* (SBT 35; London: SCM Press, 1962) 11–39, esp. 19–22; W. Schrage, *Das Verhältnis des Thomas-Evangeliums zur synoptischen Tradition und zu den koptischen Evangelienübersetzungen* (BZNW 29; Berlin: Töpelmann, 1964) 1–27; T. Säve-Söderberg, 'Gnostic and Canonical Gospel Traditions, with Special Reference to the Gospel of Thomas,' in U. Bianchi, ed., *Le Origini dello Gnosticismo. Colloquio di Messina 13–18 Aprile, 1966* (Leiden: E. J. Brill, 1967) 552–62; J. M. Robinson, 'LOGOI SOPHON: On the Gattung of Q,' in J. M. Robinson and H. Koester, *Trajectories Through Early Christianity* (Philadelphia: Fortress Press, 1971) 103–5; J.-É. Ménard, *L'Évangile selon Thomas* (NHS 5; Leiden: E. J. Brill, 1975) 25–48; P. Vielhauer, *Geschichte der urchristlichen Literatur* (Berlin: Walter de Gruyter, 1975) 633–5; J.-D. Kaestli, 'L'Evangile de Thomas: Son importance pour l'étude des paroles de Jésus et du gnosticisme chrétien,' *ETR* 54 (1979) 375–96, esp. 391–4; K. Rudolph, *Die Gnosis: Wesen und Geschichte einer spätantiken Religion* (3rd ed.; Göttingen: Vandenhoeck & Ruprecht, 1990) 167; M. Fieger, *Das Thomasevangelium: Einleitung, Kommentar und Systematik* (NTAbh, n.F. 22; Münster: Aschendorff, 1991) 3–4; R. Cameron, 'Thomas, Gospel of,' *ABD* 6 (1992) 535–40, esp. 539.

[6] This term is used by H. Koester, 'Introduction' [to the *Gospel According to Thomas*], in B. Layton, ed., *Nag Hammadi Codex II,2–7 together with XIII,2*, Brit. Lib. Or.4926(1), and P.Oxy. 1, 654, 655*, vol. 1 (2 vols., NHS 20; Leiden: E. J. Brill, 1989) 38–45, esp. 44 (in an earlier essay Koester can indeed speak about 'the Gnosticism of the Gospel of Thomas' ['One Jesus and Four Primitive Gospels,' in Robinson and Koester, *Trajectories*, 1971, 175]); cf. also C. C. Richardson, 'The Gospel of Thomas: Gnostic or Encratite?' in D. Neiman and M. Schatkin, eds., *The Heritage of the Early Church: Essays in Honor of the Very Reverend G. V. Florovsky* (Orientalia Christiana Analecta 195; Rome: Pont. Institutum Studiorum Orientalium, 1973) 65–76; S. J. Patterson, *The Gospel of Thomas and Jesus* (Foundations and Facets: Reference Series; Sonoma: Polebridge Press, 1993) 197–9.

[7] E.g. G. Quispel in his various studies between 1957 and 1972, most of which have been collected in *Gnostic Studies*, vol. 2 (Nederlands Historisch-Archaeologisch Instituut te

examined the question do not necessarily agree with each other. Some maintain that the Naassenes are the Gnostic group which produced the writing.[8] It has also been suggested that the work is Valentinian.[9] Scholars who deny the Gnostic proclivity of the *Gospel of Thomas* regard it, for example, as a Christian postbaptismal catechesis deriving its material from an independent sayings collection which is to be interpreted in light of Jewish wisdom speculation[10] or as a sayings collection which has been mainly influenced by early Jewish mysticism and Hermetism.[11]

5.1. The problem of defining Gnosticism

With regard to the relationship of the *Gospel of Thomas* to Gnosticism, the problem is not only that the evidence of the text is comprehended

---

Istanbul 34.2; Istanbul: Nederlands Historisch-Archaeologisch Instituut te Istanbul, 1975); cf. also K. Grobel, 'How Gnostic is the Gospel of Thomas?' *NTS* 8 (1961–2) 367–73; W. H. C. Frend, 'The Gospel of Thomas: Is Rehabilitation Possible?' *JTS* 18 (1967) 13–26; Y. O. Kim, 'The Gospel of Thomas and the Historical Jesus,' *The Northeast Asia Journal of Theology* 2 (1969) 17–30; S. L. Davies, *The Gospel of Thomas and Christian Wisdom* (New York: The Seabury Press, 1983); K. L. King, 'Kingdom in the Gospel of Thomas,' *Forum* 3.1 (1987) 49; B. Layton, *The Gnostic Scriptures* (Garden City: Doubleday, 1987) xvi, 360; A. D. De Conick, *Seek to See Him: Ascent and Vision Mysticism in the Gospel of Thomas* (VCSup 33; Leiden: E. J. Brill, 1996) 3–27.

[8] Grant, 'Notes,' 170–80; Schoedel, 'Naassene Themes,' 225–34; K. Smyth, 'Gnosticism in the *Gospel According to Thomas*,' *HeyJ* 1 (1960) 189–98. To be sure, there are numerous points of contact between the *Gospel of Thomas* and the so-called Naassene sermon summarized by Hippolytus (*Ref.* 5.6.3 – 11.1). Nevertheless, as Haenchen (*Botschaft*, 9–10) has pointed out, the central theological theme of the Naassene sermon, the idea of Man Adamas, as well as the syncretistic mythological framework of the text, are completely missing in the *Gospel of Thomas*. This suggests that the affinities between the two texts are not due to the fact that the *Gospel of Thomas* owes its origin to the sect of the Naassenes but that it has been used by them. Nevertheless, the thesis that *Thomas* derives from the Naassenes has recently been revived by M. Vukomanovic, 'An Inquiry into the Origin and Transmission of the Gospel of Thomas' (Ph.D. Diss., University of Pittsburgh, 1993).

[9] So L. Cerfaux, 'Les paraboles du royaume dans l'Évangile de Thomas,' *Muséon* 70 (1957) 311–27; Gärtner, *Theology*, 272. Cerfaux and Gärtner's thesis has not found followers.

[10] Davies, *Gospel of Thomas*, 145–7.

[11] De Conick, *Seek to See Him*, 28–39. De Conick's thesis seems to be an expansion and modification of that of Quispel, who in one of his more recent studies on the *Gospel of Thomas* finds three sources behind the gospel: a Jewish-Christian one, an encratite one, and a Hermetic one. The Hermetic source contains Hellenizing sayings about the knowledge of the self; see G. Quispel, 'The *Gospel of Thomas* Revisited,' in B. Barc, ed., *Colloque international sur les textes de Nag Hammadi* (Bibliothèque copte de Nag Hammadi, Section 'Études' 1; Quebec: University of Laval, 1981) 218–66.

differently by different interpreters but that no generally accepted definition of Gnosticism exists.[12] To illustrate, I cite three modern definitions of Gnosticism. All of them come from scholars who work or have worked on the *Gospel of Thomas*. The first represents an understanding which some consider to be outdated, even scientifically questionable. Despite its heresiological overtones, this sort of view still exerts its influence on some studies of Gnosticism in general and of the *Gospel of Thomas* in particular, even if it is not always explicitly spelled out. In his book, *The Theology of the Gospel of Thomas*, Bertil Gärtner states:[13]

> ... the terms 'Gnosticism' and 'Gnostic' are used here ... to denote all those syncretistic streams in the early Church which differed from the main traditions, being dominated by a different idea of God, a different concept of the world and man, and a different teaching on the Saviour, and which finally led to a split with the Church.

Thus Gärtner describes Gnosticism in such a way that, for all practical purposes, it must be seen as a general designation for all early Christian heresies.

The second view, advanced by C. C. Richardson, is more precise and balanced, and is representative of the opinions of those who regard the

---

[12] As is well known, the attempt of the so-called Messina Congress to reach a generally accepted definition of Gnosis and Gnosticism did not bring the desired result. For the English version of the definition, see U. Bianchi, ed., *Le Origini dello Gnosticismo: Colloquio di Messina 13–18 Aprile 1966* (Leiden: E. J. Brill, 1967) xxvi–xxix. Difficulty in defining Gnosticism is well illustrated by M. A. Williams, *Rethinking 'Gnosticism': An Argument for Dismantling a Dubious Category* (Princeton: Princeton University Press, 1996). As a solution to the problem, Williams himself suggests that the category 'Gnosticism' should be abandoned altogether. Bentley Layton does not reject the category 'Gnosticism' entirely but wants to reevaluate the data on which our picture of ancient Gnosticism is grounded. According to him, the primary sources for our understanding of Gnosticism are those texts deriving from heresiologists which refer to groups using the term 'Gnostics' as a self-designation and those writings of the Nag Hammadi Library which have been generally styled as 'Sethian.' Furthermore, Layton adds to this evidence some ancient patristic testimonia and summaries which speak about the groups and the writings closely related to the 'Gnostics' and the 'Sethians.' See B. Layton, 'Prolegomena to the Study of Ancient Gnosticism,' in L. M. White and O. L. Yarbrough, eds., *The Social World of the First Christians: Essays in Honor of Wayne A. Meeks* (Minneapolis: Fortress Press, 1995) 334–50.

[13] *Theology*, 12.

Gospel of Thomas as Gnostic or at least gnosticizing. It has as its point of departure a strictly dualistic view of the world and human beings:[14]

> Gnosticism is essentially a mythology of alienation, a frantic telling of tales to convince oneself that the phenomenal world is essentially evil, while the true self, the divine spark or seed entrapped in matter, is essentially divine. This stands in contrast with the Catholic view, that the phenomenal world is essentially good, although disrupted by evil, and that the true self is existentially evil, and only becomes divine by adoption.

Being the most recent, the third view is also the most restrictive of the definitions. Besides cosmological and anthropological dualism, Gnosticism is supposed to contain an account of or an explicit reference to a myth of the fall of a divine figure which results in a radical split in the godhead. April D. De Conick, who has presented this view, forcibly denies that the *Gospel of Thomas* is Gnostic. To be sure, with her definition of Gnosticism, which does not allow for much variation, the character of many other so-called Gnostic texts and systems should be re-evaluated as well.[15] According to De Conick[16]

> Gnosticism and Gnosis must be associated only with certain religious movements beginning in the late first or early second century which were characterized by the mythology of a divine figure who either falls or is forced down into the lower world. The consequent structural system involves two levels, one the realm of the Supreme God, the other the realm of a lesser god ...
> ... the lesser god whose place may be taken by a collective of angels, functions as a demiurge who is in opposition to the true God. Furthermore, the creation of man by the demiurge results in an anthropological dualism where the sparks of the true God are contained within the demiurge's material creation. A classical gnostic system, in addition to teaching the decline of a divine entity, must be characterized by three types of dualism: cosmological, theological, and anthropological.

In view of these different definitions of Gnosticism, it is no wonder that no consensus on the question of *Thomas'* relationship to Gnosticism

---

[14] Richardson, 'Thomas,' 68; for a similar definition, see C. W. Hedrick, 'Introduction: Nag Hammadi, Gnosticism, and Early Christianity – a Beginner's Guide,' in C. W. Hedrick and R. Hodgson, eds., *Nag Hammadi, Gnosticism, and Early Christianity* (Peabody: Hendrickson, 1986) 1–2.

[15] De Conick (*Seek to See Him*, 25 n. 83) states herself that several so-called Gnostic texts or movements should probably be understood as what she calls proto-Gnostic rather than Gnostic. Among them, she lists the Simonians, Satornilos, Cerinthus, and Justin's *Book of Baruch*.

[16] *Seek to See Him*, 25.

has been achieved. Depending on one's definition of Gnosticism, this question is obviously also answered in different ways.[17]

5.2. Task and approach

Conflicting views on Gnosticism do not mean that it is futile to pose the question of *Thomas'* relationship to Gnosticism. The question must only be approached in a new way. Taking into account the present confusion as to the precise characterization of Gnosticism, there is no sense in trying to start out with a general definition of Gnosticism, comparing it with the description of *Thomas'* symbolic universe and drawing conclusions from that comparison. In that approach, the point of departure, i.e. one's definition of Gnosticism, unavoidably determines or at least has a great influence on the result. In order to break the vicious circle, it is time to look at individual terms, concepts, and religious themes and motifs[18] in the *Gospel of Thomas* and to ask how their treatment correlates to their use and interpretation in other writings. It is only based on this kind of comparison, I believe, that more plausible inferences can be drawn about the place of the *Gospel of Thomas* within the traditions of early Christianity in general, and its relationship to Gnosticism in particular.

In this article I have chosen to examine the concept of the world, since it gives us a good perspective both on *Thomas'* cosmology and on its notion of the conditions of human earthly existence. As regards *Thomas'* relationship to Gnosticism, the consideration of the world can be assumed to be especially illuminating, since it plays a pivotal role both in the symbolic universe of the *Gospel of Thomas* and in that religio-philosophical thinking which according to every definition can be styled Gnostic. While examining *Thomas'* view of the world, the primary concern is those logia that explicitly mention the term **ΚΟCΜΟC**, which in *Thomas'* language is the equivalent of the

---

[17] It is symptomatic of the present situation that for Haenchen (*Botschaft*, 39–40) the idea that the real self of a human being which has fallen into the material world has its origin in the primeval light, to which it also seeks to return, is a very basic Gnostic doctrine, whereas Layton (*Gnostic Scriptures*, 360) thinks that this concept is not particularly Gnostic but grounded in 'an uncomplicated Hellenistic myth of the divine origins of the self.'

[18] In principle, one could of course examine operational models, values, and various rituals as well.

phenomenal world and worldly values. It should be noted, however, that in the symbolic universe of the writing the idea of the world is closely linked with the act of creation and the physical, human body. Therefore, attention is also to be paid to the logia which deal with these themes.

The fact that the *Gospel of Thomas* consists of collections of logia or of individual sayings deriving from various sources or traditions, as indicated by the existence of several doublets,[19] has led some scholars to assume that all attempts at finding a specifically Thomasine view of a certain theological concept are doomed to fail.[20] Although it is possible that an idea or a term may have been conceived in different ways in various sources and traditions used by the redactor(s) of the writing[21] and that Thomasine theological emphases may have undergone some development, it is nevertheless an exaggeration to claim that the choice and interpretation of the material employed in the gospel is guided by no consistent theological and ideological line of thought. On the contrary, in its chief theological emphases the *Gospel of Thomas* provides a rather coherent picture.[22]

When one selects comparative material in order to assess the possible Gnostic connections of Thomasine notions, there is no need to limit it to unequivocally Gnostic texts. Even if one is particularly interested in *Thomas'* relationship to Gnosticism, comparison with clearly non-Gnostic texts – both Christian and non-Christian – is useful, in many cases even necessary. They may provide both a good contrast and a

---

[19] For a closer examination of the doublets, see J. Ma. Asgeirsson, 'Arguments and Audience(s) in the *Gospel of Thomas* (Part I),' SBLSP 36 (1997) 47–85.

[20] So F. Wisse, 'Flee Femininity: Antifemininity in Gnostic Texts and the Question of Social Milieu,' in K. L. King, ed., *Images of the Feminine in Gnosticism* (Studies in Antiquity and Christianity; Philadelphia: Fortress Press, 1988) 305. Cf. also Davies, *Gospel of Thomas*, 146, who regards *Thomas* as 'naive and unsystematic, and hence systematic understanding of it may not be possible'; on the other hand, Davies can talk about the 'Jesusology' of *Thomas*, and he also seems to presuppose a rather consistent although complex view of the world in the *Gospel of Thomas* (see below). In his paper 'The Oracles of the *Gospel of Thomas*' (Paper Presented at the Annual Meeting of the Society of Biblical Literature, Chicago, November, 1994; for the abstract of the paper, see *AAR/SBL Abstracts 1994* [Atlanta: Scholars Press, 1994] 313–14) Davies seems to move even more clearly towards an interpretation according to which *Thomas* represents no 'coherent ideology.' It is simply a random collection of enigmatic sayings used in oracular divination.

[21] For this, see my discussion on the use of ⲡⲧⲏⲣϥ in *Thomas*, below.

[22] For this, see A. Marjanen, *The Woman Jesus Loved: Mary Magdalene in the Nag Hammadi Library and Related Documents* (NHMS 40; Leiden: E. J. Brill, 1996) 32–3.

helpful correction in case too hasty conclusions are reached on the basis of deviations from or resemblances to Gnostic texts alone. Furthermore, taking into consideration that various terms and religious themes frequently develop and gain new features and meanings, it is not problematic but rather beneficial to utilize as comparative material not only contemporary writings but older and newer texts as well. This may help to place a religious idea or concept found in a given writing, and eventually the writing itself, within the trajectory to which they relate.

With the space limitations an article such as this has, I have confined myself to four writings with which I compare *Thomas'* view of the world: the Wisdom of Solomon, the Gospel of John, the *Gospel of Philip*, and the *Apocryphon of John*. The Wisdom of Solomon is earlier than *Thomas*, John is, roughly speaking, contemporary with it, and the *Gospel of Philip* and the *Apocryphon of John*, at least in their present form, are later. In all of them the idea of the world plays a significant role. The *Gospel of Philip* and the *Apocryphon of John* represent texts which are commonly regarded as Gnostic,[23] the former generally labeled as Valentinian,[24] the latter as Sethian.[25] Apart from its interest in the concept of the world, the Wisdom of Solomon has been selected because, although not a sayings collection, it is representative of Jewish wisdom. This is of importance since it has been claimed that the *Gospel of Thomas* derives many of its theological emphases from Jewish wisdom tradition.[26] The Gospel of John constitutes an interesting piece of comparative material for our purposes, since many scholars suppose

---

[23] With regard to these writings, this identification is rejected only by those researchers who want to avoid or redefine the term 'Gnostic' altogether; see e.g. Williams, *Rethinking 'Gnosticism.'* Williams prefers to use the category 'biblical demiurgical,' which would include, however, a large percentage of the sources that are today styled Gnostic, such as the *Gospel of Philip* and the *Apocryphon of John*. Layton ('Prolegomena,' 343) does not regard Valentinian writings, such as the *Gospel of Philip*, as Gnostic, although he considers 'Valentinus and his followers ... as a distinct mutation, or reformed offshoot, of the original Gnostics.'

[24] The only scholar, to my knowledge, who has questioned this is W. G. Röhl, *Die Rezeption des Johannesevangeliums in christlich-gnostischen Schriften aus Nag Hammadi* (Europäische Hochschulschriften: Reihe 23, Theologie Bd. 428; Frankfurt: Peter Lang, 1991) 141.

[25] The term 'Sethian' is not primarily used here as a sociological category but as a tradition-historical definition accounting for thematic interrelationships between various writings. For complexities involved in the use of the term, see the articles and the discussion in B. Layton, ed., *The Rediscovery of Gnosticism*, vol. 2: *Sethian Gnosticism* (Studies in the History of Religions 41; Leiden: E. J. Brill, 1981) 563–685.

[26] The strongest advocate of this thesis is Davies, *Gospel of Thomas*.

that, although it became part of the New Testament canon, it was written in a milieu where gnosticizing tendencies were at work.[27]

5.3. Thomas *and the world: two modern interpretations*

Although there exists no special study of *Thomas'* view of the world, several scholars have addressed themselves to this topic. To illustrate scholarly discussion on this theme, I briefly present two interpretations which represent very different alternatives. It is interesting to note that with regard to the question of *Thomas'* relationship to Gnosticism these particular scholars disagree as well. Davies thinks that the *Gospel of Thomas* is not Gnostic in any 'meaningful sense' of the word,[28] whereas Haenchen maintains that *Thomas* is 'an esoteric Gnostic writing.'[29]

According to Davies, the concept of world is viewed in the *Gospel of Thomas* from two different perspectives.[30] On the one hand, it can be seen in terms of 'the world of society and of structured social obligations,'[31] and, on the other hand, it can be conceived as the object of a person's religious search, since the world, as rightly apprehended, is the kingdom of God which supplies human beings with 'the rest and immortality proper to the seventh day of creation.'[32] In order that the world and the kingdom of God may be identified in this way, 'the world ought to be considered to be in the condition of Gen 1.1 – 2.4 and, accordingly, . . . people should restore themselves to the condition of the image of God.'[33] In other words, the central message of the

---

[27] In his study of Johannine anthropology, J. A. Trumbower, *Born From Above: The Anthropology of the Gospel of John* (Hermeneutische Untersuchungen zur Theologie 29; Tübingen: J. C. B. Mohr [Paul Siebeck] 1992) 141, suggests, for instance, that the principal author of the Gospel of John 'was actually interpreting his sources . . . in a gnosticizing direction.' A gnosticizing context of the *Gospel of John* is also posited by J. D. G. Dunn, *Unity and Diversity in the New Testament: An Inquiry into the Character of Earliest Christianity* (London: SCM Press, 1977) 304–5, who does not, however, regard the author of the writing himself as Gnostic or gnosticizing. Dunn maintains that the author of the Gospel of John addressed 'a Christian community influenced by gnosticizing tendencies.' He translated his message into the language and thought patterns of his addressees without fully agreeing with their theology at every point.

[28] *Gospel of Thomas*, 147.

[29] *Botschaft*, 11.

[30] *Gospel of Thomas*, 70–2. See also S. L. Davies, 'The Christology and Protology of the *Gospel of Thomas*,' *JBL* 111 (1992) 663–82.

[31] Davies, *Gospel of Thomas*, 70.

[32] Davies, 'Christology,' 664.

[33] Ibid.

Gospel of Thomas is that the world is to be perceived from the perspective of the primordial beginning and that people should and can actualize the primordial light within themselves and become like Jesus.

For Davies, it is important that in no way can the world itself be regarded as evil in the *Gospel of Thomas*. It is created and ruled by God, not by any demonic power. Only the 'social ramifications' of the world can be seen in a negative light. Worldly concerns, such as family ties and financial interests, are indeed to be renounced according to the *Gospel of Thomas*.

Davies' dual interpretation of *Thomas'* view of the world is grounded on those texts which, on the one hand, refer to 'understanding' and 'finding' the world and which, on the other hand, stress that the one 'who has come to understand or has found' the world is 'superior to it' or should 'renounce it' (*Gos. Thom.* 56; 80; 110). Yet his explication of these logia seems forced. Without any clear evidence, and contrary to the most obvious reading of logia 56, 80, and 110, Davies postulates that the term **KOCMOC** has a different meaning in two successive sentences of these logia. Being presented as an object of understanding and seeking, it is employed with its positive connotation, while in the second part of the logion it represents negative worldly values. In addition, Davies has to assume that in logia 80 and 56 the words **CWMA** and **ΠΤWMA**[34] do not denote a negative entity as elsewhere in *Thomas* (29; 60; 87)[35] but refer to 'the body of Wisdom (seen by Christians as a body over which Christ is set as head).'[36]

Ernst Haenchen wrote his first studies on the *Gospel of Thomas* more than thirty years ago.[37] However, he made observations which are still of interest for Thomasine studies. Describing *Thomas'* view of the world, Haenchen begins with the same logia which form the cornerstone of Davies' interpretation, but he sees them in a completely

---

[34] The occurrence of the word **ΠΤWMA** ('corpse') in logion 56 causes great difficulties for Davies. Finally he has to suggest (*Gospel of Thomas*, 72) that it may be due to the fact that the later Gnostic readers of the text have replaced the original **CWMA** with **ΠΤWMA**.

[35] Davies' attempts (*Gospel of Thomas*, 73–5) to contest the negative character of the word **CWMA** in logia 29 and 87 are not convincing.

[36] Ibid., 71–2.

[37] Haenchen, *Botschaft*; Idem, 'Literatur,' 147–78, 306–38; see also E. Haenchen, 'Die Anthropologie des Thomas-Evangeliums,' in H.-D. Betz and L. Schottroff, eds., *Neues Testament und christliche Existenz: Festschrift für Herbert Braun zum 70. Geburtstag* (Tübingen: J. C. B. Mohr [Paul Siebeck], 1973) 207–27.

different light. According to Haenchen, the message of logion 56 is that the visible, material world is passing away. Rightly understood, it is nothing but a monstrous, decaying corpse, a ⲠⲦⲰⲘⲀ.[38] Unlike Davies, he thinks that the world and the kingdom of God are completely opposite to each other. One cannot hope to find the kingdom while making the world the object of one's religious search. On the contrary, as regards the direction of one's life, according to the *Gospel of Thomas*, the choice has to be made exactly between these two.[39]

The world is not only something which one has to renounce. It also represents a threat one has to be on guard against, since it can deprive a Gnostic of his or her 'kingdom' (*Gos. Thom.* 21).[40] The latter can take place if a Gnostic is lured by the temptations of the world to pursue its wealth and riches (63; 64; 110).[41] A choice for the kingdom against the world also means that a Gnostic accepts continence as an essential part of his/her lifestyle (79)[42] and that he/she gives up all family ties (101; 55; 16) and becomes ⲘⲞⲚⲀⳢⲞⲤ ('solitary'; 16; 49; 75).[43] Furthermore, Haenchen points out that, according to *Thomas*, the world is not only a theoretical threat to a Gnostic. Kingdom and the real self is not something a Gnostic possesses once for all. He/she can be drawn back to the world, without even noticing it (97).[44] Therefore it is vitally important that Gnostics be constantly told 'to fast as regards the world' (27) and to 'become passers-by' (42).[45]

One thing is conspicuous in Haenchen's presentation of *Thomas'* view of the world. He does not deal with the question of creation. Logion 12 is not included in his discussion at this point at all,[46] and the

---

[38] *Botschaft*, 50.
[39] Ibid., 51.
[40] Ibid., 51–2.
[41] Ibid., 56–7. In his essay 'Die Anthropologie des Thomas-Evangeliums' (see note 36), Haenchen tries to show that the concrete world in which the *Gospel of Thomas* originates is 'a world of the prosperous, which does not differ much from ours.' (p. 208). Most of the people who appear in the parables, for example, represent affluent strata of society. This also seems to explain why the author of the text is so preoccupied with attempting to point out how wealth can alienate a Gnostic from his/her real self.
[42] Haenchen, *Botschaft*, 55.
[43] Ibid., 58–9.
[44] Ibid., 61.
[45] Ibid., 50.
[46] Haenchen mentions logion 12 when he talks about *Thomas'* relationship to Jewish Christianity (*Botschaft*, 66), but he does not make any comment on the creation motif of the saying.

only thing in logion 89 which, according to Haenchen, is of interest to the author of the *Gospel of Thomas* relates to the fact that the worldly opposition between the internal and the external should be abolished in order that the divine unity may be established.[47] Regardless of whether or not the actual content of this estimation is accepted, Haenchen may be right in claiming that the main point of logion 89 is not the question of the creation. However, this does not negate the importance of the fact that the author of *Thomas* can include in the writing such a logion, which speaks quite unproblematically of the creation of the world, obviously by the Father himself (see the discussion below).

5.4. Thomas *and the world: text analyses*

Thomas refers to the world by using the term **κοсмос**. It appears sixteen times in the gospel (10; 16; 21; 24; 27; 28 [thrice]; 51; 56 [twice]; 80 [twice]; 110 [twice]; 111). In addition, the Coptic word **καϩ** ('earth') is in two logia employed in a way very similar to that of **κοсмос** (16; 113). Logia 12 and 89 are also of interest since they speak of creation (cf. also 77). There are also some other logia which throw light upon *Thomas'* view of the world since they describe the attitude the readers of the *Gospel of Thomas* are supposed to adopt towards worldly affairs.

As to *Thomas'* concept of the world, the relevant logia can be divided into three categories: (1) logia which refer to the world with a positive connotation, (2) logia which make the world a stage for salvific events and actions, and (3) logia which consider the world worthless and threatening.

5.4.1. The world with a positive connotation

Logion 12 contains the most explicit reference to the act of creation in the *Gospel of Thomas*. When the disciples ask Jesus who is going to be their leader after his departure Jesus states: 'James the righteous, for whose sake heaven and earth came into being.'[48] How should one

---

[47] *Botschaft*, 53.
[48] This translation as well as all later translations of the *Gospel of Thomas* by T. O. Lambdin in B. Layton, ed., *Nag Hammadi Codex II,2–7 together with XIII,2*, Brit. Lib. Or. 4926(1), and P.Oxy. 1, 654*, vol. 1 (NHS 20; Leiden: E. J. Brill, 1989) 52–93.

understand the creation motif in this description of James? The very fact that James is appointed by Jesus to be the leader of the disciples implies that his characterization, and thus the reference to the creation, are to be seen in a positive light. This is confirmed by the fact that a similar phrase is used as an honorific epithet of Israel in *4 Ezra* 7.11,[49] of patriarchs, David, and the Messiah in rabbinic writings,[50] and of the Christian church in the *Shepherd of Hermas* (1.1.6; 2.4.1).[51] These parallels not only suggest the positive nature of the expression but point to its Jewish or Jewish-Christian origin as well.[52]

It could be argued, however, that even though logion 12, as it stands by itself, offers a positive picture of James and thus also of the creation of the world, the fact that the compiler of the *Gospel of Thomas* places logion 13 immediately after it modifies its character.[53] But in which way? Admittedly, it is likely that the emphasis on a leader-centered organization among the disciples, connected with James in logion 12, is relativized in logion 13. The latter stresses that the disciples, having come to a full realization of Jesus' and their own real character, have no need of any master (see also logion 108).[54] But does this mean that, from the perspective of logion 13, James is to be seen as a negative figure and that his epithet, in which the creation motif is mentioned, must be perceived as a pejorative and, in that case, an ironical statement? This is hardly possible. In logion 13 criticism is not directed against James but against Peter and Matthew, who clearly show an inability to understand who Jesus is and what discipleship is all about. Although as a spiritual authority James is superseded by Thomas, and although with the latter a new model of discipleship is introduced, there is no reason to conclude that the author of the *Gospel of Thomas*

---

[49] J. Daniélou, *The Theology of Jewish Christianity* (Philadelphia: Westminster Press, 1964) 294–5.

[50] L. Ginzberg, *The Legends of the Jews*, vol. 5 (Philadelphia: The Jewish Publication Society of America, 1925) 67–8. *Sanh.* 4.5 also knows this phrase. However, there it is not used as an honorific title but emphasizes the uniqueness of each person.

[51] N. Brox, *Der Hirt des Hermas* (Kommentar zu den apostolischen Vätern 7; Göttingen: Vandenhoeck & Ruprecht, 1991) 82, 105–6.

[52] Smyth ('Gnosticism,' 190) has pointed out that the Naassenes can also refer to the seed of light, for whose sake the world took its beginning (Hippolytus, *Ref.* 5.8.29); but it is most likely that the Naassenes are here dependent on the *Gospel of Thomas* (see note 10).

[53] It is frequently suggested that placing logion 13 immediately after logion 12 is a kind of redactional correction made by the compiler of the writing. For this, see e.g. Koester, 'Introduction,' 40–1.

[54] See also Marjanen, 'Women Disciples in the *Gospel of Thomas*,' in this volume.

intends to declare James a *persona non grata* among Thomasine Christians. It suffices to see in logia 12 and 13 a reflection of a development from the hierarchical understanding of Christian leadership linked with James to the notion of a 'masterless' Christian self-identity connected with Thomas. If this interpretation of the relationship between logia 12 and 13 is accepted, it can hardly be maintained that the placement of logion 13 after logion 12 would mean that the reference to the creation motif in the epithet of James should be seen as a negative, ironical comment.

Logion 12 is not the only passage in *Thomas* where the event of creation is valued positively. Logion 89 reads: 'Jesus said: "Why do you wash the outside of the cup? Do you not realize that he who made (ⲦⲀⲘⲒⲞ) the inside is the same one who made the outside?"' To be sure, the main purpose of the logion is not to speak of the act of creation or the creator but to emphasize that purifying one's outside does not help one to correct the deficiency in one's inside.[55] Nevertheless, this does not negate the fact that the author of the *Gospel of Thomas* does include a logion in his writing which can refer to the event of creation as a positive deed. For if the inside of a person is made by the Father, i.e. if it stems from the light of the Father (*Gos. Thom.* 50), so also is the outside. In that case the whole person is a pure, whole product of the Father's creative act.[56]

So logia 12 and 89 suggest that the compiler of the *Gospel of Thomas* can incorporate logia in the text in which the creation of the world and the human body can be seen in a positive light. One can of course say that these particular sayings may both derive from a Jewish-Christian

---

[55] Fieger, *Thomasevangelium*, 234, argues that the outside of the cup cannot symbolize the body of a person, since the latter is normally despised in the *Gospel of Thomas* (80). Therefore, following Haenchen (*Botschaft*, 53), Fieger maintains that the main intention of the logion is only 'the abolition of the contrast between the outside and the inside and the restoration of the original unity.' Fieger's argumentation is not convincing. First, the claim that the outside of the cup cannot symbolize the body since it appears in a positive light is clearly a circular argument and not very plausible in light of the observations made on the phenomenal world in logion 12. Second, with Haenchen's and Fieger's interpretation, the question of purifying the outside of the cup which commences the logion is totally incomprehensible if the contrast between the inside and the outside is not perceived as that between the inside and the outside of a person. The source of genuine religious purity is the main theme of logion 89, not the restoration of any abstract, original unity.

[56] For this interpretation see Marjanen, '*Thomas* and Jewish Religious Practices' in this volume.

source of the gospel and do not necessarily mirror the most central emphases of the author. Be that as it may, the fact still remains that the creation logia viewed from a positive vantage point do not seem to have offended the author of the writing so much that he/she would have wanted to modify or even to remove them by redactional measures.

The third logion in which some scholars have seen an allusion to creation is 77. De Conick, for example, maintains that in this passage Jesus insists that he is the creator of the world.[57] Especially in light of 1 Cor 8.6, John 1.3, and Col 1.16, the clause ⲚⲦⲀ ⲠⲦⲎⲢϤ ⲈⲒ ⲈⲂⲞⲗ Ⲛ2ⲎⲦ ('From me did the all come forth') could refer to the event of creation.[58] In that case ⲠⲦⲎⲢϤ, usually translated 'the all,' is an equivalent of the phenomenal world which is thus viewed from a positive perspective. There are other scholars, however, who argue that the passage has nothing to do with the creation but underlines the common, divine origin of Jesus and Christians.[59] According to this position, ⲠⲦⲎⲢϤ does not then signify the creation, but becomes a collective way of speaking of the light substance which can be found in the children of light, as these Christians are called in logion 50. That Jesus can be seen as identical with them (ⲀⲚⲞⲔ ⲠⲈ ⲠⲦⲎⲢϤ 'It is I who am the all') corresponds well with a similar emphasis in logion 108, which regards the exemplary Christian identity as Jesus-like.

It is not easy to decide which interpretation of logion 77 does better justice to the internal logic of the saying and to the meaning of the terms used in it within the context of the gospel as a whole. Although the phrase ⲚⲦⲀ ⲠⲦⲎⲢϤ ⲈⲒ ⲈⲂⲞⲗ Ⲛ2ⲎⲦ ('From me etc.') may well be linked to the creation language of Jewish wisdom, which is also attested in the above-mentioned New Testament texts, another phrase ⲀⲚⲞⲔ ⲠⲈ ⲠⲦⲎⲢϤ – necessarily pantheistic in character, if understood to express the relationship between the creator and the created order – sounds quite surprising in the mouth of Jesus. Certainly, one can speak of Wisdom 'penetrating all things' (Wis 7.24), but the statement which equates Jesus/Wisdom with the created world, a view which has its closest parallel in Stoicism, in which God and the cosmos can be

---

[57] De Conick (*Seek to See Him*, 21) asserts: 'The ignorant Demiurge does not create the world in *Thomas*. Jesus as the *Phos*, the Light-Man, does.'

[58] Besides De Conick, this is maintained by Davies, *Gospel of Thomas*, 56, who emphasizes the similarities between the saying and the creation thought of the Jewish wisdom tradition.

[59] Most recently Fieger, *Thomasevangelium*, 215; but see already Haenchen, *Botschaft*, 65.

considered identical,[60] is rather unusual in Jewish or early Christian writings.[61] In addition, even though Jesus/Logos as an ultimate goal of the creation is not an uncommon idea (Col 1.16), the perfect tense of ⲡⲱⲥ in the sentence ⲁⲩⲱ ⲛ̄ⲧⲁ ⲡⲧⲏⲣϥ ⲡⲱⲥ ϣⲁⲣⲟⲉⲓ ('and unto me did the all extend') does not fit well with the creation language. Rather, one would expect a future tense.

A further difficulty with interpreting ⲛ̄ⲧⲁ ⲡⲧⲏⲣϥ ⲉⲓ ⲉⲃⲟⲗ ⲛ̄ϩⲏⲧ ('From me etc.') as a reference to the creation of the world is the fact that in the context of the *Gospel of Thomas* ⲡⲧⲏⲣϥ ('the all') does not unambiguously lend itself to having the meaning 'world.' This may be possible in logion 2; in that case, the logion may imply that the ultimate goal of one's spiritual development is to reach the point where one is not a slave of the world and its powers but rules over them.[62] Nevertheless, it is equally possible to think that ⲡⲧⲏⲣϥ does not mean anything more than 'everything' or 'all things' and that the rule over ⲡⲧⲏⲣϥ is to be understood as a characterization of a person who is in control of life in all circumstances.

In logion 67, it is quite unlikely that ⲡⲧⲏⲣϥ denotes 'world.' Despite the textual ambiguities which make it possible to find more than one overall explanation of the logion,[63] the basic purpose of the text seems clear. The passage speaks of a person whose knowledge of ⲡⲧⲏⲣϥ is contrasted with a lack of what is essentially important for salvation.[64] If ⲡⲧⲏⲣϥ is interpreted as a reference to the created world,

---

[60] See H. Sasse, 'κοσμέω κτλ.,' *TDNT* III, 876–7. As E. Schweizer, *Der Brief an die Kolosser* (EKKNT 12; Einsiedeln: Benziger, 1977) 61 n. 142, has noted, the only example of a similar view in Jewish writings is Sir 43.27.

[61] The only possible instance in early Christian writings is in the late second-century *Acts of Peter* 10, in which Peter addresses Jesus: 'You are the All, the All is you.' There is no certainty, however, that the All here denotes the created world.

[62] So O. Hofius, 'Das koptische Thomasevangelium und die Oxyrhynchus-Papyri Nr. 1, 654 und 655,' *EvT* 20 (1960) 28. Cf. also Fieger, *Thomasevangelium*, 21, who indeed thinks that ⲡⲧⲏⲣϥ has this meaning only in logion 2, whereas in logia 67 and 77 it stands for the light found in Jesus and the children of light. According to Fieger, the difference in the meaning of the word is explained by the fact that in logion 2, where the word appears only in the Coptic version, the addition of ⲡⲧⲏⲣϥ is a further gnostizising trait introduced by the Coptic translator.

[63] Whether the word after the first ⲣ̄ ⲟⲣⲱϩ is ⲟⲩⲁⲁϥ (B. Layton) or ⲟⲩⲁ (S. Emmel) depends on the way the Coptic text, written without word spaces, is divided into individual words; for this, see Layton, ed., *Nag Hammadi Codex II,2–7*, 78.

[64] The somewhat cryptic ⲡⲙⲁ ⲧⲏⲣϥ ('the entire place') at the end of the logion is best understood in light of those sayings where ⲧⲟⲡⲟⲥ or ⲙⲁ (both meaning 'place') is used to indicate the state and place of salvation (4; 18; 24; 50; 60; 64; 68).

the passage implies a contrast which is not to be expected in the context of *Thomas*. On the contrary, in the *Gospel of Thomas* knowing the real character of the phenomenal world, ⲕⲟⲥⲙⲟⲥ, is closely linked with one's self-realization (3; 56; 80), i.e. with becoming aware of one's origin in the realm of light and thus gaining the possibility of salvation. In view of this observation, another interpretation of ⲡⲧⲏⲣϥ suggests itself. In all likelihood, it simply means 'everything.' Thus logion 67 presents a paradoxical description of a person who has all knowledge but who 'by himself/herself is deficient' or who 'is in want of one thing (in the sense of the primal oneness?)' and therefore has never been granted salvation (cf. *Gos. Thom.* 70; 41).

Taking into consideration the previous discussion, it seems safest to conlude that the phrase ⲛ̄ⲧⲁ ⲡⲧⲏⲣϥ ⲉⲓ ⲉⲃⲟⲗ ⲛ̄ϩⲏⲧ ('From me etc.') in logion 77 does not provide any unambiguous evidence for examining *Thomas'* view of the world and of creation.[65] But even if it were taken so, it would not change the picture one can draw on the basis of logia 12 and 89.[66] Basically, *Thomas* may include logia in which

---

[65] This does not mean that the other interpretation of logion 77 presented above is automatically more likely. The perfect form of ⲡⲱϩ in the phrase ⲛ̄ⲧⲁ ⲡⲧⲏⲣϥ ⲡⲱϩ ϣⲁⲣⲟⲉⲓ ('unto me did the all extend') is equally difficult for those who argue that ⲡⲧⲏⲣϥ refers to the light found in Jesus and the children of light (cf. *Gos. Thom.* 50). Neither does the use of ⲡⲧⲏⲣϥ in logia 2 and 67 fit well with that interpretation. Even though logion 2 clearly posits a spiritual development from one stage to another, it can hardly be supposed that the ultimate goal of the process starting with seeking is that one is elevated to a position of supremacy over Jesus and other children of light (this is why Fieger maintains that ⲡⲧⲏⲣϥ in logion 2, by way of exception to its normal usage, stands for the cosmos and its powers; see above). In logion 67, too, ⲡⲧⲏⲣϥ can hardly be interpreted as a collective expression of the light found in Jesus and Christians. If it is, the logion presents a contrast which is very atypical of *Thomas*. In the *Gospel of Thomas* it cannot be the one who lacks something essentially important for salvation who knows about the light and its dwelling in the children of light. On the contrary, it is exactly the one who does possess that which unites him/her with the realm of light who has the knowledge of the light and its children (*Gos. Thom.* 3; 50).

On the whole, it seems that neither of the interpretations presented above satisfactorily solves all the riddles of logion 77. It may be, of course, that I have simply demanded too much consistency of the logion with respect to its own contents and to the contents of the entire gospel. For example, perhaps ⲡⲧⲏⲣϥ is employed in various ways in various logia. The problem is: when and on what criteria can an interpreter argue this kind of 'inconsistency'?

[66] The only difference which logion 77 would make, if taken as referring to the creation of the cosmos, is that it would introduce Jesus as the agent of creation. This would be a contradiction of logion 89, in which the Father is apparently assigned this role. Yet the contradiction is actually only apparent since in early Christian writings it is quite common that God is pictured as the Creator of the world and that Jesus is seen as the one through whom the actual creation takes place.

the world and the creative activity are viewed from a positive vantage point. Admittedly, the creation has no great and independent role in Thomasine theology. It is mentioned almost incidentally. Yet it is clearly there. Although this is not explicitly stated anywhere, the creator, according to the *Gospel of Thomas*, is most probably the Father (cf. logion 89).[67] The thesis that *Thomas* might encompass an idea of a separate creator god, a kind of demiurge, seems unlikely.[68]

5.4.2. The world as a stage for salvific events and actions

Like the Gospel of John, *Thomas* too regards the world as a stage for Jesus' appearance (*Gos. Thom.* 28). Even the language used in logion 28 is quite similar to that of John 1.9, 14. Clearly, both gospels presuppose an idea of the incarnation of the pre-existent Jesus.[69] The world is neither in logion 28 nor in the following logia, which are treated in this section, only the geographical location in which Jesus' appearance takes place. It also comprises the people whom Jesus seeks to approach. Jesus' appearance in the world has to do with their salvation. Yet logion 28 does not really spell out what role Jesus has in this process. Only

---

[67] See the previous note, however.

[68] It has been suggested that the mention of ΝΟΥΤΕ ('god') in logion 100 refers to the demiurge (so e.g. Wilson, *Studies in the Gospel of Thomas*, 59–60; S. G. Hall, 'Nag Hammadi,' in R. J. Coggins and J. L. Houlden, eds., *A Dictionary of Biblical Interpretation* [London: SCM Press, 1990] 485). Although this assertion cannot be completely ruled out, it is hardly the most likely interpretation of the text. Nothing elsewhere in the writing points to any interest in the person or activities of the Demiurge. It has also been argued that by placing a reference to Jesus at the end of the saying the author of the logion has lowered ΠΝΟΥΤΕ to an inferior position compared with Jesus and thus indicated that this god is not the Father of Jesus but the Demiurge. This argument is not compelling, though. There is no necessary reason to assume that the sequence of the three reflects their order of precedence in this way. Since the mention of Jesus is a clearly redactional addition, it is quite natural that it is placed at the end of the saying. In addition, ΠΝΟΥΤΕ and Jesus need not be seen as opposed to each other; they can both be considered objects of one's spiritual loyalty, whereas ΚΑΙΟΑΡ ('Caesar') represents worldly concerns. The third argument which is frequently adduced for the Demiurge thesis is that nowhere else in the *Gospel of Thomas* is the word 'god' (ΝΟΥΤΕ) used of the Father of Jesus. This is true, however, only of the Coptic version. In the Greek fragments of *Thomas* the expression ἡ βασιλεία τοῦ θεοῦ appears at least in logion 27 but probably also in logion 3. In other words, if the word 'god' is at all employed in the sense of the Demiurge, this can have happened only at the Coptic stage of transmission of the gospel.

[69] For this, see Dunderberg, '*Thomas*' I-sayings and the Gospel of John' in this volume.

obliquely can we infer that his task is in some way to remove spiritual ignorance and impassivity among people.

Another passage which deals with Jesus' mission to the world is logion 10: 'Jesus said: "I have cast fire upon the world, and see, I am guarding it until it blazes."' Even in this text it is difficult to see how Jesus' role is to be conceived. The interpretation of the logion depends on how one understands the fire the text speaks of. As some scholars have pointed out, in a late Gnostic text, *Pistis Sophia,* the same saying is explicated as a reference to the cleansing of the world's sins with fire (*PS* 368.12–14).[70] In the context of the *Gospel of Thomas,* fire can hardly be interpreted as an instrument by which the sins of the world are purified. The word 'sin' (**NOBE**) occurs only twice in the *Gospel of Thomas.* Both texts (*Gos. Thom.* 14; 104) seem to suggest that sin is no concern of Thomasine Christians but belongs to the life of those who still obey various religious obligations such as fasting, prayer, almsgiving, and dietary regulations.[71] There are, however, two other references to fire in *Thomas* which may help to throw light on this saying. In logion 82 fire is seen as a positive symbol. In fact, it is identified with the kingdom.[72] In logion 16, fire together with sword and war symbolizes the dissension Jesus' appearance engenders. It is not easy to say which one of these applications of fire would better explain its use in logion 10. Perhaps the verbal expression **NOYⲬE ̄NOYKⲰ͂T** ('cast fire') can more easily be joined to the latter idea.

It is not only Jesus whose task it is to remove the spiritual ignorance of the blind ones of the world. The same salvific function is also given to his disciples. When they come to ask Jesus to show them the place where he is in order that they should look for it (*Gos. Thom.* 24), Jesus points out that any search outside themselves is unnecessary, since they as people of light have light in themselves. However, it does not suffice that a person of light enlightens himself. The light has to spread out to others as well. The idea that Thomas Christians should see the world as their 'mission field' also appears in some other logia (33; 64; perhaps also 14).

---

[70] E.g. Grant and Freedman, *Secret Sayings,* 126; M. W. Meyer, *The Gospel of Thomas: The Hidden Sayings of Jesus* (San Francisco: Harper, 1992) 73.
[71] For this, see Marjanen, '*Thomas* and Jewish Religious Practices' in this volume.
[72] Schrage, *Verhältnis,* 50.

The difficulty of the task is underlined by the fact that the world is characterized by blindness and drunkenness (28) and by its inability to see (113). It is possible that these logia reflect concrete experiences of Thomasine Christians as they tried to preach their gospel of the kingdom, which on the one hand is part of the divine realm (49) and which on the other hand takes its place upon the earth (113), although it is visible only to those who have become aware of their belonging to the realm of light and obey its requirements (24; 27).

Jesus' incarnation and the missionary activities of his disciples do not make the world itself a better place. But that is not their concern either. Their real concern is the people who in fact have their origin in another world, in the realm of light (*Gos. Thom.* 50). The world only provides Jesus and his disciples with a stage for their actions. Otherwise, in spite of being created by the Father, it is a worthless and threatening reality.

5.4.3. The world as a worthless and threatening reality

For *Thomas*, the world as a phenomenal entity is not only destined to be destroyed at the end of the age (*Gos. Thom.* 111; cf. also logion 11), but it is already being replaced by a new reality, the kingdom, which is, however, recognizable only to those who belong to it (51; 113). Even some disciples have difficulties in realizing the new development. Even though the world still exists it is clearly decaying. In no other way can logia 56 and 80 be interpreted. Since in both cases the second part of the logion emphasizes the worthlessness of the world (cf. also 111) and since there is no obvious reason to assume that the word **ⲕⲟⲥⲙⲟⲥ** would have a different meaning in the first part of each logion, not only **ⲡⲧⲱⲙⲁ** (56) but also **ⲥⲱⲙⲁ** (80) must have the negative connotation of 'corpse.' Semantically, this is fully possible, as the comparison between Matt 24.28 ($\pi\tau\tilde{\omega}\mu\alpha$) and Luke 17.37 ($\sigma\tilde{\omega}\mu\alpha$) indicates. In addition, it is worth noting that at least five times the translators of the Sahidic New Testament render the Greek $\pi\tau\tilde{\omega}\mu\alpha$ into Coptic with **ⲥⲱⲙⲁ** (Matt 14.12;[73] 24.28; Mark 6.29; Rev 11.8, 9). The superiority of the one who has found the world worthless is emphasized by

---

[73]   To be sure, in some Greek manuscripts of Matt 14.12 there appears a variant $\sigma\tilde{\omega}\mu\alpha$.

referring to this person with a typical Jewish expression used in rabbinic literature to praise someone: ⲠⲔⲞⲤⲘⲞⲤ ⲘⲠϢⲀ ⲘⲘⲞϤ ⲀⲚ ('[he] is superior to the world,' *Gos. Thom.* 56; 80). The same phrase is found also in Hebr. 11.38.[74]

The second part of logion 111 presents another variant of the theme of the worthlessness of the world. 'Whoever finds himself is superior to the world.' This shows that to find the real character of the world is actually the reverse side of finding oneself. Both are essential elements of *Thomas'* view of salvation. In other words, salvation means not only that one discovers oneself, God, and the kingdom, but also that one is granted sight of the worthless character of the world. The same is true of the body. It is a sheer burden to the soul, to the real self of a person (*Gos. Thom.* 29; 87; 112).

It is conspicuous that the *Gospel of Thomas* contains no reflection on why and how the world (and evidently the body as well), albeit created by God, has become this discredited entity. There is no trace of any sort of mythology which would try to account for this contradictory development. The worthlessness of the world is simply presupposed.

The world not only lacks value in the perspective of a Thomasine Christian, it is actually dangerous. This is spelled out in the parable of the owner of the house, which is part of logion 21.[75] Since the man does not know when the thief may come into his house, he has to guard his house so that he is always ready *before* the thief comes. The application of the parable is surprisingly unambiguous. Jesus states: 'You, then be on your guard against the world. Arm yourselves with great strength lest the robbers find a way to come to you. For otherwise they shall find the profit you expect.' The translation of the last sentence is different from the most common recent renderings of the text.[76] The Greek word ⲬⲢⲈⲒⲀ is given the positive meaning of 'profit, good'[77] and the conjunction ⲈⲠⲈⲒ is understood elliptically 'for (if it

---

[74] Grant and Freedman, *Secret Sayings*, 75. For the references from rabbinic literature, see J. Moffatt, *A Critical and Exegetical Commentary on the Epistle to the Hebrews* (ICC; Edinburgh: T&T Clark, 1924) 189.

[75] For the interpretation of this logion, see Marjanen, *The Woman Jesus Loved*, 35–6.

[76] Lambdin (in Layton, ed., *Nag Hammadi Codex II,2–7*, 63) translates the ⲈⲠⲈⲒ clause: 'for the difficulty which you expect will (surely) materialize.' Layton (*Gnostic Scriptures*, 384) and Meyer (*Thomas*, 33) render the text: 'for the trouble you expect will come.'

[77] For this, see *Dial. Sav.* 134.7; *PS* 358.1.

were different), for otherwise.'[78] Thus the verbal expression CENAϨE ЄPOC can be translated in its most natural sense: 'they shall find it.'

Provided this interpretation is accepted, the robbers, i.e. the worldly powers, are not trying to create difficulties for the owner of the house, i.e. for a disciple, but they are trying to steal the most valuable possession he has. In this way, the peculiar genitive expression ΠЄϤΗЄI Ν̄ΤЄ ΤЄϤΜΝ̄ΤЄPO ('his house of his kingdom') becomes more understandable. The interpretative secondary addition, Ν̄ΤЄ ΤЄϤΜΝ̄ΤЄPO ('of his kingdom'),[79] clearly breaks the boundaries of the parable and brings an allegorical application to the text. Thus, it is not the concrete house (and the goods) of his disciple which the Thomasine Jesus is worried about but the kingdom,[80] i.e. salvation, which disciples carry within themselves and whose ultimate consummation is expected to take place in the future. It is that which is the target of the worldly intrusion. With this interpretation, one cannot avoid the impression that the robbers too are more than an element in the parable, and that they acquire features of worldly or even archontic powers which seek to deprive the disciples of their awareness of their heavenly origin and to prevent them from returning to the realm of light.

The command to 'fast as regards the world' brings an additional note of threat to *Thomas'* view of the world, because according to logion 27 a failure in that respect prevents a Christian from entering the kingdom, i.e. from receiving salvation. As noted above, it is generally accepted that the phrase 'to fast as regards the world'[81] is to be understood as an expression of asceticism. What this means exactly is debated, however. It is at least clear that 'fasting as regards the world' is not meant to be concrete abstinence from food. The qualification 'as regards the world' in itself shows that it has a metaphorical meaning. In addition, other texts in *Thomas* which demonstrate a critical attitude

---

[78] For this meaning, see W. Bauer, W. F. Arndt, and F. W. Gingrich, *A Greek-English Lexicon of the New Testament and Other Early Christian Literature* (Chicago: The University of Chicago Press, 1957) 283.

[79] So Wilson, *Studies in the Gospel of Thomas*, 73–4; H. Quecke, "Sein Haus seines Königreiches': Zum Thomasevangelium 85.9f.' *Muséon* 76 (1963), 47–53, esp. 48. Cf. also King, 'Kingdom,' 73, who, to be sure, does not see any mythological implications in the text but thinks its message is 'preparedness for effectively dealing with the activity of wicked persons.'

[80] Despite a clumsy way of putting it (see Quecke, 'Sein Haus,' 50), the Coptic text seems to translate a Greek version which contained a *genitivus appositivus*.

[81] For the interpretation of the phrase, see A. Guillaumont, 'ΝΗΣΤΕΥΕΙΝ ΤΟΝ ΚΟΣΜΟΝ (*P. Oxy. 1*, verso, 1.5–6),' *BIFAO* 61 (1962) 15–23.

toward fasting (6; 14; 104) and toward other Jewish religious practices (6; 14; 53; 104)[82] also suggest that logion 27 cannot require concrete fasting. In the context of the *Gospel of Thomas*, rather, it seems obvious that Christians were required to abstain from collecting (worldly) riches for themselves (110; 54). This ethos attains its clearest expression in a strong critique of merchants (64). Another conspicuous trait of *Thomas'* asceticism is the renunciation of family ties if they prove to be obstacles to the development of one's new religious identity (16; 55; 101). Whether the renunciation of earlier family ties even constituted a formal prerequisite for assuming a new religious identity among Thomasine Christians, and whether it also included sexual abstinence, are matters of debate.[83] In light of logion 114, where Mary Magdalene is to become 'male'[84] in order to reach salvation and remain a member of the group of disciples, the answer seems to be affirmative. Yet logion 114 may very well be a later addition to *Thomas'* collection and thus may reflect a more advanced development in sexual asceticism than earlier logia in which there are no direct references to sexual abstinence as a precondition for salvation, unless the remarks about the solitary (ⲘⲞⲚⲀⲬⲞⲤ) as the only ones capable of finding the kingdom and entering the bridal chamber (*Gos. Thom.* 49; 75) can be seen in this way.[85]

To summarize, in *Thomas* both the created world and the human body are regarded as worthless entities when seen from the perspective of spiritual values. Therefore the created world is considered to be already perishing and in fact it is being replaced by a 'new world' consisting of those people who represent the realm of light, the kingdom, upon the earth. Yet the powers of the world are not described as having given up the fight. They strive to gain control over the representatives of the kingdom by attempting to fetter them with traditional worldly values such as family ties and the challenge to gather material goods. In this way the world is a threat which tries to deprive a Thomasine Christian of the salvation already actualized in the present

---

[82] For this, see Marjanen, '*Thomas* and Jewish Religious Practices' in this volume.

[83] For the anti-familial language and sexual abstinence, see Uro, 'Is *Thomas* an Encratite Gospel?' in this volume.

[84] For the interpretation of the expression 'becoming male,' see Marjanen, 'Women Disciples in the *Gospel of Thomas*' in this volume.

[85] For the possible interpretations of ⲘⲞⲚⲀⲬⲞⲤ, see Uro, 'Is *Thomas* an Encratite Gospel?' in this volume.

life (*Gos. Thom.* 51) and of the profit expected in the future consummation (*Gos. Thom.* 21; 49).

5.5. Thomas' *view of the world compared with other conceptions*

5.5.1. Wisdom of Solomon

The Wisdom of Solomon is a Jewish wisdom text composed during a period when virtually no Christian literature existed. Yet the exact date of the writing is debated. Suggestions made by various scholars range from 220 BCE to 50 CE. It is most likely that it was composed closer to the end of that period.[86]

The Wisdom of Solomon is one of the first Jewish-Hellenistic writings in which the term κόσμος denotes the phenomenal world.[87] As to its view of the world, the basic point of departure is that it is created and ruled by God (1.7; 1.14; 11.17; 13.1–2, 9; 16.24).[88] There is no other power which would seriously question the absolute authority of God over the κόσμος. In light of this, there is no reason to claim that the Wisdom of Solomon serves as an example of a development in which the universe is divided into a benevolent world ruled by God and a malevolent world ruled by evil.[89] Unlike the situation in the *Gospel of Thomas*, God's role as Creator does not remain an unreflected, subsidiary theme in the Wisdom of Solomon. It is clearly an important part of the writer's conception of God, and it is even used in the writer's polemic against idolaters (13.1–9). God's special love relationship to his creation is also emphasized (11.24), and his perpetual rulership over the world is stressed time and again in the Wisdom of Solomon (1.7; 9.1–3; 12.12–18), whereas in *Thomas* the Father's existing relationship to the world is hardly considered at all. The only time when that is discussed is when the relationship of the Father to the world is characterized as a strictly invisible presence,

---

[86] For discussion of the date, see D. Winston, *The Wisdom of Solomon* (AB 43; New York: Doubleday, 1979) 20–5. Winston himself thinks that the book was written during the reign of Caligula (37–41 CE).

[87] Sasse, 'κοσμέω κτλ.,' 881–2.

[88] Certainly wisdom is seen as a kind of co-worker of God, through the agency of which he acts in the κόσμος (9.9–11; 10.1–2). It is also interesting that the ruling of the world can also be delegated to righteous human beings (9.2–3; 10.1–2).

[89] Davies (*Gospel of Thomas*, 71) makes this claim and finds support for it from Gerhard von Rad.

almost as that of an outsider, realizable only by those who are his children and who have their origin outside of the world in the realm of light (*Gos. Thom.* 113; 3). This may suggest that in the context of *Thomas* the world, albeit once created by the Father, but afterwards having become a worthless, threatening reality, is seen as having been taken over by evil powers, although this is nowhere explicitly stated.

Even in the Wisdom of Solomon the world is not without evil influence. As an example of this, the author of the writing refers to the existence of death. However, he emphasizes strongly that death is not a product of God (Wis 1.13) but that 'through the devil's[90] envy death entered the world, and those who belong to his company experience it' (2.24).[91] Nevertheless, the devil does not seem to have a strong, independent role within the world, since in 1.16 it is stated that ungodly people summoned death into the world by their words and deeds. A similar conclusion can be drawn from 10.3–8, where it is recorded that human unrighteousness brings constant misfortunes on the earth. It is also through human vanity that idols enter the world (14.14). Thus in the Wisdom of Solomon God's and his children's adversary is not really the devil nor a mysterious, threatening 'world,' as in the *Gospel of Thomas*, but ungodly, foolish people (3.10; 5.17–20; 14.9).

It is in fact significant that when evil things enter the world, this does not lead to a situation in which the κόσμος itself is somehow taken over and ruled by evil powers. On the contrary, in his battle against unrighteousness the Lord 'will arm all creation to repel his enemies' (Wis 5.17) 'and creation will join with him to fight against his frenzied foes' (5.20). Verses 5.21–23 clearly show that it is not only righteous people who join this fight but the whole created world. The same is true in the final chapters of the book which contain a colorful description of Israel's deliverance from Egypt. In 16.17 it is said that through various natural catastrophes the κόσμος came to Israel's rescue, since it 'defends the righteous.' Unlike the *Gospel of Thomas*, in the Wisdom of Solomon evil is not symbolized by the world but by the unrighteousness of the ungodly. Whereas in *Thomas* the world both stands for a created reality and symbolizes negative worldly values and

---

[90] The Greek word διάβολος is used.

[91] All the translations of the *Wisdom of Solomon* derive from *The New Oxford Annotated Bible with the Apocryphal/Deuterocanonical Books* (New Revised Standard Version; ed. by B. M. Metzger and R. E. Murphy; New York: Oxford University Press, 1991).

those evil powers which threaten to deprive Christians of their salvation, in the Wisdom of Solomon the world denotes only God's good creation.

There is an interesting common feature in the Wisdom of Solomon and the *Gospel of Thomas*. In both cases, the real self or soul of a person – or, in the case of *Thomas,* at least the real self of the children of light – seems to have its (preexistent) origin in the transcendent world of God (Wis 8.19–20; *Gos. Thom.* 50; 70; cf. also 49).[92] Yet there is a slight but significant difference in the presentation of this detail. Even though in both writings the body is described as an obvious encumbrance to the soul (Wis 9.15; *Gos. Thom.* 29), in the Wisdom of Solomon a good soul, originating from the transcendent world, can receive its dwelling in a better, undefiled body (8.19–20), whereas in *Thomas* all bodies seem to be an equal burden to the soul (29; 87).

5.5.2. Gospel of John

The Gospel of John is the writing of the New Testament which shows the greatest interest in the world, at least if that interest is measured by the number of times the word κόσμος is used. In the Gospel of John the world has several aspects, and it is viewed from various perspectives. As in *Thomas*, the term may neutrally describe the stage of Jesus' appearance (e.g. 1.9) or the people of the world in their totality (e.g. 3.16). John also knows of the creation of the world through the Logos, although this is mentioned almost in passing and only in the prologue (1.10). Nowhere else in the writing does John return to this topic.

More significant as regards John's view of the world are those passages in which this world is contrasted with the other reality to which Jesus and his Father belong (e.g. 13.1; 18.36), in which the ruler of this world is mentioned (12.31; 14.30; 16.11), in which the world is seen as being permeated by evil (17.15), and in which both Jesus and his disciples are said to be vehemently hated by the world because they do not belong to it (7.7; 15.18; 16.33; 17.14). In view of these texts, it is obvious that in the Gospel of John there is developing a conception which tends to see the world as the realm of evil. At this point, John's and *Thomas'* conceptions of the world are very similar, although the

---

[92] For the idea of a preexistent soul in the Wisdom of Solomon, see Winston, *Wisdom,* 25–32.

latter does not speak of the ruler of the world. Yet in logion 21 even *Thomas* can refer to the robbers who symbolize evil worldly powers.

Although John can speak of God's love for the world (3.16), God's interest in the world is actually limited to those disciples who by their nature have never really belonged to the world but to God (17.6,14). Unlike classical Gnostic texts, John, again in agreement with *Thomas*, does not explain how these disciples have come to the world or how the world has been subdued by the power of evil. Neither does John discuss the relationship between the body and the divine spirit of a human being.

It is interesting to note that in John the world does not seem to be a threat in the same fatal sense found in the *Gospel of Thomas*. Although the disciples of Jesus are being persecuted in and by the world,[93] there does not seem to be a real reason to be afraid that the world will deprive them of their faith and their position as the representatives of God's realm. In fact, they are comforted by Jesus saying that he has conquered the world (16.33). Even the rule of the ἄρχων τοῦ κόσμου τούτου is only temporary and in fact more or less ostensible. For John, the ruler of this world has already been judged (16.11). Nevertheless, this does not necessarily warrant the conclusion that the readers of the text have experienced the world as a lesser threat than the readers of *Thomas* have. The very fact that the author of John emphasizes the victory of Jesus over the world and its ruler may well indicate that the Johannine community perceived the whole of reality as sharply divided between the realm of God and the realm of the evil, the latter being the phenomenal world.

5.5.3. Gospel of Philip

The *Gospel of Philip* is a collection of excerpts which has no clear literary arrangement. Yet it represents a rather uniform theological perspective according to which the selection of material has been made. Therefore individual excerpts or groups of excerpts are primarily to be interpreted within the context of the writing as a whole[94] and not 'in

---

[93] In addition to the somewhat obscure concept 'world,' the 'Jews' also represent the opponents of Jesus and his disciples (cf. e.g. 8.44; 9.22).

[94] Marjanen, *The Woman Jesus Loved*, 148–9.

isolation, with comparison of other works or fragments of Valentinianism or of classic Gnosticism.'[95] The *Gospel of Philip* is somewhat later than the *Gospel of Thomas*. It is to be dated at the end of the second century or at the beginning of the third.[96] It also contains some interesting connections with *Thomas*.[97]

As in many other Valentinian texts, the world is one of the key concepts in the *Gospel of Philip*. Although the writing does not contain any mythological description of the genesis of the phenomenal world, it clearly implies one. In 75.2–14 it is stated:[98]

> The world came about through a mistake.[99] For he who created it wanted to create it imperishable and immortal. He fell short of attaining his desire. For the world never was imperishable, nor for that matter was he who made the world. For things are not imperishable, but sons are. Nothing will be able to receive imperishability if it does not first become a son. But he who has not the ability to receive, how much more will he be unable to give?

Differently from *Thomas*, the text unequivocally presupposes both the devolution of the divine and the existence of the demiurge (cf. also 71.35 – 72.1; 84.24–34). No positive values are attached to the act of creation. On the other hand, the perishableness of the created world, and its inferiority as compared with a Christian, are again features shared by *Thomas*. There are also many texts in the *Gospel of Philip* which emphasize the great qualitative difference between this world (ⲡⲉⲉⲓⲕⲟⲥⲙⲟⲥ) and the eternal realm (ⲡⲁⲓⲱⲛ) (52.26–27; 53.20–23; 53.35 – 54.5; 76.6–9) or the kingdom of heaven (72.17–22; 57.19–22).

Although the things of this world may be types of various entities of the eternal realm and they can even bear the same names, they are not the same but serve to deceive Christians into diverting their 'thoughts

---

[95] Layton, *Gnostic Scriptures*, 326.

[96] Marjanen, *The Woman Jesus Loved*, 147–8.

[97] Although not a sayings collection as such, the *Gospel of Philip* has preserved some sayings which are attributed to Jesus. Two of them have a very close parallel in the *Gospel of Thomas* (*Gos. Thom.* 19.1 = *Gos. Phil.* 64.9–11; *Gos. Thom.* 22.4 = *Gos. Phil.* 67.30–33). There are also interesting thematic connections between the two gospels (*Gos. Thom.* 29.3/*Gos. Phil.* 56.24–26; *Gos. Thom.* 50.3/*Gos. Phil.* 72.22–23; *Gos. Thom.* 108/*Gos. Phil.* 67.26–27 [cf. 61.30–31]).

[98] This translation as well as all the later translations of the *Gospel of Philip* are taken from W. W. Isenberg, 'The Gospel According to Philip' [English translation], in Layton, ed., *Nag Hammadi Codex II,2–7*, 142–215.

[99] Cf. *Gos. Truth* 17.4–21.

from what is correct to what is incorrect' (53.25–27). In 54.13–31 it is pointed out that this process of deception is launched by the worldly archons. In the same way as the *Gospel of Thomas*, the author of the *Gospel of Philip* can thus see the world as a threatening reality. This is further illustrated by 73.19–23, where it is said that 'this world is a corpse-eater. All the things eaten in it themselves die also. Truth is a life-eater. Therefore no one nourished by [truth] will die. It was from that place that Jesus came and brought food. To those who so desired he gave [life, that] they might not die.' If one, being in this world, does not himself receive the truth of the world, and resurrection (= the eternal realm; cf. 66.7–23; 67.9–27), one is in danger of being consumed by the world. If that happens, one surely ends up in 'the middle,' which according to the *Gospel of Philip* marks the ultimate death (66.15–16). Moreover, any interest of the Christians in the world is likewise fatal because those who love the world bring forth spiritual offspring which resemble the world and not the Lord (78.20–25).

5.5.4. Apocryphon of John

Generally regarded as a Sethian Gnostic text, the *Apocryphon of John* 'contains one of the most classic narrations of the Gnostic myth,'[100] in which both the origin and the character of the visible universe have a central role and find their explanation. The writing has been preserved in four Coptic manuscripts,[101] which represent two different versions of the text.[102] Two of the manuscripts found in the Nag Hammadi Library contain a long version (NHC II/1 and NHC IV/1), the other two a short version (BG 8502.2 and NHC III/1). The exact relationship between the long and short versions is unclear. Scholars debate whether the long version is an expansion of the short one or the short an abridgment of the long. In the present comparison between the *Gospel of Thomas* and the *Apocryphon of John* both the long and the

---

[100] Layton, *Gnostic Scriptures*, 23.
[101] For a synopsis of the four manuscripts, see M. Waldstein and F. Wisse, eds., *The Apocryphon of John: Synopsis of Nag Hammadi Codices II,1; III,1; and IV,1 with BG 8502,2* (NHMS 33; Leiden: E. J. Brill, 1995).
[102] Coptic texts are translations of Greek originals.

short versions are taken into account.[103] Because of the relatively good condition of NHC II/1 and BG 8502.2, references are mainly made according to these manuscripts. The fact that Irenaeus knew a version of the *Apocryphon of John*, or at least a work very similar to it, suggests that the writing was composed sometime before the last quarter of the second century.

The major difference between the views of the world in *Thomas* and the *Apocryphon of John* is undeniably the fact that in the latter the creation of the material universe (**KOCMOC**)[104] has nothing to do with the Invisible Spirit, the supreme God, but it is the result of an unfortunate mistake made by Sophia, the lowest light-being of the divine realm. The actual creator, the demiurge, is Yaldabaoth, the imperfect offspring of Sophia, whom his mother produces without the consent of her male consort and who himself does not belong to the beings of the realm of light (II/1 10.1–28; BG 37.12 – 39.10). Thus, although the creation of the world has its origin in an episode in the divine realm, there is a radical separation between the divine realm and the created cosmos. The creation of the world is not intended or accomplished by the true God, the invisible Spirit. Neither is he later

---

[103] In addition to the Coptic manuscripts, Irenaeus summarizes what seems to be a variant of the first part of the *Apocryphon of John*. Since it is impossible to decide whether he has used either of the two versions or a third one or an independent work similar to the *Apocryphon of John*, Irenaeus' summary is not taken into consideration here. For the different extant versions of the *Apocryphon of John*, see K. L. King, 'Approaching the Variants of the Apocryphon of John,' in J. D. Turner and A. McGuire, eds., *The Nag Hammadi Library After Fifty Years: Proceedings of the 1995 Society of Biblical Literature Commemoration* (NHMS 44; Leiden: E. J. Brill, 1997) 105–37.

[104] Apart from one instance in the short version (BG 26.21–27.1; III/1 7.7–9), in which **KOCMOC** denotes the sphere of influence of the aeons who emanate from the Invisible Spirit, the term refers to the world created and ruled by Yaldabaoth and his authorities (BG 20.10–11; III/1 1.21; BG 21.2; BG 42.9–10; III/1 18.8–9; II/1 30.4–7; BG 76.2–5; III/1 39.19–21). It is noteworthy that in the long version (IV/1 6.24–25; cf. also II/1 4.22) the reference to **N̄KOCMOC** of the aeons does not occur. In addition, when the author of the long version says that the power which Yaldabaoth had gained from his mother produced in him something resembling the upper world, the All, the author does not call the upper world **KOCMOC** but uses a Coptic equivalent **TCENO** (II/1 13.4–5). Thus, in the long version at least, there seems to be a conscious tendency to avoid employing the term **KOCMOC** when the upper world is spoken of.

In some passages the terms **KTICIC** ('creation') and **CWN̄T** ('creation') (II/1 1.32–33; BG 20.20–21; II/1 13.5–6; BG 44.10; II/1 28.26–29; II/1 30.4–6) are employed when the world of Yaldabaoth is described. In some cases, the use of **KTICIC** and **CWN̄T** is confined to the people inhabiting the earth (II/1 20.19–20; BG 53.10–12; II/1 28.26–29).

directly involved in the matters of the lower world at all. All his interventions take place through various intermediaries.

Yaldabaoth's world consists of the seven spheres of the planets and the depth of the abyss (II/1 11.4–6; BG 41.12–15) as well as the lowest region of all matter (II/1 20.8–9). The lowest region of all matter corresponds to the phenomenal world. Adam, the first human being created by Yaldabaoth and his rulers according to the image of the true God, is brought into this lowest region after Yaldabaoth realizes that he was deceived by Christ and the four lights of the upper world to blow the power of the pleroma he had received from his mother, Sophia, into Adam (II/1 20.7–9; BG 52.15–17). In this way Yaldabaoth hopes to hide Adam so that the representatives of the upper world cannot find him. In order to make Adam forgetful and ignorant of the power within him, i.e. his being part of the pleroma, Yaldabaoth and his authorities form a new, hylic body for him (II/1 21.4–9; III/1 26.14–19). Thus the created world and the hylic body serve to bind the real self of a human being, both in Adam and in his seed, together with the perishable world, and to prevent it from returning to the realm of light. Yaldabaoth's special weapon against the upper world is to introduce sexual desire to human beings (II/1 24.26–32). Even though his strategy is partly successful, it does not bring him any ultimate victory. Various savior figures come from the upper world, appear in the cosmos, remind the souls of their heavenly origin, and urge them to ascend back to the pleroma.

Admittedly, the *Gospel of Thomas* does not contain a myth of the devolution of the divine and the creation of the universe by the demiurge, the most essential Gnostic elements in the *Apocryphon of John*. Nevertheless, it is interesting that, as in the *Apocryphon of John*, *Thomas* too can speak of human beings as being intoxicated and blind in the world (*Gos. Thom.* 28; cf. *Ap. John* II/1 23.8; 28.26–29)[105] and of the worldly robbers who seek to deprive human beings of the

---

[105] Certainly there are also other early Christian texts in which 'drunkenness' and 'blindness' can be used as metaphors of spiritual alienation, impassivity, or lack of understanding. The most notable examples are 1 Thess 5.6–7 ('drunkenness') and 2 Cor 4.4 ('blindness'). Yet the metaphorical use of these images is especially frequent in Gnostic texts. For 'drunkenness,' see e.g. *Gos. Truth* 22.16–20; *Corpus Hermeticum* 1.27; 7.1. For 'blindness,' see e.g. *Gos. Truth* 30.14–16; *Hyp. Arch.* 86.27; 87.3–4; *Dial. Sav.* 121.21 – 122.1; *Testim. Truth* 48.2–4.

awareness of their heavenly identity (*Gos. Thom.* 21; cf. *Ap. John* II/1 21.9–12).

5.6. Conclusion

Finally, it remains to be seen what *Thomas'* view of the world reveals about its place within early Christian literature, especially with regard to its relationship to Gnosticism. Even though it is clear that Jewish Wisdom traditions have exerted a strong influence on the *Gospel of Thomas*, as regards their views on the visible world there is a notable difference between *Thomas* and Jewish wisdom, as here represented by the Wisdom of Solomon. To be sure, the creation of the world by God is maintained both by the author of the Wisdom of Solomon and by *Thomas*. Yet this does not prevent *Thomas* from regarding the world as a worthless and even a threatening entity that seeks to deprive Thomasine Christians of their salvation. Unlike the authors of the *Gospel of Philip* and the *Apocryphon of John*, however, the author of the *Gospel of Thomas* does not draw the inference from this that creation is the result of an error and has to be attributed to a perishable demiurge. *Thomas* does not even go as far as the Gospel of John, which postulates the existence of an ἄρχων who rules over 'this world.'[106] Nonetheless, there are other elements which justify the conclusion that of the four writings which I have used as comparative material, *Thomas'* view of the cosmos is closest to that of John.

Both *Thomas* and John speak relatively little of the creation of the world. As a matter of fact, in both cases the appearance of the creation motif may very well be due to the use of an earlier tradition rather than to the deliberate theological reflection of the redactor. In neither of

---

[106] It is worth noting that Paul can also speak of the god of this world (αἰών) who has blinded the minds of the unbelievers (2 Cor 4.4). However, he does not seem to use this designation in the same dualistic sense as John. In 1 Cor 8.4 Paul clearly denies the existence of any gods or idols other than the one God. In 8.6 he quotes an early Christian confession which emphasizes the creatorship and rulership of God and Christ (cf. also Rom 11.36). The *archons* of this world mentioned in 1 Cor 2.6, 8 seem to refer to the political rulers of Paul's own time. For Paul, too, this age may be penetrated by evil influences (Gal 1.4), and the creation is subjected to perishability (Rom 8.21; 1 Cor 7.31), but the world is definitely created and ruled by God. For Paul, the world does not constitute the same, almost mythological threat as it does for *Thomas* (nevertheless, cf. Eph 2.2; 6.12). The Christians are actually free from the world (1 Cor 3.22) and (the people of) the world will be judged by them (1 Cor 6.2).

these writings is the relationship between God as Creator and the evil character of the world made in any way problematic, or even discussed. Admittedly, for both *Thomas* and John the world is a stage for salvific actions on the part of the divine realm. Yet at the same time both consider the cosmos evil and stress the contrast between the divine realm and the world. *Thomas'* emphasis on the threatening character of the cosmos is somewhat lacking in John (for John, Jesus has conquered the world), although that gospel too states that Jesus and his disciples are hated by the world.

Are *Thomas'* and thus also John's views of the world then Gnostic? If a Gnostic writing has to distinguish between a good, eternal God and a perishable, malevolent creator, as is done in the *Gospel of Philip* or the *Apocryphon of John*, one has to answer no. If the fact that a writing regards the world as evil and as being in opposition to the divine realm makes its conception of the world Gnostic, one can answer yes. It is at least clear that *Thomas'* and John's views of the world have moved a long way from the view of Jewish wisdom tradition toward a Gnostic conception, as the latter is manifested in the Valentinian *Gospel of Philip* and even more plainly in the *Apocryphon of John*.

6

Is *Thomas* an encratite gospel?

Risto Uro

In addition to the claim that the *Gospel of Thomas* is 'Gnostic,' the characterization of the writing as being 'encratite'[1] or strictly ascetic has been one major way of describing the religious perspective dominant in the gospel. Some scholars state emphatically that *Thomas* is *not* Gnostic but rather encratite. The most devoted advocate of this view is Gilles Quispel, who has argued for this position in numerous studies over a period of forty years.[2] In an article of 1981,[3] Quispel summarizes and modifies his earlier research by claiming that *Thomas* used different sources, such as some Jewish Christian gospels and a 'Hermetic Anthology.' The author of the gospel himself was encratite, however,

---

[1] I use 'encratism' in the same sense as in the *Anchor Bible Dictionary*, where it is defined as 'the advocacy of a harsh discipline of the body, especially in regard to sexual activity, diet, and the use of alcoholic beverages.' O. C. Edwards, Jr, 'Encratism,' *ABD* 2 (1992) 506–7. More specifically, the term has sometimes been understood to refer to a sect founded by Tatian (see Irenaeus, *Adv. haer.* 1.28.1), but it is more reasonable to take it as a strict form of asceticism practiced by several early Christian groups; see A. D. De Conick, *Seek to See Him: Ascent and Vision Mysticism in the Gospel of Thomas* (VCSup 33; Leiden: E. J. Brill, 1996) 3 n. 3.

[2] See e.g. his *Makarius, das Thomasevangelium und das Lied von der Perle* (NovTSup 15; Leiden: E. J. Brill, 1967); *Gnostic Studies*, vol. 2 (Nederlands Historisch-Archaeologisch Instituut te Istanbul 34.2; Istanbul: Nederlands Historisch-Archaeologisch Instituut te Istanbul, 1975); 'The *Gospel of Thomas* Revisited,' in B. Barc, ed., *Colloque international sur les textes de Nag Hammadi* (Bibliothèque copte de Nag Hammadi, Section 'Études' 1; Québec: University of Laval; Louvain: Peeters, 1981) 218–66; 'The Study of Encratism: A Historical Survey' in U. Bianchi, ed., *La traditizione dell'enkrateia: motivazioni ontologiche e protologiche. Atti de Colloquio Internazionale Milano, 20–23 aprile, 1982* (Rome: Edizioni dell'ateneo) 35–81. Quispel has been followed by De Conick, *Seek to See Him*. See also A. D. De Conick and J. Fossum, 'Stripped Before God: A New Interpretation of Logion 37 in the Gospel of Thomas,' *VC* 45 (1991) 123–50. For further advocates of the encratite origin of the gospel, see the literature in De Conick, ibid., 3–27.

[3] '*Gospel of Thomas* Revisited.'

which means that he rejected 'women, wine, meat, and therefore taught that only bachelors go to heaven.'[4]

'Gnostic' and 'encratite' are not of course mutually exclusive alternatives.[5] There are many who think that *Thomas* is both. Stevan Davies, on the other hand, has argued that *Thomas* is *neither* Gnostic *nor* encratite and has thus distanced himself from both of these categories that are frequently used in Thomasine studies.[6] In response to many scholars who have stressed *Thomas'* encratite character, he states that the 'abhorrence of sex' plays no or a minimal role in the gospel. According to Davies, the *Gospel of Thomas* is less encratite than, for example, the Q material, and consequently far less encratite than the apocryphal Acts of the Apostles or the Desert Fathers.[7]

Davies' position has not, however, received much following.[8] The majority of scholars, irrespective of how 'Gnostic' they think *Thomas* to be, see traits of radical sexual asceticism in the gospel. There is also general agreement among scholars that the *Gospel of Thomas* originated in eastern Syria, where such ascetic tendencies flourished at an early stage among Christian groups, and where traditions under the name of the apostle 'Judas Thomas (Didymos)' were transmitted.[9]

Generally speaking, one can hardly deny that the *Gospel of Thomas* is an important document for the history of early Christian asceticism. *Thomas'* ethos is distinguishably world-denying, and the frequent use of

---

[4]   Ibid., 234.

[5]   C. C. Richardson, 'The Gospel of Thomas: Gnostic or Encratite?,' in D. Neiman and M. Schatkin, eds., *The Heritage of the Early Church: Essays in Honor of the Very Reverend G. V. Florovsky* (OrChrA 195; Rome: Pont. Institutum Studiorum Orientalium, 1973) 68.

[6]   *The Gospel of Thomas and Christian Wisdom* (New York: The Seabury Press, 1983).

[7]   Ibid., 21–2. This position is repeated in Davies' later article 'The Christology and Protology of the *Gospel of Thomas*,' *JBL* 111 (1992) 663–82 with reference to *Thomas'* disapproval of fasting in sayings 14 and 104 (ibid., 674).

[8]   Note, however, J. J. Buckley, 'An Interpretation of Logion 114 in the Gospel of Thomas,' *NovT* 27 (1985) 245–72. Like Davies, Buckley observes that 'on the whole, *Gos. Thom.* seems quite uninterested in asceticism' (ibid., 270).

[9]   For the origin of the *Gospel of Thomas* in the Syrian encratite tradition, see e.g. D. A. Baker, 'The "Gospel of Thomas" and the Syriac "Liber Graduum,"' *NTS* (1965–66), 49–55; A. F. J. Klijn, *Edessa, die Stadt des Apostels Thomas: Das älteste Christentum in Syrien* (Neukirchener Studienbücher 4; Neukirchen-Vluyn: Neukirchener Verlag, 1965) 64–82; L. W. Barnard, 'The Origins and Emergence of the Church in Edessa during the First Two Centuries' *VC* 22 (1968) 161–75; J. J. Gunther 'The Meaning and Origin of the Name "Judas Thomas"' *Muséon* 93 (1980) 113–48; P. Perkins, *The Gnostic Dialogue: The Early Church and the Crisis of Gnosticism* (New York: Paulist Press, 1980) 99–112; H. J. W. Drijvers, 'Facts and Problems in Early Syriac-Speaking Christianity,' *SecCent* 2.3 (1982) 157–75.

asexual imagery and anti-familial language gives a clear ascetic flavor to the gospel. Yet the characterizations of the *Gospel of Thomas* as an 'ascetic' or 'encratite' document are in need of refinement. During the last two decades there has been a growing interest in the study of asceticism in various religious traditions, and scholars have become more conscious of the diversity of ascetic behavior and its motives.[10] Such recent analyses teach us that 'asceticism' is an important cultural phenomenon, which in a loose sense can be defined, to use Geoffrey Harpham's words, as 'any act of self-denial undertaken as a strategy of empowerment or gratification.'[11] Although he also uses the term in a narrower sense to refer to a specific historical ideology, 'a product of early Christian ethics and spirituality,'[12] the wider definition is helpful to us. Without entering into a detailed theoretical discussion about different cultural and social functions of asceticism, one may conclude that recent research on different types of ascetic behavior and traditions has broadened our understanding of this phenomenon.[13] Asceticism should not be restricted to its most bizarre and fanatic forms of behavior but, to borrow Harpham's language again, should be seen rather as a kind of computer operating system which is

> a fundamental operating ground on which the particular culture, the word processing program itself, is overlaid. Where there is culture there is asceticism: cultures structure asceticism, each in its own way, but do not impose it.[14]

In light of this cultural understanding of asceticism, it is not enough to

---

[10] V. L. Wimbush, 'The Ascetic Impulse in Early Christianity: Some Methodological Challenges,' *StPatr* 25 (1993), 462–78, esp. 462. The diversity and richness of ascetic traditions have been aptly demonstrated in a recent massive collection of articles, V. L. Wimbush and R. Valantasis, eds., *Asceticism* (Oxford: Oxford University Press, 1995).

[11] *The Ascetic Imperative in Culture and Criticism* (Chicago: The University of Chicago Press, 1987) xiii.

[12] Ibid.

[13] From a different perspective, a group of scholars who worked on the *Ascetic Behavior in Greco-Roman Antiquity* project and produced a sourcebook under the same title, ended up with the following definition of ascetic behavior: It 'represents a range of responses to social, political, and physical worlds often perceived as oppressive or unfriendly, or as stumbling blocks to pursuit of heroic personal or communal goals, life styles, and commitments' (V. L. Wimbush, ed., *Ascetic Behavior in Greco-Roman Antiquity: A Sourcebook* [Studies in Antiquity & Christianity; Minneapolis: Fortress Press, 1990]) 2.

[14] *The Ascetic Imperative*, xi. Harpham's metaphor has also been employed in R. Valantasis, 'A Theory of the Social Function of Asceticism,' in V. L. Wimbush and R. Valantasis, eds., *Asceticism* (Oxford: Oxford University Press, 1995) 544–52, esp. 546–7.

recognize the ascetic traits of the *Gospel of Thomas* and to locate the document in the 'ascetic' or 'encratite' Syrian Thomas tradition. We have to advance our research on more specific questions about the *nature* of *Thomas'* ascetic language. What kind of asceticism does the *Gospel of Thomas* represent? How does it seem to operate in the contemporary cultural context? What social strategies and attitudes does the 'ascetic imperative' of the gospel involve? What kind of compromises or ambivalence, inherent in all asceticism,[15] does *Thomas'* asceticism imply?

The present essay is an attempt to answer these questions. The main focus is on sexual asceticism, which has often been seen as a prominent element in several sayings of the gospel.[16] Most of these can conveniently be structured under the following three themes: (1) anti-familial sayings, (2) sayings on 'becoming one/the two becoming one,' and (3) those on the 'solitary.'

6.1. Anti-familial sayings

The *Gospel of Thomas* records many sayings which have been viewed as showing disregard for normal family ties or as reflecting the ethos of 'homelessness' (*Gos. Thom.* 16; 42; 55; 79; 86; 99; 101; 105).[17] Most of

---

[15] Cf. Harpham, *The Ascetic Imperative*, xii: 'Despite the fanaticism of its early Christian practitioners, who constantly extolled the value of "single-mindedness," asceticism is always marked by ambivalence, by a compromised binarism.'

[16] The question of dietary regulations in *Thomas* is not discussed in detail. It suffices to note that I find no clear evidence for vegetarianism or rejection of wine in the gospel. The idea of 'eating the dead' in *Gos. Thom.* 11 (cf. 60) hardly suggests the contrary, since it may simply contrast normal eating (dead animals) with the possibility of eating what is living (cf. 111; similarly Davies, 'Christology and Protology,' 672). Logion 28 contains a negative statement about people being intoxicated, but drunkenness is a commonplace as a metaphor for religious impenitence (e.g. 1 Thess 5.5–8; *Gos. Truth* 22.17–20). Moreover, being intoxicated can also be used as a positive metaphor in the gospel (*Gos. Thom.* 13; cf. 108). Fasting is explicitly rejected in logion 14 (cf. also 104; for fasting in *Thomas*, see Marjanen, '*Thomas* and Jewish Religious Practices' in this volume). For the opposite view of dietary regulations in *Thomas*, see M. Lelyveld, *Les logia de la vie dans l'évangile selon Thomas: A la recherche d'une tradition et d'une rédaction* (NHS 34; Leiden: E. J. Brill, 1987) 21–2; De Conick, *Seek to See Him*, 7.

[17] See also R. Uro, 'Asceticism and Anti-familial Language in the *Gospel of Thomas*,' in H. Moxnes, ed., *Constructing Early Christian Families: Family as Social Reality and Metaphor* (London: Routledge, 1997), 216–34. Part of the material of this article has been incorporated in this essay.

these have parallels in the Synoptic gospels, and the general tone of these sayings resembles one we can recognize already in the 'Q' material. Jesus' message brings dissension upon earth (*Gos. Thom.* 16/Q 12.49–53). The 'son of man' has no place to lay his head (*Gos. Thom.* 86/Q 9.58), and disciples must be ready to hate father and mother to be worthy of Jesus (*Gos. Thom.* 55; 101; 105; Q 14.26). As in Mark and the other Synoptics, but probably not in Q, *Thomas* presents Jesus himself as expressing the same negative attitude towards his own family as he demands from his disciples (*Gos. Thom.* 79; 99/Mark 3.31–35parr; Luke 11.27–28).

Thomas' heavy emphasis on the anti-familial traditions used in the Synoptic gospels could be taken as an indication of the encratite character of the gospel.[18] On the other hand, *Thomas*, although rich in material dealing with social conflicts in the family household, has surprisingly little interest in the marital relationship itself. The dissension within families anticipated in the *Gospel of Thomas* is never that between married couples. In this respect, the canonical Gospel of Luke appears to be more 'encratite' than *Thomas* (cf. e.g. the addition of 'wife' in Luke 14.26 or the formulation of Jesus' answer to the Sadducees in Luke 20.34–36).[19] In Luke's version of the parable of the Great Feast, marriage is one of the excuses presented by those invited (Luke 14.20). We cannot be quite certain about the Q form of the parable, since Matthew's version differs considerably from Luke's. In any case, it is interesting that the Thomasine version of the parable mentions marriage only indirectly – the guest has to arrange

---

18   *Thomas'* anti-familial ethos and similarity with the Q material has led some scholars to assume that the traditions of *Thomas* were transmitted mainly by itinerant radicals. See especially S. J. Patterson, *The Gospel of Thomas and Jesus* (Sonoma: Polebridge Press, 1993). Patterson does not stress that *Thomas'* wandering charismatics were celibate, even though he seems to imply this (see ibid., 153). For De Conick, the members of the Thomasine community were clearly those who 'were abstaining from the world and were renouncing it completely by becoming poor wandering celibates with restricted diets' (*Seek to See Him*, 135). For a discussion on this issue, see Uro, 'Anti-familial Language,' 217–19.

19   For the ascetic tendencies in Luke's writings, see T. K. Seim, *The Double Message: Patterns of Gender in Luke & Acts* (Nashville: Abingdon, 1994). The Lukan pericope in 20.34–36 became a key passage to many later ascetics, for example to Marcion; for Marcion's interpretation of the pericope, see D. E. Aune, *The Cultic Setting of Realized Eschatology in Early Christianity* (NovTSup 28; Leiden: E. J. Brill, 1972) 202–11.

his *friend's* wedding dinner, not his own – and the emphasis is on the business activities of those who receive the invitation (see *Gos. Thom.* 64).[20]

In any case, the anti-familial language of *Thomas* focuses on the rejection of the biological family and parenthood as a source of honor and replaces them with different sorts of family metaphors. There are two parallel sayings in *Thomas*, of which the latter seems to contrast ordinary parents with the idea of true 'motherhood':

> (55) Jesus said, 'Whoever does not hate his father and his mother cannot become a disciple to me. And whoever does not hate his brothers and sisters and take up his cross in my way will not be worthy of me.'[21]

> (101) <Jesus said,> 'Whoever does not hate his [father] and his mother as I do cannot become a [disciple] to me. And whoever does [not] love his [father and] his mother as I do cannot become a [disciple to] me. For my mother [. . .], but [my] true [mother] gave me life.'[22]

The doublet is one of those cases which, according to Quispel, proves that *Thomas* used at least two written sources, one Jewish-Christian and the other encratite.[23] He thinks that the latter version of the saying, including the additional statement about 'mother,' derives from the encratite source used by the author and should be understood as an injunction against procreation and marriage. Quispel refers to the encratites condemned by Clement of Alexandria in the third chapter of *Stromateis*. According to Clement, they teach that one 'should not bring others . . . to live in this wretched world, nor give any sustenance to death' (*Strom.* 3.45). In the same context Clement also attempts to

---

[20] One may also note that the Lukan version of the parable was used by the encratites criticized by Clement of Alexandria in *Strom.* 2.12.90.

[21] Unless otherwise noted, I cite the translation by T. O. Lambdin in B. Layton, ed., *Nag Hammadi Codex II, 2–7 together with XIII,2*, Brit. Lib. Or.4926(1), and P.Oxy. 1, 654, 655*, vol. 1 (NHS 20; Leiden: E. J. Brill, 1989) 53–93.

[22] Unfortunately the last sentence of *Gos. Thom.* 101 is partially damaged and remains defective, but the words '[my] true [mother]' are based on a well-grounded reconstruction. A possible reconstruction of the preceding lacuna is given with hesitation by Layton (in consultation with S. Emmel) and can be translated 'For my mother [gave falsehood];' *Nag Hammadi Codex II,2–7*, 88.

[23] '*Gospel of Thomas* Revisited,' 224–5, 257.

prove that the encratites 'pervert the sense of books' when they use a saying of the Lord, which he elsewhere knows as a saying from the *Gospel of the Egyptians*:

> When Salome asked the Lord: 'How long shall death hold sway?' He answered: 'As long as you women bear children.'[24]

This makes Quispel think that *Gos. Thom.* 101 also derives from the *Gospel of the Egyptians*. Both sayings reflect 'the same gloomy view, namely, that man shall continue to die as long as women bring forth children.'[25]

The issue of the numerous doublets of *Thomas* is certainly pertinent and may reveal different sources used in the process of composition. But Quispel's identification of *Thomas'* encratite source as the gospel mentioned in Clement's *Stromateis* is speculative and has been widely criticized.[26] There are also problems in his 'encratite' reading of the end of *Gos. Thom.* 101, in which there is a lacuna. Quispel is compelled to read the last sentence of the logion as 'my mother [gave me death]' to create a better connection between *Thomas* and the teaching of the encratites mentioned by Clement, but there is no indication how this would work in Coptic. Moreover, the contrast between 'my mother' and '[my] true mother,' rather than being a direct statement against marriage, reflects the idea of Jesus' (and the disciples') heavenly origin. *Gos. Thom.* 15 may indicate this kind of thinking:

> When you see one who was not born of woman, prostrate yourselves on your faces and worship him. That one is your father.

The cryptic saying in *Gos. Thom.* 105 ('He who knows the father and the mother will be called the son of a harlot') may express this idea of

---

[24] Translation by H. Chadwick in J. E. L. Oulton and H. Chadwick, *Alexandrian Christianity: Selected Translations of Clement and Origen with Introductions and Notes* (LCC 2; Philadelphia: Westminster Press, 1954) 61.

[25] '*Gospel of Thomas* Revisited,' 257.

[26] See e.g. F. T. Fallon and R. Cameron, 'The Gospel of Thomas: A Forschungsbericht and Analysis,' *ANRW* II 25.6 (1988) 4216–9; De Conick, *Seek to See Him*, 175–80; J. Ma. Asgeirsson, 'Arguments and Audience(s) in the *Gospel of Thomas*,' SBLSP 36 (1997) 47–85.

'heavenly origin' in a sharpened way.[27] The language can be compared to other sayings which proclaim the true identity of the disciples as 'children of the living father' (e.g. *Gos. Thom.* 49; 50). In the *Gospel of Thomas*, the divine origin of Jesus is closely related to the true identity of the disciples, since salvation is understood as a process of becoming like Jesus or even better as becoming him in a process of union (*Gos. Thom.* 108). This notion may explain why Jesus' rejection of his fleshly family plays such a central role in *Thomas*. Radical sexual asceticism is not, therefore, the only or even the major reason for the prominence of this theme in the gospel.

Among the sayings that reflect the Synoptic ethos of 'homelessness,' *Gos. Thom.* 79 presents the most explicit negative statement against childbearing.

> (79) A woman from the crowd said to him, 'Blessed are the womb which bore you and breasts which nourished you.' [2]He said to [her], 'Blessed are those who have heard the word of the father and truly kept it. [3]For there will be days when you (pl.) will say, 'Blessed are the womb which has not conceived and the breasts which have not given milk.''

The saying has two parallels in the Synoptic gospels. The episode about a woman in the crowd is also found in Luke 11.27–28 (*Gos. Thom.* 79.1–2), material usually labelled as peculiar to Luke.[28] The end of

---

[27] Quispel (*Makarius*, 99) explains this difficult saying by referring to the encratites' teaching that marriage should be regarded as 'corruption' (φθορά) and 'fornication' (πορνεία); see Irenaeus, *Adv. haer.* 1.28.1. One should not, however, overlook the fact that the saying does not speak of marriage but of family lineage. Scholars have sometimes referred to John 8.41–42, which has been considered to imply that according to 'the Jews' Jesus was born 'of fornication'; R. M. Grant and D. N. Freedman, *The Secret Sayings of Jesus* (London: Collins, 1960) 180–1. Some traditions about Jewish attacks on the legitimacy of Jesus' birth have been preserved (Origen, *Cels.* 1.28). In light of such traditions, one could interpret *Gos. Thom.* 105 as reflecting outsiders' reproaches that Jesus' disciples (like their Master himself), who claimed to be of heavenly origin, were in fact 'children of a harlot.'

[28] Scholars have sometimes argued that the Luke 11.27–28 was derived from Q and that Matthew omitted it and replaced it with the Markan story on True Relatives (Mark 3.31–35/Matt 12.46–50), but no waterproof arguments can be presented for this view. The International Q Project (a group of more than thirty scholars who worked on the reconstruction of Q in the context of SBL and the Institute for Antiquity and Christianity, Claremont, CA), though sensitive to parallels in *Thomas* in general, concluded that the inclusion of this section cannot be decided with certainty; see M. C. Moreland and J. M. Robinson, 'The International Q Project Work Sessions 23–27 May, 22–26 August, 17–18 November 1994,' *JBL* 114 (1995) 475–85.

Thomas' saying (79.3) has a parallel in the Lukan passion narrative (Luke 23.29) as part of the section which addresses the daughters of Jerusalem (23.27–31). When compared with Luke, *Gos. Thom.* 79 appears to be a combination of these two passages, but the relationship between the Lukan versions and the Thomasine saying may be more complex than that.[29]

Does the composition of *Gos. Thom.* 79.1–3 reflect a definite stance in favor of sexual asceticism and celibacy? Many have answered in the affirmative. Wolfgang Schrage, for example, argues that the omission of Luke's 'the barren' may reveal *Thomas'* intention to emphasize voluntary celibacy.[30] Peter Nagel sees in *Gos. Thom.* 79 an early example of an ascetic interpretation of Jesus' apocalyptic word (cf. Mark 13.17).[31] One could also take notice of the word μενοῦν in Luke 11.28, which has no equivalent in *Thomas*. This particle is probably to be understood in the corrective sense ('yes, but rather')[32] and therefore has the effect of softening the contrast between maternal honor and true discipleship. In *Thomas*, biological motherhood is clearly contrasted with discipleship.

One can hardly deny that *Gos. Thom.* 79.3 adds an ascetic element to the story of the Woman in the Crowd. But we should be cautious about making this saying more 'encratite' than it is. The absence of 'the

---

29 The Woman in the Crowd (Luke 11.27–28) may be a thematic variant of the tradition on True Relatives (Mark 3.31–35 parr; *Gos. Thom.* 99), and it is therefore likely that the Coming Days in Luke 23.29 and *Gos. Thom.* 79.3 is a separate tradition, not the original part of the saying. The catchwords 'blessed are the womb ... and the breasts' have provided a formal reason for joining these two traditions. It is, however, unclear whether the combination of these two traditions is Lukan redaction. The specifically Lukan phraseology in v. 27a ('As he said this') is lacking in *Thomas*, but on the other hand the words 'hear the word of God and keep it' (cf. Luke 8.21) have a Lukan flavor. The similar expression in *Thomas* may therefore reveal a Lukan redaction. The latter suggestion does not, however, solve the question of a possibly independent tradition history behind the Thomasine saying, since the influence of the Lukan redaction may have occurred after the two units were joined. An argument for the independence of *Gos. Thom.* 79 from the Lukan redaction has been made by Patterson, *Gospel of Thomas*, 59–60. For the opposite view, see W. Schrage, *Das Verhältnis des Thomas-Evangeliums zur synoptischen Tradition und den koptischen Evangelienübersetzungen: Zugleich ein Beitrag zur gnostischen Synoptikerdeutung* (BZNW 29; Berlin: Töpelmann, 1964) 164–8, and (with some hesitation) K. R. Snodgrass, 'The Gospel of Thomas: A Secondary Gospel,' *SecCent* 7 (1989–90) 36–7.

30 Schrage, *Verhältnis*, 165; similarly J. A. Fitzmyer, *The Gospel According to St. Luke, X–XXIV; Introduction, Translation and Notes* (AB 28B, Garden City: Doubleday, 1985) 1494.

31 P. Nagel, *Die Motivierung der Askese in der alten Kirche und der Ursprung des Mönchtums* (TU 95; Berlin: Akademie-Verlag 1966) 26.

32 Fitzmyer, *Luke, X–XXIV*, 928–9

barren' in *Thomas* may be due simply to the parallelism between 79.1 and 79.3 ('Blessed . . . the womb'), which would make further elements disturbing. Luke's 'softening' word (μενοῦν) is to be ascribed to the evangelist's redaction,[33] and it may not have been preserved in or have been part of the tradition that *Thomas* used.

More importantly, we should note that the eschatological language of Luke 23.29 (ἰδοὺ ἔρχονται ἡμέραι) has not completely disappeared in the Thomasine saying, which similarly speaks of the 'coming days.'[34] Of course, an apocalyptic or historical context, such as in Luke 23.27–31, is not present. The 'timelessness' of the *Gospel of Thomas* does not give a clear indication of the historical situation of the speaker,[35] and it is therefore difficult to place the saying on any fixed time-axis. In any case, the reference to a future situation at least leaves a possibility that marriage and childbearing may be part of the present experience of *Thomas'* audience. Even if the saying predicts that there will be a time when the disciples understand the preciousness of ascetic life, it is not an explicit exhortation to abolish marriage.

6.2. Becoming one

An important group of sayings in *Thomas* focuses on the themes of 'becoming one and the same' (*Gos. Thom.* 4; 22; 23) or 'making the two one' (22; cf. also 11 and 106). These sayings have often called forth ascetic interpretations and have been understood to imply the ideal of sexual continence. The language of these sayings is, however, cryptic and open to more than one interpretation.

It is difficult to recognize what kind of mythology constitutes the symbolic world behind the sayings. It is often suggested that these sayings

---

[33] Cf. the Lukan redaction in Luke 8.19–21 (Mark 3.31–35), where Luke similarly makes it clear that Jesus' own family is not excluded from God's family. For an analysis, see Seim, *The Double Message*, 66–8.

[34] For a similar emphasis, see Buckley, 'Interpretation of Logion 114,' 261–2.

[35] It has sometimes been argued that the 'living Jesus' of *Gos. Thom.* 1 refers to 'the risen Jesus' and that *Thomas* presents a post-resurrection revelation (e.g. B. Gärtner, *Ett nytt evangelium? Thomasevangeliets hemliga Jesusord* [Stockholm: Diakonistyrelsens bokförlag, 1960] 86–8). *Thomas'* indifference to story-time has, however, rightly been emphasized by H. Koester, 'One Jesus and Four Primitive Gospels,' in J. M. Robinson and H. Koester, *Trajectories through Early Christianity* (Philadelphia: Fortress Press, 1971) 167–8; and J. M. Robinson, 'Jesus from Easter to Valentinus (or to the Apostles' Creed),' *JBL* 101 (1982) 23.

reflect the image of the asexual Primordial Man based on Hellenistic Jewish exegesis of Gen 1–2, which can be found in Philo and later rabbinic literature.[36] The passage most often referred to is *Op. Mund.* 134, where Philo draws a contrast between the man formed of clay (Gen 2.7) and 'the man who came into being after the image of God' (Gen 1.27) being 'neither male nor female, by nature incorruptible (οὔτ' ἄρρεν οὔτε θῆλυ, ἄφθαρτος φύσει).' Read against such a background, *Thomas* envisages the original, incorruptible realm of asexuality as the final goal of human life. This would also explain why the 'end' and the 'beginning' fall together in the gospel (*Gos. Thom.* 18; see also 19; 49; 77). Such language could motivate ascetic behavior,[37] but the practical consequences of the myth are not necessarily one-dimensional. It is well known that Philo himself, in spite his high esteem for certain ascetic groups such as the Therapeutae (*Cont.* 68), could also strongly support the Stoic view of marriage and procreation as the responsibility of every free man (see e.g. *Praem. poen.* 108; *Spec. leg.* 3.36).[38]

Moreover, the language of 'becoming one' is not one-dimensional itself. Such Valentinian texts as the *Gospel of Philip* or the *Excerpts from Theodotus* can use a similar idea with respect to the eschatological reunion of the elect or one's 'image' with the 'male' angelic counterpart (esp. *Exc. Theod.* 21–2). Neither of these texts represent an unambiguous encratite stance, however.[39] It is not, of course, a legitimate

---

[36] A. F. J. Klijn, 'The "Single One" in the Gospel of Thomas' *JBL* 81 (1962) 271–8; H. C. Kee, ' "Becoming a Child" in the Gospel of Thomas,' *JBL* 82 (1963) 307–14; W. A. Meeks, 'The Image of the Androgyne: Some Uses of the Symbol in Earliest Christianity,' *HR* 13 (1974) 165–208; D. R. MacDonald, *There is No Male and Female* (HDR 20; Philadelphia: Fortress Press, 1987). For Philo's exegesis of Adam's creation, see R. A. Baer, *Philo's Use of the Categories Male and Female* (ALGHJ 3, Leiden: E. J. Brill, 1970). Baer argues that although Philo can occasionally suggest the myth of the androgynous man (see *Op. Mund.* 151–2), the 'man after the image of God' is to be understood more in terms of asexuality than of bisexuality or androgyny.

[37] See e.g. G. S. Gasparro, 'Asceticism and Anthropology: Enkrateia and "Double Creation" in Early Christianity,' in V. L. Wimbush and R. Valantasis, eds., *Asceticism* (Oxford: Oxford University Press, 1995) 127–56.

[38] For the co-existence of 'Cynic' and 'Stoic' views of marriage in Philo as well in many other first- and second-century authors, see W. Deming, *Paul on Marriage and Celibacy: The Hellenistic Background of First Corinthians 7* (SNTSMS 83; Cambridge: Cambridge University Press) 50–107.

[39] The question of marriage vs. celibacy in the *Gospel of Philip* is debated. I follow here recent analyses which emphasize that the author of the document does not take a clear stance on this issue. See E. Pagels, 'The "Mystery of Marriage" in the *Gospel of Philip*

procedure to read the (probably more developed) Valentinian concept into the *Gospel of Thomas*. But it is not far-fetched to suggest a similar complexity of myth for the *Gospel of Thomas*, since the idea of one's heavenly counterpart may be reflected elsewhere in the gospel (cf. *Gos. Thom.* 84).[40]

The ideas of 'the two becoming one' and 'image' (ϨΙΚШΝ) appear in the same context in the much-discussed logion 22:

> When you make the two one, and when you make the inside like the outside and the outside like the inside, and the above like the below, [5]and when you make the male and the female one and the same (ΟΥΑ ΟΥШΤ), so that the male not be male nor the female female; [6]and you fashion eyes in the place of an eye, and a hand in place of a hand, and a foot in place of a foot, and an image (ΟΥϨΙΚШΝ) in place of an image; [7]then will you enter [the kingdom].[41]

It is well known that the saying has significant parallels in *2 Clement* and in the *Gospel of Egyptians* cited by Clement of Alexandria in his *Stromateis* (3.13.92).

> For the Lord himself, when asked by someone when his kingdom will come, said: 'When the two shall be one, and the outside as the inside, and the male

---

Revisited,' in B. A. Pearson, *The Future of Early Christianity: Essays in Honor of Helmut Koester* (Minneapolis: Fortress Press, 1991) 442–54; A. Marjanen, *The Woman Jesus Loved: Mary Magdalene in the Nag Hammadi Library and Related Documents* (NHMS 40; Leiden: E. J. Brill, 1996) 154–6. For the view that *Gos. Phil.* presupposes 'spiritual marriage,' that is, a marriage involving no sexual intercourse, see M. A. Williams, 'Uses of Gender Imagery in Ancient Gnostic Texts,' in C. W. Bynum, S. Harrell, and P. Richman, eds., *Gender and Religion: On the Complexity of Symbols* (Boston: Beacon, 1986) 196–227, esp. 205–11; *Rethinking 'Gnosticism': An Argument for Dismantling a Dubious Category* (Princeton: Princeton University Press, 1996) 148–50. For the *Excerpta ex Theodoto*, see R. P. Casey, 'Introduction,' in R. P. Casey, ed., *The Excerpta ex Theodoto of Clement of Alexandria* (SD 1; London: Christophers, 1934) 3–38. These fragments may even include an anti-ascetic interpretation of the 'Salome' passage of the *Gospel of Egyptians* (*Exc. Theod.* 67.2–3), unless it does not represent Clement's own theology (cf. *Strom.* 3.6.45).

[40] *Gos. Thom.* 84 has often been connected with the idea of man's heavenly counterpart, even though the term 'image' has clearly been understood in *Thomas* differently from in the Valentinian texts; see e.g. Quispel, *Makarius*, 49–50; J.-É. Ménard, *L'Évangile selon Thomas* (NHS 5; Leiden: E. J. Brill, 1975) 184–5; S. J. Patterson in J. S. Kloppenborg, M. W. Meyer, S. J. Patterson, and M. G. Steinhauser, *Q–Thomas Reader* (Sonoma: Polebridge Press, 1990) 97–8; De Conick, *Seek to See Him*, 148–50.

[41] Lambdin's translation modified by the present author.

with the female, neither male nor female.' . . . When you do these things, he said, 'the kingdom of my Father will come.' (*2 Clement* 12.2, 6)[42]

When Salome asked when she would know the answer to her questions, the Lord said: 'When you trample on the robe of shame, and when the two shall be one, and the male with the female, and there is neither male nor female.' (*Strom.* 3.13.92)[43]

According to Clement of Alexandria, the latter saying from the *Gospel of Egyptians* was used by Julius Cassianus, who came from the Valentinian school and taught docetism and extreme asceticism. Obviously, the Lord's words were used by Cassianus to support his encratite position, but in Clement's view he missed the real meaning of the saying. The saying should be understood, according to Clement, as referring to 'wrath (θυμός)' and 'desire (ἐπιθυμία),' which are male and female impulses in humans respectively. 'Therefore when someone gives in neither to wrath nor to desire – which indeed . . . overshadow and cover rationality – but takes off the mist of these things by repentance after having been made ashamed, he ought to unite spirit and soul by obedience to the Word.'[44]

The author of *2 Clement* also offers an interpretation of the Lord's words, in which he gives paraenetic meanings to every element of his version of the saying. 'Neither male nor female' is explained to refer to cessation of sexual attraction between man and woman so that 'a brother seeing a sister should not have any thought of her as of a female, and that a sister seeing a brother should not have any thought of him as of a male' (12.5). It seems clear that the author is thinking of the present situation of his Christian congregation (cf. 'when you *do* these things' in 12.6). He may have wanted to encourage his community to live as brothers and sisters in the family of God,[45] but it is difficult to conclude how ascetic or what kind of communal life the

---

[42] It is unclear which part of 12.6 should be taken as belonging to the saying quoted. The use of the word φησίν (cf. 7.6) and the peculiar expression 'the kingdom of my Father' indicate, however, that the author was drawing on a citation rather than using his own language; see T. Baarda '2 Clem 12 and the Sayings of Jesus,' in J. Delobel, ed., *Logia: Les paroles de Jésus – The Sayings of Jesus* (BETL 59; Leuven: Peeters/Leuven University Press, 1982) 547–9.

[43] Translation by Chadwick in Oulton & Chadwick, *Alexandrian Christianity*, 83.

[44] *Strom.* 3.13.93. Translation modified from MacDonald, *No Male and Female*, 38–9.

[45] T. Baarda, '2 Clem 12,' 536.

author had in mind.[46] The present and the future realization of the eschaton are however intertwined as the author presents proper Christian conduct and the suspension of sexual desire as conditions of 'the day of God's appearing' (12.1, 6).[47]

2 *Clement* and the *Stromateis* of Clement of Alexandria demonstrate the various ways in which Jesus' words on 'the two becoming one' could be interpreted in early Christianity.[48] These range from the strict encratite interpretation by Julius Cassianus implied by Clement of Alexandria to the non-encratite and allegorical reading of Clement himself. In terms of asceticism, the exposition by the author of *2 Clement* represents something like a middle position between these two. Are there any clues showing how the saying was understood by the author who composed the saying in *Gos. Thom.* 22?

There are two distinctly Thomasine elements in the saying. First, it is introduced by Jesus' teaching on infants entering the kingdom (22.1–2), and second, in addition to the dissolution of the opposites and 'the two becoming one' (22.4–5), *Thomas* has a number of anthropological pairs (eyes, hands, feet) and the unification of 'images' (22.6). All these elements result in the view that according to logion 22 entering the kingdom means (1) becoming child-like, (2) the dissolution of the opposites, including male and female sexes, and (3) putting on a new body or 'image.' The imagery is not unambiguous, but it shows obviously enough that the author is speaking of the new state of being in which old anthropological differences, such as the sexes or the body/soul (inside/outside) dichotomy, have disappeared, but which nevertheless still involves some kind of (pneumatic?) body. It is difficult to say how much of this new being could be seen as being realized in the present situation of the Thomasine Christian. One may illustrate this problem by referring to another saying on 'becoming one,' *Gos. Thom.* 4, which provides a good example of the futuristic perspective not completely lacking in the gospel:

---

[46] There are no strong ascetic tendencies in the homily; cf., however, *2 Clem.* 8.5–6, and Baarda, '2 Clement 12,' 543; H. Koester, *Synoptische Überlieferung bei den apostolischen Vätern* (Berlin: Akademie-Verlag, 1957) 104. K. P. Donfried (*The Setting of Second Clement in Early Christianity* [NovTSup 38; Leiden: E. J. Brill, 1973] 154) argues that the author speaks against 'indiscriminate sexual behavior' occurring in his church.

[47] See Donfried, ibid.

[48] Cf. also *Gos. Phil.* 67.31–5.

The man old in days will not hesitate to ask a small child of seven days old about the place of life, and he will live. For many who are first will become (ⲚⲀⲢ̄) last (Gr. adds: [. . . and] the last will be first), and they will become one and the same (Ⲛ̄ⲤⲈⲰⲰⲠⲈ ⲞⲨⲀ ⲞⲨⲰⲦ).

As in logion 22, the little child is the model for the Thomasine Christian but 'becoming one and the same' is something that will finally come true only in the future. The saying does not tell when this final goal is reached. The answer to this question is left open, perhaps on purpose. But it would be unwise to conclude that this 'openness' excludes all kinds of eschatological reservations from *Thomas'* theology.[49] The saying invites eschatological interpretations quite easily.

One may raise objections to this reading. Scholars have often connected *Gos. Thom.* 22.4–7 (and/or a primitive version of this saying) with Christian baptism.[50] One could therefore argue that the asexuality anticipated in the saying was seen as being realized in baptism, or even that virginity was a condition for baptism in the Thomasine community (cf. also *Gos. Thom.* 75; for this logion see below). Admittedly, there are elements which appear to support the baptismal context of logion 22. The language of 'no male and female' occurs already in the passage that is often regarded as a pre-Pauline baptismal formula (Gal 3.28).[51] The metaphors of 'stripping off' and 'being without shame,' although not found in logion 22 (cf. however the *Gospel of Egyptians*), do appear in *Gos. Thom* 21.4 ('stripping') and 37 ('stripping without shame'), and could be associated with the early Christian practice of baptismal nudity.[52] Moreover, the imagery of putting on a new 'body' could be seen as a Thomasine version of early Christian baptismal language, in which those baptized have

---

[49] Cf. e.g. Davies (*Gospel of Thomas*, 135), who categorically states that 'Thomas, of course, does not apply an eschatological reservation.' Similarly De Conick and Fossum, 'Stripped Before God,' 134; Patterson, *Gospel of Thomas*, 170.

[50] Meeks, 'Image of the Androgyne,' 193–4; Davies, *Gospel of Thomas*, 131–2; K. L King, 'Kingdom in the Gospel of Thomas,' *Forum* 3.1 (1987) 68; MacDonald, *No Male and Female*.

[51] For Gal 3.28 as a Pre-Pauline baptismal formula, see MacDonald, *No Male and Female*, 1–16, and further literature cited there. This common exegesis has been challenged by G. Dautzenberg, ' "Da ist nicht männlich und weiblich," ' *Kairos* 24 (1982) 181–206.

[52] See especially J. Z. Smith, 'Garments of Shame,' *HR* 5 (1966) 217–38.

'put on Christ' (Gal 3.28) or 'the new self' (Col 3.10; cf. also 1 Cor 12.13).[53]

Nonetheless, some caution is warranted. The water symbolism is lacking in the relevant sayings (contrast e.g. the openly sacramental language in the *Gospel of Philip*). The imagery of 'stripping off' in *Gos. Thom.* 21.4 and 37 does not necessarily refer to the baptismal ritual but is open to other interpretations as well (e.g. the 'garment' can easily be understood merely as a metaphor for the physical body without baptismal connotations[54]). The language of the baptismal formulas could also be applied in non-sacramental contexts. But even if the saying in *Gos. Thom.* 22.4–7 preserves a baptismal reunification formula, as is often suggested, it is still unclear whether one should suggest strictly encratite requirements for baptism, such as was the case in the teaching of Marcion (see e.g. Tertullian, *Adv. Marc.* 1.29), or whether the ethical consequences of the rite were understood more loosely as an encouragement to diminish the power of sexual desire (cf. *2 Clement*).

One may of course argue that the 'eschatological reservation' is annulled by Jesus in logion 51, which states that the 'repose of the dead' and the 'new world' have already come. It is clear that *Thomas*, at least in its present form,[55] does not assume the apocalyptic doctrine of the general resurrection[56] and ridicules those who teach that the kingdom will be some concrete reality within the visible world (*Gos. Thom.* 3). But on the other hand there are surprisingly many future expressions with respect to the final 'salvation' in *Thomas*,[57] and these may not all be explained as purely rhetorical language or 'logical'

---

[53] See Davies, *Gospel of Thomas*, 117–37.

[54] For such an argument, see De Conick and Fossum, 'Stripped Before God,' 123–50. They are probably right in questioning the baptismal setting of such passages as *Gos. Phil.* 66.16–20; *Odes of Solomon* 11.10–12; 21.3–4; 25.8–9, but are overly convinced that the passages represent 'the kind of encratite soteriology which was espoused by the group behind the *Gospel of Thomas*' (ibid., 128).

[55] The Greek version of saying 5 (*P. Oxy.* 654.31) may, however, indicate the resurrection of the dead: '[For there is nothing] hidden which [will] not [become] manifest, nor buried (θεθαμμένον) that [will not be raised].' See H. W. Attridge, 'The Greek Fragments' [of the *Gospel According to Thomas*] in B. Layton, ed., *Nag Hammadi Codex II, 2–7 together with XIII,2*, Brit. Lib. Or.4926(1), and P.Oxy. 1, 654, 655*, vol. 1 (NHS 20; Leiden: E. J. Brill, 1989) 115, 126.

[56] For the resurrection and *Thomas*, see G. J. Riley, *Resurrection Reconsidered: Thomas and John in Controversy* (Minneapolis: Fortress Press, 1995).

[57] See e.g. *Gos. Thom.* 4; 11; 18; 23; 27; 44; 49; 57; 60; 70; 75; 79; 106; 111.

futures.[58] This demonstrates that the tension between present and future is not completely eliminated.[59] Rather, the eschatological language of the gospel has an ambiguity which can be compared to that in many other early Christian writings. *Thomas'* peculiarity is that 'salvation' is understood as a *process* of 'seeking and finding,' a pattern that has its roots in wisdom literature.[60] The emphasis is individualistic and certainly non-apocalyptic. But the present situation of *Thomas'* audience can be characterized as a state of being 'in-between' rather than one of final consummation.

6.3. Standing solitary

A group of three sayings speaks of the disciples as 'solitary' (*monachos*). These sayings have played an important role in the argument that the *Gospel of Thomas* derives from strictly encratite Christianity.

> Men think, perhaps, that it is peace which I have come to cast upon the world. They do not know that it is dissension which I have come to cast upon the earth: fire, sword, and war. For there will be five in a house: three will be against two and two against three, the father against the son, and the son against the father. And they will stand solitary (ⲁⲩⲱ ⲥⲉⲛⲁⲱ̄ⲅⲉ ⲉⲣⲁⲧⲟⲩ ⲉⲩⲟ ⲙ̄ⲙⲟⲛⲁⲭⲟⲥ). (*Gos. Thom.* 16)

> Blessed are the solitary (ⲛⲙⲟⲛⲁⲭⲟⲥ) and elect, for you will find the kingdom. For you are from it and to it you will return. (*Gos. Thom.* 49)

> Many are standing at the door, but it is the solitary (ⲙ̄ⲙⲟⲛⲁⲭⲟⲥ) who will enter the bridal chamber. (*Gos. Thom.* 75)

The meaning of the term *monachos* has been discussed in numerous studies and a full treatment of the philological problems is not possible

---

[58] B. Lincoln has interpreted the tension between the present and future expressions of salvation as referring to different levels of initiation into *Thomas'* community, which are equivalent to the different levels of seeking presented in *Gos. Thom.* 2. At the top of the community stood the Perfects ('those who marvel and reign over the all'), who had attained the androgynous state; see 'Thomas-Gospel and Thomas-Community: A New Approach to a Familiar Text,' *NovT* 19 (1977) 65–76. It is however less than certain whether one can establish such a clear hierarchy behind *Thomas'* veiled language.

[59] *Pace* Koester, 'One Jesus,' 173.

[60] J. S. Kloppenborg calls this 'a process of "sapiential research"' (*The Formation of Q: Trajectories in Ancient Wisdom Collections* [Studies in Antiquity and Christianity; Philadelphia: Fortress Press, 1987] 305).

here.[61] The word was not used as a noun by Classical Greek writers, and it does not appear in Philo or in the Septuagint (note, however, the appearance of the word in the Greek translations of the Old Testament by Aquila, Symmachus and Theodotion).[62] Later it came to mean 'monk' in the monastic terminology of Pachomius and Athanasius. The earliest known text in which *monachos* clearly appears as a name of a recognized social type is found in a papyrus containing a petition of Aurelius Isidorus of Karanis, dated to June 324 CE (P.Coll. Youtie 77).[63]

In view of what we know about the history of ascetic and monastic movements, it is not reasonable to suggest that the original Greek version of the *Gospel of Thomas* assumed the existence of monastic or hermit 'monks' in the later senses of the word. *Monachos*, although a Greek loan-word, has not been preserved in the Greek fragments of the gospel, and it has sometimes been suggested that it derives from a fourth-century Coptic editor and not from (the) earlier Greek author(s).[64] The most common interpretation, however, is that the term should be understood in light of the Syriac word *iḥidaya*, which

---

[61] For the discussion, see A. Adam, 'Grundbegriffe des Mönchtums in sprachlicher Sicht,' *ZKG* 65 (1953–54) 209–39; M. Harl, 'A propos des logia de Jésus: Le sens du mot MONAXOΣ,' *Revue des Études Grecques* 73 (1960) 464–74; F.-E. Morard, 'Monachos, Moine: Histoire du terme grec jusqu'au 4e siècle,' *Freiburger Zeitschrift für Philosophie und Theologie* 20 (1973) 332–411; 'Monachos: une importation sémitique en Egypte?' in E. A. Livingstone, ed., *Papers Presented to the Sixth International Conference on Patristic Studies Held in Oxford 1971* (TU 115 [= *StPatr* 12], Berlin: Akademie-Verlag, 1975) 242–6; 'Encore quelques réflexions sur monachos,' *VC* 34 (1980) 395–401.

[62] For the use of the word by later Greek Bible translators, see the helpful table in Morard, 'Monachos, Moine,' 348. The most discussed passages are Gen 2.18, in which Aquila and Symmachus use the word *monachos* for Hebrew לבד, and Ps 68.7, in which Symmachus and Thedotion use the same Greek word as an equivalent of יחיד. The latter ('solitary') was understood by the rabbis to refer to bachelors, and the verse in Ps 68.7 was interpreted (under the influence of Aquila's translation) to refer to consecrated celibates by Church Fathers (see Morard, ibid., 352–3). Since Symmachus and Theodotion are said to have been Ebionites, Quispel argues that יחיד 'was used to indicate the bachelor in Jewish Christian circles' (*'Gospel of Thomas* Revisited,' 238). However, the Jewish-Christian background of Symmachus is uncertain, and Theodotion's origins are even more obscure.

[63] E. A. Judge, 'The Earliest Use of Monachos for "Monk" (P.Coll. Youtie 77) and the Origins of Monasticism,' *JAC* 20 (1977) 72–89.

[64] Cf. Judge, 'The Earliest use of Monachos' 87: 'we must recognize the possibility that the Greek loan-word was adapted by the Coptic author (whether from a prior work, or from current usage in the first two cases above) because at the time he was writing he knew that *monachos* was the name of a recognized social type in Egypt.' Note also Williams, *Rethinking 'Gnosticism,'* 146.

was used by fourth-century Syrian writers to denote consecrated celibates, both male and female, living in Christian communities (in addition, it was also a Christological title; cf. 'the *only* Son' in John 1.14, 18; 3.16, 18).[65] This kind of exegesis would make the Thomasine sayings on 'solitary' sound like strictly encratite statements: only virgins can remain faithful (16) or will find the kingdom (49). *Gos. Thom.* 75, in particular, is often referred to when *Thomas'* encratite nature has been stressed: only a person who is unattached or single can enter the bridal chamber!

One can hardly deny that sayings like *Gos. Thom.* 75 were favored by later Syrian ascetics. On the other hand, it does not seem methodologically sound to read all of the later technical meanings of *iḥidaya* into the *monachos* of the *Gospel of Thomas*, which by any dating is much earlier than the Syriac texts which use this word. It is therefore unlikely that the 'solitary' in *Thomas* formed a clearly-defined celibate group among the larger group of Christians.[66] Moreover, the meaning of the 'bridal chamber' in the saying is elusive. There is no indication of a specific sacramental interpretation of the symbol in *Thomas* (in contrast to the use of the symbol in the *Gospel of Philip*).[67] This renders uncertain the suggestion that we are dealing with an initiation rite

---

[65] For *iḥidaya* in Syrian Christianity, see E. Beck, 'Ein Beitrag zur Terminologie des ältesten syrischen Mönchtums,' *Studia Anselmina* 38 (1956) 254–67; A. Vööbus, *History of Asceticism in the Syrian Orient*, vol. 1: *The Origin of Asceticism, Early Monasticism in Persia* (Corpus Scriptorum Christianorum Orientalium 184, Louvain: Van den Bempt, 1958) 106–8; R. Murray, 'The Exhortation to Candidates for Ascetical Vows at Baptism in the Ancient Syriac Church,' *NTS* (1974–75) 59–80; idem, *Symbols of Church and Kingdom: A Study in Early Syriac Tradition* (Cambridge: Cambridge University Press, 1975) 16–17; S. H. Griffith, 'Asceticism in the Church of Syria: The Hermeneutics of Early Monasticism' in V. L. Wimbush and R. Valantasis, eds., *Asceticism* (Oxford: Oxford University Press, 1995) 220–45. The meaning of *monachos* in the *Gospel of Thomas* is often associated with that of the Syriac term; see e.g. Quispel, *Makarius*, 108; Murray, 'Exhortation to Candidates,' 70–2; Morard, 'Monachos, Moine,' 377; Griffith, 'Asceticism,' 229; De Conick, *Seek to See Him*, 4–5.

[66] Scholars usually suggest that the *iḥidaye* (or the *bnay/bnat qyama* often associated with the 'singles' by Syrian Fathers) formed an inner circle of elite Christians in Syriac-speaking churches. See e.g. Griffith, 'Asceticism,' 223, 230.

[67] For the ritual aspects of 'bridal chamber' in the *Gospel of Philip*, see e.g. E. Segelberg, 'The Coptic-Gnostic Gospel according to Philip and its Sacramental System,' *Numen* 7 (1960) 189–200; H.-G. Gaffron, 'Studien zum koptischen Philippusevangelium unter besonderer Berücksichtigung der Sakramente' (Th.D. diss., Rheinishe Friedrich-Wilhelms-Universität, Bonn, 1969) 212–19; W. W. Isenberg, 'Introduction' [to the *Gospel According to Philip*] in B. Layton, ed., *Nag Hammadi Codex II,2–7 together with XIII,2*, Brit. Lib. Or.4926(1), and P.Oxy. 1, 654, 655*, vol. 1 (NHS 20; Leiden: E. J. Brill, 1989) 136–7.

through which celibate persons only could enter the community. Perhaps one should understand the 'bridal chamber' in *Thomas* simply as a metaphor for the kingdom based on Jesus' parable on the Ten Virgins (Matt 25.1–13).[68] If so, logion 75 is just another way of expressing the thought that the elect and solitary will find the kingdom (49).

The saying in *Gos. Thom.* 16 (cf. Q 12.51–53) gives the most detailed context for the use of *monachos* in the gospel. In this saying 'solitary' refers to those who have been involved in conflicts within their households. As we have seen, this theme is related to the question of the disciples' true identity as the 'children of the light' (*Gos. Thom.* 50). One can therefore imagine several ways of understanding the word *monachos* as referring to those who have been compelled to break away from family to become followers of Jesus in *Thomas'* community. In a social context where such conflicts were frequent, 'solitary' could become, by way of generalization, an honorary title for those who regarded themselves as the 'elect of the living father' and who did not consider themselves as belonging to this world (cf. 'poor' in *Gos. Thom.* 54). In this sense, *monachos* has indisputable anti-familial overtones, but a clear-cut encratite interpretation does not do justice to the multi-dimensional imagery of the gospel. The term probably also carries at least partly different connotations than 'one' or 'single one,' which refer to the ideas of unification rather than to those of separation.[69]

One may finally take note of the *Dialogue of the Savior*, where the word *monachos* appears twice together with 'elect' (120.26; 121.18–20) in striking parallel to *Gos. Thom.* 49.[70] The dialogue presents a treatise on eschatology and the dissolution of bodily existence, creating a tension between present and future[71] not unlike what we have found in the *Gospel of Thomas*. The writing does not have an overall encratite

---

[68] Similarly Quispel, *Makarius*, 26.

[69] Cf. however *Gos. Thom.* 23, in which 'standing as a single one' is closely parallel with the expression 'standing solitary' in logion 16; for the question, see Morard, 'Monachos, Moine,' 366–72; 'Monachos,' 242–6.

[70] See Morard, 'Quelques réflexions,' 395–401. There are also other interesting parallels between the *Gospel of Thomas* and the *Dialogue of the Savior;* cf. for example the 'place of life (ⲠⲘⲀ Ⲙ̄ⲠⲰⲚⲈ̣)' in *Dial. Sav.* 132.7 (cf. *Gos. Thom.* 4: ⲠⲦⲟⲠⲟⲥ Ⲙ̄ⲠⲰⲚⲈ̣) and the idea of 'entering the bridal chamber' in 138.19 (cf. *Gos. Thom.* 75).

[71] This tension has been pointed out in H. Koester and E. Pagels, 'Introduction' [to the *Dialogue of the Savior*] in S. Emmel, ed., *Nag Hammadi Codex III,5: The Dialogue of the Savior* (NHS 26; Leiden: E. J. Brill, 1984) 11–15.

character, even though it discusses the Lord's words on 'praying in the place where there is no woman' (144.15–21; cf. also *Gos. Thom.* 114). The 'dissolution of the works of womanhood' is explained to mean that women 'will cease [giving birth].'[72] This may, of course, indicate sexual asceticism, as was the case among the opponents of Clement of Alexandria, who appealed to a similar slogan (see *Strom.* 3.63.1–2).[73] But given the tension between present and future eschatology in the *Dialogue of the Savior*, it is not clear whether the author intends the cessation of childbearing to be part of the final 'dissolution' or whether it is meant to be an exhortation to the author's contemporary audience.[74] In other words, one may surmise that the use of the term in this document involves an openness similar to that which we have seen in the *Gospel of Thomas*.

6.4. Conclusions

The three themes discussed above do not of course cover all the sayings or motifs that are relevant to the question of sexual asceticism in the *Gospel of Thomas*. It has, for example, been argued that in *Gos. Thom.* 7 the 'lion' appears as a metaphor for passion and sexual desire, and that it is blessed as an element in man which may 'be redeemed by being obedient to – "devoured" by – his more spiritual master.'[75] Scholars

---

[72] The whole passage runs as follows: The Lord said, 'Pray in the place where there is no woman.' Matthew said: ' "Pray in the place where there is [no woman]," he tells us, meaning, "Destroy the works of womanhood," not because there is any other [manner of birth], but because they will cease [giving birth].' Mary said, 'They will never be obliterated.' The Lord said, '[Who] knows that they will [not] dissolve and . . .? (Trans. by Emmel in S. Emmel, ed. *Nag Hammadi Codex III,5: The Dialogue of the Savior* [NHS 26; Leiden: E. J. Brill, 1984] 89–91). Unfortunately the Lord's response to Mary's comment (or question) is badly damaged, which leaves the final interpretation of the saying open.

[73] Marjanen, *Woman Jesus Loved*, 89–90.

[74] Similarly Koester and Pagels ('Introduction,' 15) who argue, although on somewhat different grounds, that 'the author's interpretation of the "dissolution of the works of womanhood" does not suggest a metaphysically motivated sexual asceticism.' F. Wisse, referring to the *Testimony of Truth* (30.18 – 31.5), supports a strongly encratite reading of the passage, but it would be more reasonable to interpret the saying in the context of the *Dialogue of the Savior*; see his 'Flee Feminity: Antifeminity in Gnostic texts and the Question of Social Milieu,' in K. L. King, ed., *Images of the Feminine in Gnosticism* (Studies in Antiquity and Christianity; Philadelphia: Fortress Press, 1988) 297–307. For an ascetic reading of the dialogue, see also Perkins, *Gnostic Dialogue*, 107–12.

[75] H. M. Jackson, *The Lion Becomes Man: The Gnostic Leontomorphic Creator and the Platonic Tradition* (SBLDS 81; Atlanta: Scholars Press, 1985) 212.

have also often regarded 'fasting as regards the world' in logion 27 as involving sexual abstinence (cf. also *Strom.* 3.15.99).[76]

Yet such individual sayings do not change the overall picture presented in this essay. In spite of the clear ascetic inclination, one can recognize a certain ambiguity in *Thomas'* relation to the issue of marriage versus celibacy. *Thomas* praises those who have broken with their families and have become 'solitary,' but never directly rejects marriage and sexual intercourse. In many sayings, we cannot be sure whether the state of asexuality presupposed by *Thomas* is a matter of the final destination or whether it is anticipated by means of an unconditional demand for sexual abstinence and rejection of marriage. In my judgment, the ambiguity is best explained by the suggestion that *Thomas* does not derive from a strictly encratite sect in which celibacy was the condition of entrance to the community, even though encratite tendencies must have occurred in *Thomas'* environment. Such tendencies should not be regarded as unusual, however. Ascetic proclivities of various degrees were popular among many Christian groups since the time of the apostle Paul. Sexual abstinence was widely admired in the late Hellenistic world, and a negative attitude toward sexual desire and the human body was a commonplace at least in many educated circles.[77] For many Christians from the late first century onwards, the crucial question was not so much whether sexual abstinence was good or bad but rather how much abstinence was *enough* for proper Christian conduct.[78] Perhaps the ambivalence of the gospel reflects an ongoing discussion on the matter in *Thomas'* community.[79]

The ambiguity with respect to sexual asceticism I have described is in

---

[76] For analyses of the saying, see Marjanen, 'Is *Thomas* a Gnostic Gospel?' and idem, '*Thomas* and Jewish Religious Practices' in this volume.

[77] This is aptly demonstrated by D. B. Martin, *The Corinthian Body* (New Haven: Yale University Press, 1995).

[78] To pick one example, cf. P. Brown's comment on Tertullian: 'for a rigorist such as Tertullian, marriage itself was no more than a school of continence. When Tertullian spoke of *castitas* he did not mean virginity; he meant sexual activity whittled away to minimum in marriage and abandoned totally after marriage.' (Brown refers to Tertullian's *De monogamia* 3.1 and 17.5.) P. Brown, *The Body and Society: Men, Women, and Sexual Renunciation in Early Christianity* (New York: Columbia University Press, 1988) 149.

[79] Cf. Pagels' interpretation of the *Gospel of Philip*: 'The author ... was well aware of the controversies raging between various teachers and groups on matters of marriage versus celibacy. ... Yet the author of *Gos. Phil.* expresses, precisely through his ambiguity on this topic, a deliberate refusal to take sides on this issue' (' "Mystery of Marriage," ' 446). The *Gospel of Thomas*, however, is classified by Pagels as belonging among those writings which express an unambiguous attitude toward the matter (ibid., 447).

accord with many other traits of the gospel. In *Thomas*, the cosmos appears as a worthless but also threatening reality (e.g. 21; 27; 56; 80; 111). On the other hand, the world is considered as created by God (cf. 12; 89).[80] The 'body' may also be disparaged as 'poverty' (cf. 29) and said to be 'wretched,' if dependent upon a 'body' (cf. 87). However, 'flesh' can serve as the place of Jesus' appearance (28). 'Drunkenness' can be used both as a positive and as a negative metaphor (cf. 28 and 13).[81] One could go on with this list.

The different emphases or inconsistencies may, of course, be considered in terms of separate layers in the gospel.[82] One cannot exclude the possibility that some sayings or elements in *Thomas* reflect a development toward a more encratite communal situation. Such an argument has indeed been made by Antti Marjanen in this volume with respect to the much-debated logion 114. On the other hand, there are good reasons to think that the composer of the main bulk of the Thomasine sayings represented a much more ambiguous and less encratite attitude than is usually considered. This 'Thomas' would hardly have approved the later, radically encratite writings written in his name.[83]

---

[80] For a full discussion of the issue, see Marjanen, 'Is *Thomas* a Gnostic Gospel?' in this volume.

[81] See above, note 16.

[82] These observations should not, however, lead to a completely 'atomistic' reading of the gospel; pace Wisse, ' "Flee feminity",' 303–5. and S. L. Davies, 'The Oracles of the *Gospel of Thomas*,' (Paper Presented at the Annual Meeting of the Society of Biblical Literature, Chicago, November, 1994), which signifies a drastic change of opinion as compared to Davies' earlier studies on *Thomas*.

[83] For a comparison between the *Gospel* and the *Book of Thomas*, see R. Uro, 'The Secret Words to Judas Thomas: The *Gospel* and the *Book of Thomas*' (Paper Presented at the Annual Meeting of the Society of Biblical Literature, New Orleans, November, 1996).

7

Thomas and Jewish religious practices

Antti Marjanen

7.1. Early Christianity and Jewish religious practices

First- and second-century Christianity reacted in various ways to the central religious practices of the Jewish faith as it gradually separated from its mother religion and sought to find its own identity.[1] Prayer was quite commonly accepted, although in some Christian groups there were critical opinions even about that.[2] Circumcision was altogether rejected or at least spiritualized except in the most extreme Jewish-Christian groups. After the destruction of the temple in Jerusalem, offering sacrifices could not have a concrete meaning to anybody, not even to the Jews themselves. Nevertheless, the author of the Letter to the Hebrews still refers to the sacrifices of the Old Testament and sees them as a provisional means of atonement which was replaced by the permanent arrangement occasioned by the sacrificial death of Jesus (9.10).

---

[1] In this article a religious practice refers to religious rituals and obligations which were obeyed by Jews according to the regulations found in the Old Testament or in later Jewish traditions. In this introductory chapter mainly those practices are dealt with which appear in the *Gospel of Thomas*.

[2] Clement of Alexandria (*Strom.* 7.7.41) refers to the followers of Prodicus, who denied the usefulness of prayer; see E. Segelberg, 'Prayer Among the Gnostics? The Evidence of Some Nag Hammadi Documents,' in M. Krause, ed., *Gnosis and Gnosticism: Papers Read at the Seventh International Conference on Patristic Studies* (NHS 7; Leiden: E. J. Brill, 1977) 65–79, esp. 65. Segelberg finds a critical attitude to prayer also in the *Gospel of Philip*. It is especially prayer of petition, which seeks to receive worldly blessings, that is condemned by the author (ibid., 57). Cf. also the negative view of prayer in the *Gospel of Thomas* (see below).

Views on fasting and almsgiving also varied greatly among early Christians. For example, in the Matthean community they were an essential part of Christian life (Matt 6.1–4, 16–18; see also *2 Clem.* 16.4), even though the evangelist passes strictures on their false practice. The situation is very similar in the *Didache* (8.1; 15.4). The readers are encouraged to fast and to give alms regularly. It is only the choice of the fast days which differs from the Jewish custom. While Jewish 'hypocrites' fast on Mondays and Thursdays, Christians are told to abstain from food on Tuesdays and Fridays (8.1). Paul speaks only twice about fasting (2 Cor 6.5; 11.27). In both cases it seems to be an inevitable part of the role of an apostle, but not necessarily a general religious obligation required of every Christian. Almsgiving is not mentioned at all by Paul. Admittedly, he refers to performing acts of mercy and to supporting the poor. Nevertheless, he does not regard them as a regular Christian duty but as a special charism (Rom 12.8) or as an exceptional expression of solidarity shown to one's Christian brothers and sisters in cases of emergency (Rom 15.26–27; 2 Cor 8.13–14).

Early Christians adopted divergent attitudes to sabbath observance as well. In the Epistle to the Colossians it is asserted that sabbath regulations belonged to the time prior to Christ (2.16–17; cf. also Ignatius, *Magn.* 9.1). The *Epistle of Barnabas* suggests that the Old Testament sabbath commandments did not actually mean the regular weekly observance of the sabbath but anticipated the eschatological rest which God himself will prepare after the last judgment (15.1–9). According to Justin Martyr, the new law demands that one perpetually keep the sabbath. The purpose of the sabbath observance is nevertheless completely reinterpreted: it means to repent and to avoid sin (*Dial.* 12.3, cf. also *Ptolemy's Letter to Flora* [Epiphanius, *Panarion* 33.5.12]). In the Matthean community Jewish sabbath regulations do not seem to have been repudiated or reinterpreted altogether. The way the sabbath controversies are described by Matthew at the beginning of chapter 12 suggests that the observance of the sabbath still has some value to him or at least to some of his readers even though, according to Matthew, it does not restrain anybody from showing mercy and doing good (Matt 12.5–8,12). It is also possible that in his eschatological discourse, in which the evangelist shows Jesus urging his disciples to pray that their flight 'may not be in winter or *on the sabbath*' (24.20), he sympathizes with those Christians who have to compromise with their religious convictions if fleeing on a sabbath.[3] Even in the second century there were Jewish Christians who still kept the sabbath (Eusebius, *Hist. eccl.* 3.27.5).

Jewish dietary regulations were also variously received by early Christians. Among some, they seemed to have no significance whatsoever (Mark 7.19; Col 2.16; Hebr 9.10). In other Christian circles discussion about dietary rules centered on the question of whether or not it was permitted to eat blood and meat sacrificed to idols (Acts 15.29; cf. also 1 Cor 8; Rev 2.14, 20). Traditional Jewish dietary and purity regulations were strictly kept only in the most extreme Jewish-Christian groups (*Ps.-Clem. Hom.* 13.4).

To summarize, early Christian writings display five different models of reaction to traditional Jewish religious practices. First, a religious obligation is adopted and observed as such (e.g. prayer in most of the writings). Second, a religious practice is accepted in principle but its concrete observance is modified (e.g. fasting in *Didache* or in Paul). Third, the traditional name of a religious practice is preserved but it is deprived of its initial contents and given a metaphorical meaning which has nothing to do with the original concrete practice (e.g. sabbath observance in Justin's writings). Fourth, Jewish religious obligations are explicitly and polemically rejected; polemics may show, however, that among the readers of the writings the attitude to practices is still ambivalent or wrong from the perspective of the author. Fifth, in certain writings Jewish religious practices are not mentioned at all; this probably indicates indifference towards them.

The *Gospel of Thomas* belongs to those early Christian writings in which Jewish religious practices receive a lot of attention. With the exception of temple offerings, all the previously-mentioned obligations appear in *Thomas*. The writing refers to fasting, prayer, and almsgiving in logia 6, 14, 104, and 27. It speaks about dietary and purity regulations in logia 14 and 89, and the question of sabbath observance comes up in logion 27 and circumcision in logion 53. The purpose of

---

[3] Another, less likely interpretation of this verse is that it expresses the wish not to have to flee on the sabbath and thus to become more easily recognizable as Christians, since the Jews would in any case stay at home; see e.g. W. Grundmann, *Das Evangelium nach Matthäus* (ThHKNT; 4th ed.; Berlin: Evangelische Verlagsanstalt, 1975) 506. This interpretation does not take into consideration the all-embracing character of the tribulation Matthew is portraying. It is not only Christians who are threatened, but all people (Matt 24.16, 22).

this article is to examine which of the previously-delineated attitudes towards Jewish religious practices are displayed in these logia. Furthermore, it will be asked why so much attention is paid to these obligations in the *Gospel of Thomas*, and what this fact may reveal about the sociohistorical circumstances of the Christians who used and preserved these sayings.

7.2. Fasting, prayer, and almsgiving

The four logia of the *Gospel of Thomas* where fasting, prayer, and almsgiving are mentioned, read as follows:[4]

His disciples questioned him and said to him, 'Do you want us to fast? How shall we pray? Shall we give alms? What diet shall we observe?' [2]Jesus said, 'Do not tell lies, [3]and do not do what you hate, [4]for all things are plain in the sight of heaven. [5]For nothing hidden will not become manifest, [6]and nothing covered will remain without being uncovered.' (*Gos. Thom.* 6)

Jesus said to them, 'If you fast, you will give rise to sin for yourselves; [2]and if you pray, you will be condemned; [3]and if you give alms, you will do harm to your spirits. [4]When you go into any land and walk about in the districts, if they receive you, eat what they will set before you, and heal the sick among them. [5]For what goes into your mouth will not defile you, but that which issues from your mouth – it is that which will defile you.' (*Gos. Thom.* 14)

They said to Jesus, 'Come, let us pray today and let us fast.' [2]Jesus said, 'What is the sin that I have committed, or wherein have I been defeated? [3]But when the bridegroom leaves the bridal chamber, then let them fast and pray.' (*Gos. Thom.* 104)

<Jesus said,> 'If you do not fast as regards the world, you will not find the kingdom. [2]If you do not rest (sabbatize) as regards the sabbath, you will not see the Father.'[5] (*Gos. Thom.* 27)

Just as in *Gos. Thom.* 6.1 and 14.1–3, fasting, prayer, and almsgiving appear together in Matt 6.2–18 and *2 Clem* 16.4. Yet no literary connection between the three writings need be assumed. The three

---

4   Unless otherwise advised, all translations of the *Gospel of Thomas* are taken from T. O. Lambdin, 'The Gospel According to Thomas' [English translation] in B. Layton, ed., *Nag Hammadi Codex II,2–7 together with XIII,2*, Brit. Lib. Or.4926(1), and P.Oxy. 1,654,655*, vol. 1 (NHS 20; Leiden: E. J. Brill, 1989) 52–93.
5   For the translation of logion 27, see the discussion below, pp. 175–8.

practices are in a different order in each passage. The fact that fasting, prayer, and almsgiving are joined together in the Book of Tobit (12.8) shows that the combination has its origin already in Jewish ethical tradition.[6]

The answer Jesus gives to the questions of the disciples in *Gos. Thom.* 6.1 is astonishing. *Gos. Thom.* 6.2–6 does not say anything direct about fasting, prayer, almsgiving, and dietary regulations, i.e. about those things which the disciples are concerned with, whereas 14.1–3 addresses itself to these topics and gives the impression of being fairly well-suited to be an answer to the questions presented in 6.1. Therefore it has been suggested that Jesus' original response to the inquiry of the disciples is now found in *Gos. Thom.* 14.1–3, and that the present answer has been copied from or at least shaped according to logion 5.[7]

Among the first to advance this kind of solution was Gilles Quispel.[8] He assumed that the final redactor separated logia 6 and 14 and formed a new answer to the questions of the disciples based on the latter part of logion 5. But what would motivate the redactor to replace the original answer with a new, more ambiguous one? This would be especially unusual in that the old answer is also preserved, even if it is moved to a new context. Quispel does not give any satisfactory explanation, and therefore his theory of intentional redaction as a solution to the problem of logia 6 and 14 does not appear plausible.

Other scholars attempting to solve the difficulty involving logia 6 and 14 do not assume a deliberate editorial reworking of source material. Rather, they surmise that the separation of logia 6 and 14 is the result of a mechanical process. According to Stevan Davies, the rearrangement of the material is due to a tired scribe who inadvertently left out the right answer (14.1–3) and instead copied another one taken from logion 5. When he later realized his oversight he added Jesus' original response before logion 15.[9] Davies' suggestion is not very

---

[6]   So also J. Schröter, 'Thomas and Judaism' (Paper Presented at the Annual Meeting of the Society of Biblical Literature, New Orleans, November, 1996).

[7]   Since the Greek manuscript of the *Gospel of Thomas* (P.Oxy. 654) contains logion 6 in the same form as the Nag Hammadi manuscript, this theory has to presuppose that the separation of the question in logion 6 from the answer in logion 14 took place before the text was translated into Coptic.

[8]   *Makarius, das Thomasevangelium und das Lied von der Perle* (NovTSup 15; Leiden: E. J. Brill, 1966) 35–6.

[9]   S. L. Davies, *The Gospel of Thomas and Christian Wisdom* (New York: The Seabury Press, 1983) 153.

convincing. It presupposes a copyist who handles the material far too carelessly and whose attempt to correct the mistake does not help at all but simply adds to the confusion. It is difficult to imagine a scribe who could work in such a reckless manner.

Another solution involving an involuntary accident has been proposed by Birger Pearson.[10] He assumes that the separation of logia 6 and 14 was caused by an accident through which the pages of the Greek manuscript of *Thomas* at some point of its transmission became disordered. In other words, the question of logion 6 which was at the end of a page and the answer of logion 14 which began the next page no longer followed each other, but the material presently found between *Gos. Thom.* 6.1 and *Gos. Thom.* 14 was incorporated between them. This postulate is supported by the fact that there indeed were some books and manuscripts in antiquity which became disarranged.[11] Pearson's theory is thus possible but will remain merely a conjecture unless we discover a Greek manuscript of the *Gospel of Thomas* which is unaffected by the hypothetical transposition of the pages. Besides, the question of the disciples (6.1) is perhaps not as incompatible with the answer of Jesus (6.2–6) as Quispel, Davies, and Pearson give us to understand. As we shall see, the discussion about fasting, prayer, and almsgiving in Jewish wisdom tradition is also connected with the exhortation not to lie or to do what one hates. Therefore I shall try to interpret logion 6 in its present form and see how it was perceived by those readers for whom Jesus' words in 6.2–6 were a response to the questions of the disciples in 6.1.

If the question in *Gos. Thom.* 6.1 is understood in such a way that it speaks about the right manner of fasting, prayer, and almsgiving, as the Greek version of the logion suggests,[12] then these religious practices are not rejected *per se*. It is only important that while observing them the

---

[10] Pearson presented his view in a private discussion at the 1995 Annual Meeting of the Society of Biblical Literature in Philadelphia.

[11] Several scholars have explored this phenomenon in connection with the discussion about the possible disorder of the Gospel of John; see e.g. J. Becker, *Das Evangelium des Johannes, Kapitel 1–10* (Ökumenischer Taschenbuchkommentar zum Neuen Testament 4/1; Gütersloher Taschenbücher Siebenstern 505; Gütersloh: Gerd Mohn, 1979) 30–2.

[12] The beginning of the Greek version of logion 6 has been reconstructed by H. W. Attridge as follows: [ἐξ]ετάζουσιν αὐτὸν ο[ἱ μαθηταὶ αὐτοῦ καὶ λέ]γουσιν· πῶς νηστεύ[σομεν, καὶ πῶς προσευξό]μεθα, καὶ πῶς [ἐλεημοσύνην ποιήσομεν κ]αὶ

disciples should not lie and do what they hate.[13] The last part of the answer emphasizes that the disciples cannot be accepted by God on the basis of outward obedience unless their internal attitude is right. Pretense and lack of real commitment cannot be hidden 'in the sight of heaven.' Understood in such a way, the point of the logion comes quite close to that of Matthew in the Sermon on the Mount. Criticism is not directed against the religious obligations as such but against their hypocritical fulfillment.

Jesus' answer in logion 6.2–6 can also be conceived in another way. It is possible that despite the form the questions of the disciples take, Jesus' reply does not deal with how the three religious practices are to be observed but with their necessity and justification in general. In the Coptic version of the logion, the first question of the disciples, which refers to fasting, does in fact speak about the justification of this practice. According to its wording, the disciples do not ask, 'How shall we fast?' but 'Do you want us to fast?' Even if the Greek version has preserved the original reading at this point, the possibility of interpreting Jesus' answer as a statement which questions the validity of the three religious practices cannot be ruled out. In other words, Jesus may give a 'right' answer to questions which are wrongly put. This is not unusual in the *Gospel of Thomas* (cf. logion 113). In several logia Jesus also has to correct an obvious misunderstanding of the disciples (13; 51; 52; 99; perhaps also 91). If the questions of the disciples (6.1) and the answer of Jesus (6.2–6) are seen in this light, one can infer that fasting, prayer, and almsgiving *are* lies and hateful deeds which have to be avoided altogether.

Provided that logion 6 can be perceived in this way, it also becomes understandable why the beginning of Jesus' response, which clearly alludes to Tob 4.15, nevertheless at one point deviates from that text.

τί παρατηρήσ[ομεν περὶ τῶν βρωμάτω]ν; see H. W. Attridge, 'The Greek Fragments' [of the *Gospel According to Thomas*] in B. Layton, ed., *Nag Hammadi Codex II,2–7 together with XIII,2*, Brit. Lib. Or.4926(1), and P. Oxy. 1, 654, 655,* vol. 1 (NHS 20; Leiden: E. J. Brill, 1989) 116. Apart from the last lacuna, an identical reconstruction is offered by J. A. Fitzmyer, 'The Oxyrhynchus Logoi of Jesus and the Coptic Gospel according to Thomas,' TS 20.4 (1959); reprinted in idem, *Essays on the Semitic Background of the New Testament* (London: Geoffrey Chapman, 1971) 385. Hence, unlike the Coptic version, all the questions of the Greek version begin with the interrogative word πῶς ('how').

[13] Exhortations not to lie (Sir 7.12–13) and not to do (to any one) what one hates (Tob 4.15) are both well known in Jewish wisdom tradition.

Whereas Tob 4.15 states: 'Do not do *to anybody* what you hate,' *Gos. Thom.* 6.3 leaves out the expression 'to anybody.' This alteration shows that Jesus' purpose is not to instruct the disciples not to separate the religious practices from right behavior but to reject such practices altogether.

In principle, both interpretations of logion 6 presented here are possible. In light of the other logia dealing with Jewish religious practices, however, the latter interpretation is more likely.

If the latter interpretation of logion 6 is accepted, it is interesting to notice that the two wisdom texts (Sir 7.12; Tob 4.15) which are alluded in the logion appear in literary contexts in which Jewish religious obligations are mentioned. Sir 7.10 speaks about prayer and almsgiving, and Tob 4.7–11, 16 refers to almsgiving. However, whereas those wisdom traditions maintain that exhortations to pray (Sir 7.10), to give alms (Sir 7.10; Tob 4.7–11), to fast (Tob 12.8), not to lie (Sir 7.12), and not to do to anybody what one hates (Tob 4.15) are maxims of equal importance to a follower of wisdom, *Thomas* admonishes his readers not to fast, not to pray, and not to give alms, because in so doing one lies and does what one hates. This may be an intentional paradox by means of which the writer invites those familiar with Jewish wisdom to a new understanding of the old tradition.

If logion 6 is basically open to two interpretations, *Gos. Thom.* 14.1–3 says explicitly what I suggested in the second interpretation of logion 6. Fasting, prayer, and almsgiving not only are unnecessary but are also harmful. Fasting is characterized as sin, prayer leads to condemnation, and almsgiving is detrimental to one's spirit. In other words, the one who fasts, prays, and gives alms risks his/her salvation. A negative attitude to these Jewish religious obligations can hardly be expressed more distinctly.[14]

Logia 104 and 27.1, which also speak about fasting – logion 104 speaks about prayer as well – seem to complicate the picture. They appear to contain some kind of encouragement to fast and pray. But what kind and for whom? In logion 104 it is at least clear that Jesus

---

[14] If *Gos. Thom.* 14.1–3 originally was Jesus' response to the questions of the disciples in 6.1 and only by accident was separated from them, as Pearson has suggested (see note 9), there is of course no need to discuss whether *Thomas*' view of fasting, prayer, and almsgiving in logion 6 represents an emphasis on the right inner disposition of a disciple (my first interpretation; cf. Matt 6) or a complete repudiation of these practices (my second interpretation). The latter is clearly the only possible interpretation.

does not think it is necessary for him to fast and pray. Actually, he suggests that only those who have committed sins or have been defeated in their spiritual life are in need of these religious exercises. But who are these people?

The reference to prayer and fasting after the departure of the bridegroom from the bridal chamber reminds us of Jesus' words in Mark 2.20. As many commentators maintain, this verse (like 2.19b) is a corrective of 2.19a and explains why the Christian community fasts although Jesus himself did not do so during his lifetime.[15] Fasting is thus necessary after the death of Jesus. Can a similar interpretation be applied to *Gos. Thom.* 104? Can Jesus' answer in logion 14 be understood in such a way that the disciples have to fast and pray after Jesus has departed from them?[16] This interpretation is not plausible for two reasons.

First, Jesus' order to fast and to pray is not directed to the questioners, that is, to the disciples.[17] In his reply, Jesus does not use the second person plural but the third.[18] Either 'they' refers to a group of people who remain unidentified, or the third person plural simply stands for the passive voice. Hence the text does not say: 'When the bridegroom leaves the bridal chamber, you shall fast and pray,' but: 'When the bridegroom leaves the bridal chamber, then let *them* fast and pray' or 'then let *fasting and prayer be done.*'

Second, in the context of the *Gospel of Thomas*, the idea of bridegroom and bridal chamber is not most readily connected with Jesus and his presence with the disciples. Without going into detail as to the problematic question of the use of bridal chamber imagery in early Christian literature, it suffices to say that in *Thomas* the bridal chamber is a symbol of religious salvation and deliverance. This is suggested by logion 75 in which Jesus says: 'Many are standing at the

---

[15]   E.g. E. Schweizer, *Das Evangelium nach Markus* (NTD 1; 6th ed.; Göttingen: Vandenhoeck & Ruprecht, 1983) 33.

[16]   So S. J. Patterson, *The Gospel of Thomas and Jesus* (Foundations and Facets: Reference Series; Sonoma: Polebridge Press, 1993) 80–1. Patterson realizes that this interpretation is in conflict with logia 6 and 14 but he explains this by assuming that the last sentence of Jesus' answer in logion 104 is a later scribal addition to the text of the *Gospel of Thomas*.

[17]   J. Sieber, 'A Redactional Analysis of the Synoptic Gospels with regard to the Question of the Sources of the Gospel according to Thomas' (Ph.D. Diss., Claremont Graduate School, 1965) 98. To be sure, the beginning of the logion does not explicitly mention who the questioners are. The situation, however, is the same as in logia 91 and 100, and at least in the latter the questioners are most likely the disciples.

[18]   Segelberg, 'Prayer Among the Gnostics?' 59.

door, but it is the solitary who will enter the bridal chamber.' In the *Gospel of Philip*, the bridal chamber constitutes a ritual through which salvation is gained and the final consummation is anticipated (65.1–26; 67.27–30; cf. also Irenaeus, *Adv. haer.* 1.21.3). Moreover, the author of the *Gospel of Philip* can also call those Christians who have experienced the ritual 'children of the bridal chamber' (72.20–21). In the *Gospel of Thomas* there is no clear indication whether the bridal chamber refers to a concrete ritual or is used as a mere metaphor. Be that as it may, it is at any rate evident that the bridal chamber symbolizes the state a Thomasine Christian attains after having been chosen for salvation.

If entering the bridal chamber is a metaphor for salvation, what does the departure from it signify? If the bridal chamber is regarded as a ritual, this motif could refer to the time after the reception of salvation experienced in the bridal chamber. In that case, fasting and prayer would belong to the highest stage of one's Christian existence. This does not, however, fit well with that part of Jesus' words which indicates that only sinners and the spiritually less advanced need to fast and pray. Therefore, it seems best to understand Jesus' response to the disciples as a paradoxical statement according to which 'masterless' Christians[19] need never practice fasting and prayer because after having entered the bridal chamber they should not leave it at all.[20] But whenever some do and thus commit sin and become defeated in the midst of worldly allurements, they are in need of fasting and prayer.

Logion 27, which also refers to fasting, contains two statements that are formally parallel to each other. Both of them begin with a negative conditional clause, which is followed by a main clause that expresses a sanction in case the negative condition of the protasis is fulfilled. The first statement (27.1) says that the prerequisite for finding the kingdom is νηστεύειν κόσμον (Coptic version: ΝΗⲤⲦⲈⲨⲈ ⲈⲠⲔⲞⳞⲘⲞⳞ), and the second (27.2) stresses the fact that the Father cannot be seen without 'sabbatizing' the sabbath. Since the question of sabbath observance will be taken up later, we shall not examine the second part

---

19   For the expression, see Marjanen, 'Women Disciples in the *Gospel of Thomas*' in this volume.
20   Cf. R. M. Grant and D. N. Freedman, *The Secret Sayings of Jesus* (London: Collins, 1960) 180.

of the logion here. At this point, we shall try to see how the phrase
ΝΗϹΤΕΥΕ ΕΠΚΟϹΜΟϹ in logion 27 could be understood.

In the Greek version of logion 27, νηστεύειν is accompanied by an
accusative direct object τὸν κόσμον instead of the genitive, which one
would normally expect. This has led to numerous attempts to emend
the text.[21] All these emendations are unnecessary, however. Although
somewhat unusual in connection with νηστεύειν, the accusative can
be understood as an accusative of respect.[22] Thus νηστεύειν τὸν
κόσμον can be rendered as 'to fast as regards the world.' This
understanding of the phrase was confirmed when the Coptic version of
the *Gospel of Thomas* was discovered. The Coptic preposition ε- before
the word **ΚΟϹΜΟϹ** is an obvious translation of the accusative of
respect.[23]

How then, is the 'fasting as regards the world' to be understood? The
very fact that the verb **ΝΗϹΤΕΥΕ**/νηστεύειν is followed both in the
Coptic and Greek versions by a qualifier (**ΕΠΚΟϹΜΟϹ**/τὸν κόσμον)
shows that the verb is not utilized in its concrete, ritual meaning of 'to
fast from food' but figuratively as 'to abstain from something which is
related to the world.' What is this something? As I have argued above,
'to fast as regards the world' has a definite ascetic dimension. In the
context of the *Gospel of Thomas*, logion 27 suggests that finding the
kingdom presupposes an ascetic, world-denying lifestyle, according to
which pursuit of worldly riches and maintenance of traditional family

---

[21] For these attempts, see A. Guillaumont, 'ΝΗΣΤΕΥΕΙΝ ΤΟΝ ΚΟΣΜΟΝ (P. Oxy. 1,
verso, 1.5–6)' *BIFAO* 61 (1962) 15–16.

[22] This understanding has almost become a consensus among scholars nowadays. A
somewhat different interpretation of the accusative has been advanced by Schröter
('Thomas and Judaism'), who suggests that the use of the accusative object in connection
with νηστεύειν points to the author's desire to avoid the use of a genitive, since it may
give the impression of the object being partitive, even though he/she wants to emphasize
the necessity of total abstinence from the world. Schröter's proposal is not very
convincing. The use of the genitive in connection with νηστεύειν is not due to the fact
that the action expressed by the verb would affect the object only in part but to the fact
that the genitive is generally employed with the verbs signifying restraint from something
(*genetivus separationis*).

[23] It is possible but not necessary that a Syriac formulation underlies both versions or at least
the Greek one, as Guillaumont, 'ΝΗΣΤΕΥΕΙΝ ΤΟΝ ΚΟΣΜΟΝ,' 15–23, and A.
Baker, '"Fasting to the World,"' *JBL* 84 (1965) 291–4, have suggested. For the whole
topic of the original language of *Thomas*, see F. T. Fallon and R. Cameron, 'The Gospel
of Thomas: A Forschungsbericht and Analysis,' *ANRW* II 25.6 (1988) 4228–30.

relations and values are obstacles to the development of one's genuine religious identity.[24]

To summarize, logion 27 follows the pattern of interpretation which borrows a traditional Jewish concept but gives it another, metaphorical meaning (i.e. model no. 3), whereas the three other logia we have treated in this section (6; 14; 104) represent a complete, even polemical rejection of Jewish religious obligations (model no. 4).

7.3. Dietary and purity regulations

There are two logia in the *Gospel of Thomas* which deal with dietary and purity regulations (14; 89). Logion 14 (see the translation, p. 166) begins with a complete rejection of fasting, prayer, and almsgiving (14.1–3). After that follows Jesus' instruction about the way his disciples ought to act while receiving food from the people they meet during their travels (14.4–5).[25] The dietary regulations are not viewed in an equally negative way as fasting, prayer, and almsgiving. While one who fasts, prays, and gives alms may, according to *Thomas*, even risk his/her salvation, dietary regulations do not seem to be anything worse than an unnecessary burden. Clearly they need not be obeyed. In that respect, *Thomas* is aligned with most of the early Christian authorities, including Paul, Mark, Matthew, and Luke.

One can of course ask whether by placing the instruction about dietary regulations in the context of stern warnings against fasting, prayer, and almsgiving, Thomas wants to give the impression to his readers that the food rules, too, are not only useless but harmful.

---

[24] See Marjanen, 'Is *Thomas* a Gnostic Gospel?' in this volume. The ascetic character of the phrase 'to fast as regards the world' should not be exaggerated, however. This has been done by A. D. De Conick, who insists that logion 27 'is most appropriately understood as promoting the overall encratite lifestyle encouraged throughout *Thomas* ... The phrase, "fast from the world," describes the adopted lifestyle of the followers of *Thomas*. They were abstaining from the world and were renouncing it completely by becoming poor wandering celibates with restricted diets'; see *Seek to See Him: Ascent & Vision Mysticism in the Gospel of Thomas* (VCSup 33; Leiden: E. J. Brill, 1996) 135. Likewise, in the context of the *Gospel of Thomas* those who 'fast as regards the world' can hardly be seen as Christians 'who have made themselves eunuchs,' as Clement of Alexandria understood the expression (*Strom.* 3.15.99).

[25] This part of the logion forms a clear parallel to Luke 10.8 (*Gos. Thom.* 14.4); Mark 7.15, and Matt 15.11 (*Gos. Thom.* 14.5). It goes beyond the scope of this study to assess the exact tradition-historical relationship between these texts. For various interpretations, see Uro, '*Thomas* and Oral Gospel Tradition' in this volume.

However, this remains nothing but a conjecture, since logion 14 does not actually contain any explicit polemic against dietary regulations.[26]

What logion 14.4–5 says about dietary regulations, logion 89 states with regard to Jewish purity rules:

> Jesus said, 'Why do you wash the outside of the cup? Do you not realize that he who made the inside is the same one who made the outside?'

Logion 89 consists of two questions. The first cannot be interpreted in any other way than that it fully undermines the significance of all purity ordinances. Jesus' second question gives the reason for this kind of stance. If the inside of a person is made by the Father, i.e. it stems from the light of the Father (50), it has its influence on that person's outward behavior. Purifying the outside, on the other hand, does not help anybody to rectify the deficiency in his/her inside.

Dietary and purity regulations belong to that category of Jewish religious obligations which, according to *Thomas*, can easily be dismissed (model no. 4). *Thomas'* attitude toward them again provides a good example of the internalization of faith which is typical of the writing.

7.4. Sabbath observance

The only passage in which the demand for sabbath observance occurs is logion 27 (for the translation, see above p. 166). As noted earlier, the logion comprises two conditional sentences which are formally parallel to each other. It is in the second that sabbath observance is mentioned (27.2). 'Sabbatizing the sabbath' is presented as the precondition for *visio Dei*, seeing the Father. Of all the Jewish religious obligations referred to in the *Gospel of Thomas*, the demand for sabbath observance in *Gos. Thom.* 27.2 has called forth the most diverse opinions on how it is to be perceived. There are scholars who think that it represents a literal demand to celebrate the Jewish sabbath. According to them, σαββατίζειν τὸ σάββατον/ΕΙΡΕ ⲘⲠⲤⲀⲘⲂⲀⲦⲞⲚ ⲚⲤⲀⲂⲂⲀⲦⲞⲚ means basically nothing less than τὰ σάββατα σαββατίζειν in Lev

---

[26] *Pace* M. Fieger, *Das Thomasevangelium: Einleitung, Kommentar und Systematik* (NTAbh, n.F. 22; Münster: Aschendorff, 1991) 76.

23.32 (LXX) and 2 Chron 36.21 (LXX).[27] Others maintain that 'sabbatizing the sabbath' is a metaphorical expression which no longer has anything to do with the concrete keeping of the sabbath. Rather, it symbolizes pursuing inner rest and giving up all worldly concerns,[28] or it is read 'as a protest against piety without substance.'[29] Some scholars have tried to cut the Gordian knot by pointing out that both in Greek and in Coptic 'sabbath' was regularly used to mean not only the seventh day of the week but also the entire period of seven days. Thus the phrase has been rendered in such a way that the protasis of the sentence reads: 'If you keep not the (entire) week as sabbath.'[30] A further variant of the figurative interpretation is developed by T. Baarda. In a recent article he seeks to show that, as in some Gnostic and other early Christian writings, τὸ σάββατον here denotes the demiurge or his world. Thus, in parallel with the first sentence of logion 27, 'sabbatizing the sabbath' means 'being at rest with respect to the sabbath, i.e. the world or its Demiurge.'[31]

As most scholars have pointed out, there is a clear parallelism between the two parts of logion 27.[32] This is the most important starting point when the meaning of *Gos. Thom.* 27.2 is considered. Taking the parallelism seriously results in three important corollaries. First, there is no indication in the text that the parallelism between the two parts of the logion means that the first part refers to fasting in metaphorical terms but the second part presents the keeping of the sabbath as a concrete, ritual act. On the contrary, the parallelism obliges the reader to think that when νηστεύειν is understood in a

---

[27] So e.g. K. Grobel, 'How Gnostic is the Gospel of Thomas?' *NTS* 8 (1961–62) 373; more recently also De Conick, 'Seek to See Him,' 129–35.

[28] This kind of spiritualizing interpretation is presented e.g. by M. W. Meyer, *The Gospel of Thomas: The Hidden Sayings of Jesus* (San Francisco: Harper, 1992) 81; cf. also Fieger, *Thomasevangelium*, 110.

[29] Patterson, *Gospel of Thomas*, 148.

[30] Most recently, this has been proposed by Paterson Brown, 'The Sabbath and the Week in Thomas 27,' *NovT* 34 (1992) 193. The same suggestion was also made earlier; for the evidence, see T. Baarda, '"If You Do Not Sabbatize the Sabbath ...": The Sabbath as God or World in Gnostic Understanding (*Ev. Thom.*, Log. 27),' in R. van den Broek, T. Baarda, and J. Mansfeld, eds., *Knowledge of God in the Graeco-Roman World* (EPRO; Leiden: E. J. Brill, 1988) 199–200; reprinted in T. Baarda, *Essays on the Diatessaron* (Contributions to Biblical Exegesis and Theology 11; Kampen: Pharos, 1994) 169.

[31] Baarda, ibid., 178–201.

[32] This is seen most clearly in the Greek version of the logion. The Coptic version offers a somewhat different picture; see note 34.

non-ritual way as meaning 'to abstain from,' so also σαββατίζειν should be seen as meaning 'to rest from.'

Second, if the accusative τὸν κόσμον is quite correctly taken as an accusative of respect, the accusative τὸ σάββατον should be regarded in the same way.[33] Thus the logion could be rendered as follows: '<Jesus said,> "If you do not fast as regards the world, you will not find the kingdom. If you do not rest (sabbatize) as regards the sabbath, you will not see the Father." '[34]

Third, on the basis of synonymous parallelism between the two parts of the logion, there has to be a correspondence between κόσμος and σάββατον. Presumably, this means that σάββατον denotes something similar to κόσμος, i.e. 'world' or 'worldly values.' In light of this, it is interesting that Baarda has called attention to a Nag Hammadi text (*Interp. Know.* 11.18–19) where the sabbath (**ⲡⲥⲁⲃⲃⲁⲧⲟⲛ**) is identified with the world (**ⲡⲕⲟⲥⲙⲟⲥ**).[35] Despite the somewhat poor condition of the manuscript, the reading is established beyond any reasonable doubt. The text reads: **ⲁⲃⲁⲗ̣ ϩⲙ̄ ⲡ[ⲧ̄ⲣ̄ϥ̄ⲁ̄]ⲡϥ̄ ⲙ̄ⲛ̄ ⲧⲉⲥϩⲓⲙ̣[ⲉ] ϩⲁⲡϩⲓⲛⲏ[ϥ ⲛ̄ ⲡϩⲓⲥ]ⲉ ⲙ̄ⲛ̄ ⲡⲥ[ⲁ]ⲃ̣ⲃ̣[ⲁ]ⲧⲟⲛ ⲉⲧⲉ ⲡⲉ̣[ⲉⲓ ⲡⲉ ⲡⲕⲟ]ⲥⲙⲟⲥ** ('From [being counted] with the female, sleep [brought labor] and the [sabbath] which [is the] world').[36] Thus what seems to be implicit in *Gos. Thom.* 27 is explicit in another Nag Hammadi writing deriving from the second century.

Based on these observations, 'sabbatizing the sabbath' in logion 27 no longer has anything to do with concrete sabbath observance. Rather,

[33] This is emphasized by Baarda, ibid., 196–7.

[34] The translation follows the Greek version. The Coptic rendering **ⲉⲧⲉⲧⲛ̄ⲧⲙ̄ⲉⲓⲣⲉ ⲙ̄ⲡⲥⲁⲙⲃⲁⲧⲟⲛ ⲛ̄ⲥⲁⲃⲃⲁⲧⲟⲛ** ('If you do not keep the sabbatical [= real] sabbath') seems to have lost the idea of the formal parallelism between the two parts of the saying and presents a spiritualizing interpretation which demands the keeping of a real sabbath. Even so, there is no doubt that the keeping of the real sabbath is not a demand for better fulfillment of the requirements of a Jewish religious obligation but suggests an alternative to it. The precise content of this alternative is not easy to determine, but we are certainly not far from the truth if we assume that keeping the real sabbath is something like abstaining from worldliness.

[35] ' "If You Do Not Sabbatize the Sabbath . . .," ' 189–91. Baarda's endeavor to demonstrate that this sabbath is the Demiurge, however, is not convincing (180–8). Apart from one late text by Tertullian (*Adv. Val.* 20.2) in which the Demiurge is called *sabbatum*, all his other attempts to find passages in which the sabbath is identified with the Demiurge appear to be speculative.

[36] The text and the translation are found in J. D. Turner, 'The Interpretation of Knowledge' [Transcription and Translation], in C. W. Hedrick, ed., *Nag Hammadi Codices XI, XII, XIII* (NHS 28; Leiden: E. J. Brill, 1990) 54–5.

it symbolizes abstinence from the world and from worldly values.[37] In his *Letter to Flora*, Ptolemy interprets sabbath observance in a similar vein: 'to keep the sabbath [means] that we desist from evil works' (Epiphanius, *Panarion* 33.5.12). The same is true of Justin Martyr (*Dial.* 12.3). Thus all three, *Thomas*, Ptolemy, and Justin, represent a similar view of sabbath observance. All of them can speak about keeping the sabbath, but none of them means the same thing that the Jews do. They use the concept but give it a completely new, non-ritual content (model no. 3).

7.5. Circumcision

His disciples said to him, 'Is circumcision beneficial or not?'
    [2]He said to them, 'If it were beneficial, their father would beget them already circumcised from their mother. [3]Rather, the true circumcision in spirit has become completely profitable.' (*Gos. Thom.* 53)

Jesus' answer to the question of the usefulness of circumcision is clear and simple. Bodily circumcision is of no use. The reason for this is the rationalization that if circumcision were to bring any advantage to children they would be born as circumcised. A similar argument is often found in anti-Jewish polemic. In some rabbinic sources a story is told according to which a king called Rufus comes to Rabbi Akiba and asks him: 'If God is so pleased with circumcision, why does the child not come out of the womb circumcised?'[38] In his *Dialogue With Trypho*, Justin Martyr argues similarly: 'For if circumcision were necessary God would not have made Adam uncircumcised' (*Dial.* 19.3).

Thomas' Jesus does not even give circumcision that salvation-historical value which Paul grants it when he states that through their circumcision the Jews obtained the privilege of being the first to hear the gospel (Rom 3.1–2). In the Valentinian *Gospel of Philip*, too, bodily circumcision is seen in a somewhat positive light: the circumcision of Abraham teaches a Valentinian Christian to see the necessity of the mortification of the flesh (82.26–29).

Despite the negative attitude the author of the *Gospel of Thomas* has

---

[37] A similar conclusion is reached by Schröter, 'Thomas and Judaism.'
[38] The text is derived from *Tanchuma* B 7 (18a). The translation is taken from W. D. Stroker, *Extracanonical Sayings of Jesus* (SBL Resources for Biblical Study 18; Scholars Press: Atlanta, 1989) 34.

toward circumcision, he/she does not want to abandon the term altogether. This is demonstrated by the final part of Jesus' reply (53.3). At this point *Thomas* proves to be part of that tradition in which the 'circumcision of heart' brought about by the Spirit is considered the prerequisite for hearing the word, awakening faith, faithful service of God, and putting off the body of flesh. This tradition is represented by Paul (Rom 2.25–29; Phil 3.3), possibly Stephen and the Hellenists already before Paul,[39] the Epistle to the Colossians (2.11), the Epistle to Barnabas (9.1–5), the *Odes of Solomon* (11.1–3), Justin Martyr (*Dial.* 113.7), and *Ptolemy's Letter to Flora* (Epiphanius, *Panarion* 33.5.11).

The author of the *Gospel of Thomas* does not explain what he means by the 'true circumcision in spirit.' This suggests that during the period in which logion 53 was composed the expression already had such a fixed meaning that there was no need to define it in explicit terms. This perhaps indicates that *Gos. Thom.* 53 does not belong to the earliest stage within the development of the 'circumcision of heart' tradition. With regard to some of the most crucial themes of *Thomas*, the most interesting parallels may be Col 2.11, in which circumcision by Christ is seen as 'putting off the body of flesh,' and *Odes Sol.* 11.1–7, which says:[40]

> My heart was pruned and its flower appeared, then grace sprang up in it, and it produced fruits for the Lord. [2]For the Most High circumcised me by His Holy Spirit, then he uncovered my inward being toward him, and filled me with his love. [3]And his circumcising became my salvation, and I ran in the Way in his peace, in the Way of truth. [4]From the beginning until the end I received his knowledge. [5]And I was established upon the rock of truth, where he had set me. [6]And speaking waters touched my lips from the spring of the Lord generously. [7]And so I drank and became intoxicated, from the living water that does not die.

It is possible that the 'true circumcision in spirit' in *Gos. Thom.* 53 should be understood as 'putting off the body of flesh,' a body which is seen in the *Gospel of Thomas* as a great burden,[41] or as 'uncovering the

---

[39] For this, see H. Räisänen, 'The "Hellenists" – A Bridge Between Jesus and Paul?' in idem, *The Torah and Christ* (Publications of the Finnish Exegetical Society 45; Helsinki: Finnish Exegetical Society, 1986) 242–306, esp. 286–90.

[40] The translation is taken from J. H. Charlesworth, 'Odes of Solomon,' in idem, ed., *The Old Testament Pseudepigrapha*, vol. 2 (London: Darton, Longman, and Todd, 1985) 744.

[41] Cf. also the imagery of 'putting on' and 'stripping off' in logia 21, 22, and 37. For an analysis of these sayings, see Uro, 'Is *Thomas* an Encratite Gospel?' in this volume.

inward being toward the Most High,' which results in becoming intoxicated from the spring of the Lord (cf. *Gos. Thom.* 13). Whether or not this is a right interpretation of the 'true circumcision in spirit' in logion 53 cannot be definitively settled. One thing is obvious, however. Again, *Thomas'* view of a Jewish religious obligation follows model no. 3: the practice itself is rejected but the term is preserved and given a completely new meaning.

7.6. Conclusion

The attitude that the author of the *Gospel of Thomas* adopts toward the concrete observance of Jewish religious practices is very unresponsive. He/she sees no need to pray, to fast in the literal sense, to give alms, or to obey any dietary or purity regulations. With regard to these religious obligations, the author thus belongs to those early Christians who reject their Jewish legacy altogether (model no. 4). On the level of vocabulary, the author may give a positive connotation to fasting, sabbath observance, and circumcision, but in all cases these religious practices undergo such a radical reinterpretation that they no longer have anything left of their original concrete meaning (model no. 3).

Thus none of the traditional Jewish religious practices has a favorable reception in the *Gospel of Thomas*. It is significant that they are not only regarded as expendable, but some of them – prayer, fasting, and almsgiving – can also be seen as harmful for one's spiritual existence. Taking this into account, it is not surprising that the author is critical of the Old Testament as well. This is demonstrated by logion 52. The twenty-four dead prophets mentioned in the passage are most likely the twenty-four books of the Old Testament according to the reckoning found in *4 Ezra* 14.45 and the Talmud.[42] This means that in the same way as the Jewish religious practices are dead institutions, so also the Jewish scriptures seem to be incapable of providing life to their readers.

These observations compel one to ask one final question: if *Thomas'* view of the most central elements of the Jewish faith is so negative, why do these elements still have such significant space devoted to them in

---

[42] B. Gärtner, *Ett nytt evangelium? Thomasevangeliets hemliga Jesusord* (Stockholm: Diakonistyrelsens bokförlag, 1960) 139; cf. also Meyer, *Gospel of Thomas*, 90.

the writing? There is one evident reason. Apparently, the *Gospel of Thomas* is being read in an environment in which the themes of the Jewish-Christian controversy are not yet settled issues, or else they have become pertinent problems for some other reason. At any rate, among the readers there are people who are somehow bound to their Jewish heritage. Therefore the logia dealing with Jewish religious practices are utilized to confront and to instruct them in order that they might abandon that form of Christianity (or Judaism) which is characterized by pious observance of various religious obligations, and that they might assume the Thomasine version of Christianity with its emphasis on self-knowledge and rejection of worldly values.

It is difficult to say whether this challenge arises as a natural consequence when new Jewish or Jewish-Christian people seek to join the group of Thomasine Christians, or whether it is a sign of a new religious development within the Thomasine community at large. Jesus' comments on Jewish religious practices are almost invariably replies to the questions of the disciples, who need to get additional, new information (6; 53) or to have their misunderstandings corrected (27; 89; 104). No outsider enters into a dialogue with Jesus in connection with these logia. This may indicate two things.

First, just as the disciples need new (critical) instructions about Jewish religious practices, so do the Thomasine Christians themselves. Second, the discussion about religious practices is not a matter of teaching outsiders but of teaching the inner circle of Thomasine Christians. Consequently, the extensive use of the logia dealing with Jewish religious obligations may mark a general change in the spiritual atmosphere of the Thomasine Christians. If this is so, it is interesting to ask whether and in what way this change is related to the transition which logia 12 and 13 seem to mirror. As I have suggested elsewhere, the placement of logion 13 after logion 12 may reflect a development from the hierarchical understanding of Christian leadership that is connected with the name of James to the notion of a 'masterless' Christian self-identity that is linked with the name of Thomas.[43] One can now see in this transition an additional factor. It is entirely possible that the figure of James, the hierarchical understanding of Christian leadership, and the observance of Jewish religious practices belonged

---

[43] Marjanen, *The Woman Jesus Loved*, 40; see also Marjanen, 'Women Disciples in the *Gospel of Thomas*' in this volume.

together and represented one stage within the religious development of the Thomasine community, whereas the figure of Thomas, the idea of 'masterless' Christian self-identity, and a critical attitude toward Jewish religious practices constituted a new option. While this must remain a hypothesis, it demonstrates intentional patterns within the writing, and points to a clearer purpose for its composition.

Bibliography

Achtemeier, P. J. 'Omne verbum sonat: The New Testament and the Oral Environment of Late Western Antiquity.' *JBL* 109 (1990) 3–27.

Adam, A. 'Grundbegriffe des Mönchtums in sprachlicher Sicht.' *ZKG* 65 (1953–4) 209–39.

al-Din Attar, F. *Muslim Saints and Mystics: Episodes from the Tadkhirat al-Auliya'.* Trans. by A. J. Arberry. Persian Heritage Series. London: Routledge and Kegan Paul, 1979.

Andersen, Ø. 'Oral Tradition.' In H. Wansbrough, ed. *Jesus and the Oral Gospel Tradition.* JSNTSup 64. Sheffield: Sheffield Academic Press, 1991. 17–58.

Arai, S. ' "To Make Her Male": An Interpretation of Logion 114 in the Gospel of Thomas.' *StPatr* 24 (1993) 373–6.

Asgeirsson, J. Ma. 'Arguments and Audience(s) in the *Gospel of Thomas* (Part I).' *SBLSP* 36 (1997) 47–85.

Attridge, H. W. 'Greek Equivalents of Two Coptic Phrases: CG I,1.65.9–10 and CG II,2.43.26.' *BASP* 18 (1981) 27–32.

–. 'The Greek Fragments' [of the *Gospel According to Thomas*]. In B. Layton, ed. *Nag Hammadi Codex II, 2–7 together with XIII,2*, Brit. Lib. Or.4926(1), and P.Oxy. 1, 654, 655.* Vol. 1. *Gospel According to Thomas, Gospel According to Philip, Hypostasis of the Archons, and Indexes.* NHS 20. Leiden: E. J. Brill, 1989. 96–128.

Attridge, H. W., and G. W. MacRae. 'The Gospel of Truth.' In H. W. Attridge, ed. *Nag Hammadi Codex I (The Jung Codex).* 2 Vols. NHS 22–23. Leiden: E. J. Brill, 1985. 1.55–117; 2.39–135.

Aune, D. E. *The Cultic Setting of Realized Eschatology in Early Christianity.* NovTSup 28. Leiden: E. J. Brill, 1972.

Baarda, T. '2 Clem 12 and the Sayings of Jesus.' In J. Delobel, ed. *Logia: Les paroles de Jésus – The Sayings of Jesus.* BETL 59. Leuven: Peeters/Leuven University Press, 1982. 529–56.

–. ' "Jesus Said: Be Passers-by:" On the Meaning and Origin of Logion

42 of the Gospel of Thomas.' In T. Baarda, *Early Transmission of Words of Jesus: Thomas, Tatian and the Text of the New Testament.* Amsterdam: VU, 1983. 179–205.

–. ' "If You Do Not Sabbatize the Sabbath … :" The Sabbath as God or World in Gnostic Understanding (*Ev. Thom.*, Log. 27).' In R. van den Broek, T. Baarda, and J. Mansfeld, eds. *Knowledge of God in the Graeco-Roman World.* EPRO. Leiden: E. J. Brill, 1988. 178–201. Reprinted in idem, *Essays on the Diatessaron.* Contributions to Biblical Exegesis and Theology 11. Kampen: Pharos, 1994. 147–71.

Baer, R. A. *Philo's Use of the Categories Male and Female.* ALGHJ 3. Leiden: E. J. Brill, 1970.

Baker, D. A. 'The "Gospel of Thomas" and the Syriac "Liber Graduum." ' *NTS* (1965–6) 49–55.

–. 'Fasting to the World.' *JBL* 84 (1965) 291–4.

Balogh, J. ' "Voces Paginarum": Beiträge zur Geschichte des lauten Lesens und Schreibens.' *Philologus* 82 (1927) 84–109, 202–42.

Barnard, L. W. 'The Origins and Emergence of the Church in Edessa during the First Two Centuries.' *VC* 22 (1968) 161–75.

Barth, G. 'Das Gesetzverständnis des Evangelisten Matthäus.' In G. Bornkamm, G. Barth and H. J. Held, *Überlieferung und Auslegung im Matthäusevangelium.* WMANT 1. Neukirchen: Neukirchener Verlag, 1960. 54–154.

Bartholomew, G. L. 'Feed My Lambs: John 21.15–19 as Oral Gospel.' *Semeia* 39 (1987) 69–96.

Bauckham, R. 'The Beloved Disciple as Ideal Author.' *JSNT* 49 (1993) 21–44.

Bauer, W. *Griechisch-deutsches Wörterbuch.* 6th rev. edition, ed. by K. Aland and B. Aland. Berlin: Walter de Gruyter, 1988.

Bauer, W., W. F. Arndt, and F. W. Gingrich. *A Greek-English Lexicon of the New Testament and Other Early Christian Literature.* Chicago: The University of Chicago Press, 1957.

Beck, E. 'Ein Beitrag zur Terminologie des ältesten syrischen Mönchtums.' *Studia Anselmina* 38 (1956) 254–67.

Becker, J. *Das Evangelium des Johannes, Kapitel 1–10.* Ökumenischer Taschenbuchkommentar zum Neuen Testament 4.1. Gütersloher Taschenbücher Siebenstern 505. Gütersloh: Gerd Mohn, 1979.

Bekker-Nielsen, H., P. Foote, A. Haarder, and H. F. Nielsen, eds. *Oral Tradition, Literary Tradition: A Symposium.* Odense: Odense University Press, 1977.

Berger, K. *Formgeschichte des Neuen Testaments*. Heidelberg: Quelle & Meyer, 1984.

Bianchi, U., ed. *Le Origini dello Gnosticismo: Colloquio di Messina 13–18 Aprile 1966*. Leiden: E. J. Brill, 1967.

Bienert, W. A. 'The Picture of the Apostle in Early Christian Tradition.' In W. Schneemelcher, ed. *New Testament Apocrypha*. Vol. 2. *Writings Relating to the Apostles, Apocalypses, and Related Subjects*. English trans. ed. by R. McL. Wilson. Cambridge: James Clarke; Louisville: Westminster Press/John Knox Press, 1992. 5–27.

Booth, R. P. *Jesus and the Laws of Purity: Tradition History and Legal History in Mark 7*. JSNTSup 13. Sheffield: Sheffield Academic Press, 1986.

Boring, M. E. *Sayings of the Risen Jesus*. SNTSMS 46. Cambridge: Cambridge University Press, 1982.

Botha, P. J. J. 'Greco-Roman Literacy as Setting for New Testament Writings.' *Neot* 26 (1992) 195–215.

–. 'The Verbal Art of Pauline Letters: Rhetoric, Performance and Presence.' In S. E. Porter and H. O. Thomas, eds. *Rhetoric and the New Testament: Essays from the 1992 Heidelberg Conference*. JSNTSup 90. Sheffield: Sheffield Academic Press, 1993. 409–59.

Bovon, F. 'Le privilège pascal de Marie-Madeleine.' *NTS* 30 (1984) 50–62.

Brown, Paterson. 'The Sabbath and the Week in Thomas 27.' *NovT* 34 (1992) 193.

Brown, Peter. *The Body and Society: Men, Women, and Sexual Renunciation in Early Christianity*. New York: Columbia University Press, 1988.

Brown, R. E. 'The Gospel of Thomas and St John's Gospel.' *NTS* 9 (1962–3) 155–77.

–. *The Gospel According to John: Introduction, Translation, and Notes*. 2 Vols. AB 29–29A. Garden City: Doubleday, 1966–1970.

–. *The Community of the Beloved Disciple*. New York: Paulist Press. 1979.

Brox, N. *Der Hirt des Hermas*. Kommentar zu den apostolischen Vätern 7. Göttingen: Vandenhoeck & Ruprecht, 1991.

Buckley, J. J. 'An Interpretation of Logion 114 in the Gospel of Thomas.' *NovT* 27 (1985) 245–72.

Bultmann, R. *The History of the Synoptic Tradition.* 2nd ed. English trans. by J. Marsh. Oxford: Blackwell, 1968.

–. *Das Evangelium des Johannes.* 21st ed. KEK 2. Göttingen: Vandenhoeck & Ruprecht 1986 [1941].

Cameron, R. *Sayings Traditions in the Apocryphon of James.* HTS 34. Philadelphia: Fortress Press, 1984.

–. 'Thomas, Gospel of.' *ABD* 6 (1992) 535–40.

Carlston, C. 'The Things that Defile (Mark vii.14) and the Law in Matthew and Mark.' *NTS* 15 (1968–9) 75–96.

Casey, R. P. 'Introduction.' In R. P. Casey, ed. *The Excerpta ex Thedoto of Clement of Alexandria.* SD 1. London: Christophers, 1934. 3–38.

Castelli, E. 'Virginity and Its Meaning for Women's Sexuality in Early Christianity.' *Journal of Feminist Studies in Religion* 2 (1986) 61–88.

Catchpole, D. 'The Mission Charge in Q.' *Semeia* 55 (1991) 147–73. Reprinted in idem, *The Quest for Q.* Edinburgh: T&T Clark, 1993. 151–88.

Cerfaux, L. 'Les paraboles du royaume dans l'Évangile de Thomas.' *Muséon* 70 (1957) 307–27.

Charlesworth, J. H. 'Odes of Solomon.' In J. H. Charlesworth, ed. *The Old Testament Pseudepigrapha.* Vol. 2. London: Darton, Longman, and Todd, 1985. 725–71.

–. *The Beloved Disciple: Whose Witness Validates the Gospel of John?* Valley Forge: Trinity Press International, 1995.

Charlesworth, J. H., and C. E. Evans. 'Jesus in the Agrapha and Apocryphal Gospels.' In B. Chilton and C. E. Evans, eds. *Studying the Historical Jesus: Evaluations of the State of Current Research.* NTTS 19. Leiden: E. J. Brill, 1994. 479–533.

Collins, J. J., and G. W. E. Nickelsburg. 'Introduction.' In J. J. Collins and G. W. E. Nickelsburg, eds. *Ideal Figures in Ancient Judaism: Profiles and Paradigms.* SBLSCS 12. Chico: Scholars Press 1980. 1–12.

Crossan, J. D. *In Fragments: The Aphorisms of Jesus.* San Francisco: Harper & Row, 1983.

–. *The Historical Jesus: The Life of a Mediterreanean Jewish Peasant.* San Francisco: Harper, 1991.

Crum, W. E. *A Coptic Dictionary.* Oxford: Clarendon Press, 1939.

Culpepper, R. A. *Anatomy of the Fourth Gospel: A Study in Literary Design.* Philadelphia: Fortress Press, 1987.

–. *John, the Son of Zebedee: The Life of a Legend.* Studies on Personalities of the New Testament. Columbia: University of South Carolina Press, 1994.

Daniélou, J. *The Theology of Jewish Christianity.* Philadelphia: Westminster Press, 1964.

Dart, J. 'The Two Shall Become One.' *Theology Today* (1978) 321–5.

Dauer, A. 'Das Wort des Gekreuzigten an seine Mutter und den "Jünger den er liebte": Eine traditionsgeschichtliche und theologische Untersuchung zu Joh 19,25–27.' *BZ* 11 (1967) 222–39; *BZ* 12 (1968) 80–93.

Dautzenberg, G. ' "Da ist nicht männlich und weiblich." ' *Kairos* 24 (1982) 181–206.

Davies, S. L. *The Gospel of Thomas and Christian Wisdom.* New York: The Seabury Press, 1983.

–. 'The Christology and Protology of the *Gospel of Thomas*.' *JBL* 111 (1992) 663–82.

–. 'The Oracles of the *Gospel of Thomas*.' Paper Presented at the Annual Meeting of the Society of Biblical Literature. Chicago, November, 1994.

–. '[Review of] G. Riley, *Resurrection Reconsidered*.' *JBL* 116 (1997) 147–8.

Davies, W. D., and D. C. Allison. *The Gospel According to Saint Matthew.* Vol. 2. *Commentary on Matthew VIII–XVIII.* ICC. Edinburgh: T&T Clark, 1991.

De Conick, A. D. *Seek to See Him: Ascent and Vision Mysticism in the Gospel of Thomas.* VCSup 33. Leiden: E. J. Brill, 1996.

De Conick, A. D., and J. Fossum. 'Stripped Before God: A New Interpretation of Logion 37 in the Gospel of Thomas.' *VC* 45 (1991) 123–50.

de Solages, B. 'L'Évangile de Thomas et les évangiles canoniques: l'ordre des péricopes.' *BLE* 80 (1979) 102–8.

Deming, W. *Paul on Marriage and Celibacy: The Hellenistic Background of First Corinthians 7.* SNTSMS 83. Cambridge: Cambridge University Press, 1995.

Dewey, J., ed. *Orality and Textuality in Early Christian Literature.* Semeia 65. Atlanta: Scholars Press, 1994.

Dodd, C. H. *The Interpretation of the Fourth Gospel.* Cambridge: Cambridge University Press, 1960.

Donfried, K. P. *The Setting of Second Clement in Early Christianity.* NovTSup 38. Leiden: E. J. Brill, 1973.

Downing, F. G. 'Word-Processing in the Ancient World: The Social Production and Performance of Q.' *JSNT* 64 (1996) 29–48.

Drijvers, H. J. W. 'Facts and Problems in Early Syriac-Speaking Christianity.' *SecCent* 2.3 (1982) 157–75.

Dunderberg, I. *Johannes und die Synoptiker: Studien zu Joh 1–9.* AASF DHL 69. Helsinki: The Finnish Academy of Science and Letters, 1994.

–. 'John and Thomas in Conflict?' In J. D. Turner and A. McGuire, eds. *The Nag Hammadi Library After Fifty Years: Proceedings of the 1995 Society of Biblical Literature Commemoration.* NHMS 44. Leiden: E. J. Brill, 1997. 361–80.

Dundes, A. 'Foreword.' In J. M. Foley, ed. *The Theory of Oral Composition: History and Methodology.* Bloomington: Indiana University Press, 1988.

Dunn, J. D. G. *Unity and Diversity in the New Testament: An Inquiry into the Character of Earliest Christianity.* London: SCM Press, 1977.

–. *Christology in the Making: A New Testament Inquiry into the Origins of the Doctrine of Incarnation.* London: SCM Press, 1980.

–. 'Jesus and Ritual Purity: A Study on the Tradition-history of Mark 7,15.' In F. Refoulé, ed. *A cause de l'Évangile: études sur les synoptiques et les Actes offerts au P. Jacques Dupont.* LD 123. Paris: Cerf, 1985. 251–76.

Edwards, Jr., O.C. 'Encratism.' *ABD* 2 (1992) 506–7.

Emmel, S., ed. *Nag Hammadi Codex III,5: The Dialogue of the Savior.* NHS 26. Leiden: E. J. Brill, 1984.

Erlemann, K. 'Papyrus Egerton 2: "Missing Link" zwischen synoptischer und johanneischer Tradition.' *NTS* 42 (1996) 12–34.

Fallon, F. T., and R. Cameron. 'The Gospel of Thomas: A Forschungsbericht and Analysis.' *ANRW* II 25.6 (1988) 4195–251.

Fieger, M. *Das Thomasevangelium: Einleitung, Kommentar und Systematik.* NTAbh, n.F. 22. Münster: Aschendorff, 1991.

Finnegan, R. *Oral Poetry: Its Nature, Significance and Social Context.* Cambridge: Cambridge University Press, 1977.

–. *Literacy and Orality: Studies in the Technology of Communication.* Oxford: Basil Blackwell, 1988.

Fitzmyer, J. A. 'The Oxyrhynchus LOGOI of Jesus and the Coptic Gospel According to Thomas.' *TS* 20 (1959) 505–60. Reprinted in idem, *Essays on the Semitic Background of the New Testament.* London: Geoffrey Chapman, 1971. 355–433.

–. *The Gospel According to St. Luke: Introduction, Translation and Notes.* 2 Vols. AB 28A-28B. Garden City: Doubleday, 1981–5.

Fleddermann, H. 'John and the Coming One: Matt 3.11–12/Luke 3.16–17.' *SBLSP* 23 (1984) 377–84.

Foley, J. M. 'Introduction.' In J. M. Foley, ed. *Oral Tradition in Literature.* Columbia: University of Missouri Press, 1986. 1–18.

–. *The Theory of Oral Composition: History and Methodology.* Bloomington: Indiana University Press, 1988.

Frend, W. H. C. 'The Gospel of Thomas: Is Rehabilitation Possible?' *JTS* 18 (1967) 13–26.

Frey, J. 'Appendix: Erwägungen zum Verhältnis der Johannesapokalypse zu den übrigen Schriften des Corpus Johanneum.' In M. Hengel, *Die johanneische Frage: Ein Lösungsversuch.* WUNT 67. Tübingen: J. C. B. Mohr (Paul Siebeck), 1993. 326–429.

Gaffron, H.-G. 'Studien zum koptischen Philippusevangelium unter besonderer Berücksichtigung der Sakramente.' Th.D. diss., Rheinische Friedrich-Wilhelms-Universität, Bonn, 1969.

Gamble, H. Y. *Books and Readers in Early Church: A History of Early Christian Texts.* New Haven: Yale University Press, 1995

Gärtner, B. *Ett nytt evangelium? Thomasevangeliets hemliga Jesusord.* Stockholm: Diakonistyrelsens bokförlag, 1960. English trans. by E. J. Sharpe as *The Theology of the Gospel of Thomas.* London: Collins, 1961. *The Theology of the Gospel According to Thomas.* New York: Harper, 1961.

Gasparro, G. S. 'Asceticism and Anthropology: Enkrateia and "Double Creation" in Early Christianity.' In V. L. Wimbush and R. Valantasis, eds. *Asceticism.* Oxford: Oxford University Press, 1995. 127–56.

Gaston, L. *No Stone on Another: Studies in the Significance of the Fall of Jerusalem in the Synoptic Gospels.* NovTSup 23. Leiden: E. J. Brill, 1970.

Gerhardsson, B. *Memory and Manuscript: Oral Tradition and Written Transmission in Rabbinic Judaism and Early Christianity.* ASNU 22. Lund: C. W. K. Gleerup. Copenhagen: Munksgaard, 1961.

–. *The Gospel Tradition*. ConBNT 15. Lund: C. W. K. Gleerup, 1986.

Gilliard, F. D. 'More Silent Reading in Antiquity.' *JBL* 112 (1993) 689–94.

Ginzberg, L. *The Legends of the Jews*. 5 Vols. Philadelphia: The Jewish Publication Society of America, 1909–38.

Goody, J., ed. *Literacy in Traditional Societies*. Cambridge: Cambridge University Press, 1968.

–. *The Interface between the Written and the Oral*. Cambridge: Cambridge University Press, 1987.

Grant, R. M. 'Notes on the Gospel of Thomas.' *VC* 13 (1959) 170–80.

Grant, R. M., and D. N. Freedman. *The Secret Sayings of Jesus*. London: Collins, 1960.

Grenfell, B. P., and A. S. Hunt. *New Sayings of Jesus and Fragment of a Lost Gospel from Oxyrhynchus*. Egypt Explorations Fund: Graeco-Roman Branch. New York: Oxford University Press, American Branch, 1904.

Griffith, S. H. 'Asceticism in the Church of Syria: The Hermeneutics of Early Monasticism.' In V. L. Wimbush and R. Valantasis, eds. *Asceticism*. Oxford: Oxford University Press, 1995. 220–45.

Grobel, K. 'How Gnostic is the Gospel of Thomas?' *NTS* 8 (1961–2) 367–73.

Gronewald, M. 'Unbekanntes Evangelium oder Evangelienharmonie: Fragment aus dem "Evangelium Egerton."' *Kölner Papyri* 6 (1987) 136–7.

Grundmann, W. *Das Evangelium nach Matthäus*. ThHKNT. 4th ed. Berlin: Evangelische Verlagsanstalt, 1975.

Guillaumont, A. ΝΗΣΤΕΥΕΙΝ ΤΟΝ ΚΟΣΜΟΝ (P. Oxy. 1, verso, 1.5–6)' *BIFAO* 61 (1962) 15–23.

Guillaumont, A., H.-C. Puech, G. Quispel, W. Till, and Y. 'A. al Masīh, eds. *The Gospel According to Thomas: Coptic Text Established and Translated*. Leiden: E. J. Brill. New York: Harper, 1959.

Gunther, J. J. 'The Meaning and Origin of the Name "Judas Thomas."' *Muséon* 93 (1980) 113–48.

Güttgemanns, E. *Offene Fragen zur Formgeschichte des Evangeliums*. 2nd. ed. BEvT 54. Munich: Chr. Kaiser, 1978 [1971]. English trans. by W. G. Dotz as *Candid Questions Concerning Gospel Form*

Criticism: A Methodological Sketch of the Fundamental Problematics of Form and Redaction Criticism. PTMS 26. Pittsburgh: Pickwick, 1979.

Haenchen, E. *Die Botschaft des Thomas-Evangeliums.* Berlin: Töpelmann, 1961.

—. 'Literatur zum Thomasevangelium.' *TRu* n.F. 27 (1961–2) 147–78; 306–38.

—. 'Die Anthropologie des Thomas-Evangeliums.' In H. D. Betz and L. Schottroff, eds. *Neues Testament und christliche Existenz: Festschrift für H. Braun zum 70. Geburtstag.* Tübingen: J. C. B. Mohr (Paul Siebeck), 1973. 207–27.

Hall, S. G. 'Nag Hammadi.' In R. J. Coggins and J. L. Houlden, eds. *A Dictionary of Biblical Interpretation.* London: SCM Press, 1990. 485.

Harl, M. 'A propos des logia de Jésus: Le sens du mot ΜΟΝΑΧΟΣ.' *Revue des Études Grecques* 73 (1960) 464–74.

Harpham, G. G. *The Ascetic Imperative in Culture and Criticism.* Chicago: The University of Chicago Press, 1987.

Harris, W. V. *Ancient Literacy.* Cambridge: Harvard University Press, 1989.

Havelock, E. A. *The Literate Revolution in Greece and Its Cultural Consequences.* Princeton: Princeton University Press, 1982.

Hawkin, D. J. 'The Function of the Beloved Disciple Motif in the Johannine Redaction.' *Laval théologique et philosophique* 33 (1977) 135–50.

Hedrick, C. W. 'Introduction: Nag Hammadi, Gnosticism, and Early Christianity – A Beginner's Guide.' In C. W. Hedrick and R. Hodgson, eds. *Nag Hammadi, Gnosticism, and Early Christianity.* Peabody: Hendrickson, 1986. 1–11.

—. 'Thomas and the Synoptics: Aiming at a Consensus.' *SecCent* 7.1 (1989–90) 39–56.

Henaut, B. J. *Oral Tradition and the Gospels: The Problem of Mark 4.* JSNTSup 82. Sheffield: Sheffield Academic Press, 1993.

Henderson, I. 'Didache and Orality in Synoptic Comparison.' *JBL* 111 (1992) 283–306.

Hoffmann, P. *Studien zur Theologie der Logienquelle.* NTAbh 8. Münster: Aschendorff, 1972.

Hofius, O. 'Das koptische Thomasevangelium und die Oxyrhynchus-Papyri Nr. 1, 654 und 655.' *EvT* 20 (1960) 21–42; 182–92.

Hübner, H. *Das Gesetz in der synoptischen Tradition: Studien zur These einer progressiven Qumranisierung und Judaisierung innerhalb der synoptischen Tradition.* Witten: Luther-Verlag, 1973.

Hummel, R. *Auseinandersetzung zwischen Kirche und Judentum im Matthäusevangelium.* Munich: Chr. Kaiser, 1963.

Isenberg, W. W. 'Introduction' [to the *Gospel According to Philip*]. In B. Layton, ed. *Nag Hammadi Codex II,2–7 together with XIII,2*, Brit. Lib. Or.4926(1), and P.Oxy. 1, 654, 655.* Vol. 1. *Gospel According to Thomas, Gospel According to Philip, Hypostasis of the Archons, and Indexes.* NHS 20. Leiden: E. J. Brill, 1989. 131–9.

–. 'The *Gospel According to Philip*' [English translation]. In B. Layton, ed. *Nag Hammadi Codex II,2–7 together with XIII,2*, Brit. Lib. Or.4926(1), and P.Oxy. 1, 654, 655.* Vol. 1. *Gospel According to Thomas, Gospel According to Philip, Hypostasis of the Archons, and Indexes.* NHS 20. Leiden: E. J. Brill, 1989. 142–215.

Jackson, H. M. *The Lion Becomes Man: The Gnostic Leontomorphic Creator and the Platonic Tradition.* SBLDS 81. Atlanta: Scholars Press, 1985.

Jacobson, A. D. *The First Gospel: An Introduction to Q.* Sonoma: Polebridge Press, 1992.

Johnson, S. R. 'The *Gospel of Thomas* 76.3 and Canonical Parallels: Three Segments in the Tradition History of the Saying.' In J. D. Turner and A. McGuire, eds. *The Nag Hammadi Library After Fifty Years: Proceedings of the 1995 Society of Biblical Literature Commemoration.* NHMS 44. Leiden: E. J. Brill, 1997. 308–26.

Judge, E. A. 'The Earliest Use of Monachos for "Monk" (P.Coll. Youtie 77) and the Origins of Monasticism.' *JAC* 20 (1977) 72–89.

Kaestli, J.-D. 'L'Évangile de Thomas: Son importance pour l'étude des paroles de Jésus et du gnosticisme chrétien.' *ETR* 54 (1979) 375–96.

Karpp, H. 'Viva vox.' In A. Stuiber and A. Hermann, eds. *Mullus: Festschrift Theodor Klauser.* JAC Ergänzungsband 1. Münster: Aschendorff, 1964. 190–8.

Kee, H. C. ' "Becoming a Child" in the Gospel of Thomas.' *JBL* 82 (1963) 307–14.

Kelber, W. H. *The Oral and the Written Gospel: The Hermeneutics of Speaking and Writing in the Synoptic Tradition, Mark, Paul, and Q.* Philadelphia: Fortress Press, 1983.

–. 'The Authority of the Word in St. John's Gospel: Charismatic Speech, Narrative Text, Logocentric Metaphysics.' *Oral Tradition* 2 (1987) 108–31.

–. 'Narrative as Interpretation and Interpretation of Narrative: Hermeneutical Reflections on the Gospels.' *Semeia* 39 (1987) 107–33.

–. 'In the Beginning Were the Words: The Apotheosis and Narrative Displacement of the Logos.' *JAAR* 58 (1990) 69–98.

Kim, Y. O. 'The Gospel of Thomas and the Historical Jesus.' *The Northeast Asia Journal of Theology* 2 (1969) 17–30.

King, K. L. 'Kingdom in the Gospel of Thomas.' *Foundations & Facets Forum* 3.1 (1987) 48–97.

–. 'The Apocryphon of John: One Work or Many Versions?' In J. D. Turner and A. McGuire, eds. *The Nag Hammadi Library After Fifty Years: Proceedings of the 1995 Society of Biblical Literature Commemoration.* NHMS 44. Leiden: E. J. Brill, 1997. 105–37.

Klijn, A. F. J. 'The "Single One" in the Gospel of Thomas.' *JBL* 81 (1962) 271–8.

–. *Edessa, die Stadt des Apostels Thomas: Das älteste Christentum in Syrien.* Neukirchener Studienbücher 4. Neukirchen-Vluyn: Neukirchener Verlag, 1965.

Kloppenborg, J. S. *The Formation of Q: Trajectories in Ancient Wisdom Collections.* Studies in Antiquity and Christianity. Philadelphia: Fortress Press, 1987.

Kloppenborg, J. S., M. W. Meyer, S. J. Patterson, and M. G. Steinhauser. *Q-Thomas Reader.* Sonoma: Polebridge Press, 1990.

Koch, K. *Was ist Formgeschichte? Methoden und Bibelexegese.* 3rd rev. ed. Neukirchen-Vluyn: Neukirchener Verlag, 1974.

Körtner, U. H. J. *Papias von Hierapolis: Ein Beitrag zur Geschichte des frühen Christentums.* FRLANT 133. Göttingen: Vandenhoeck & Ruprecht, 1983.

Koester, H. *Synoptische Überlieferung bei den apostolischen Vätern.* Berlin: Akademi Verlag, 1957.

–. 'One Jesus and Four Primitive Gospels.' In J. M. Robinson and H. Koester, *Trajectories through Early Christianity.* Philadelphia: Fortress Press, 1971. 158–204.

–. 'Dialog und Sprachüberlieferung in den gnostischen Texten von Nag Hammadi.' *EvT* 39 (1979) 532–56.

–. 'Gnostic Writings as Witnesses for the Development of the Sayings

Tradition.' In B. Layton, ed. *The Rediscovery of Gnosticism. Proceedings of the International Conference on Gnosticism at Yale, New Haven, Connecticut, March 28–31, 1978.* Vol. 1. *The School of Valentinus.* Studies in the History of Religions 41. Leiden: E. J. Brill, 1980. 238–61.

–. *Introduction to the New Testament.* Vol 2. *History and Literature of Early Christianity.* Philadelphia: Fortress Press; Berlin: Walter de Gruyter, 1982.

–. 'Gnostic Sayings and Controversy Traditions in John 8.12–59.' In C. W. Hedrick and R. Hodgson, eds. *Nag Hammadi, Gnosticism, and Early Christianity.* Peabody: Hendrickson, 1986. 97–110.

–. 'Introduction' [to the *Gospel According to Thomas*]. In B. Layton, ed. *Nag Hammadi Codex II,2–7 together with XIII,2*, Brit. Lib. Or.4926(1), and P.Oxy. 1, 654, 655.* Vol. 1. *Gospel According to Thomas, Gospel According to Philip, Hypostasis of the Archons, and Indexes.* NHS 20. Leiden: E. J. Brill, 1989. 38–49.

–. *Ancient Christian Gospels: Their History and Development.* London: SCM Press. Philadelphia: Trinity Press International, 1990.

Koester, H., and E. Pagels. 'Introduction' [to the *Dialogue of the Savior*]. In S. Emmel, ed. *Nag Hammadi Codex III,5: The Dialogue of the Savior.* NHS 26. Leiden: E. J. Brill, 1984. 1–17.

Kotila, M. *Der umstrittene Zeuge: Studien zur Stellung des Gesetzes in der johanneischen Theologiegeschichte.* AASF DHL 48. Helsinki: The Finnish Academy of Science and Letters, 1988.

Kügler, J. *Der Jünger, den Jesus liebte: Literarische, theologische und historische Untersuchungen zu einer Schlüsselgestalt johanneischer Theologie und Geschichte, mit einem Exkurs über die Brotrede in Joh 6.* SBB 16. Stuttgart: Katholisches Bibelwerk 1988.

Kümmel, W. G. 'Äussere und innere Reinheit des Menschen bei Jesus.' In H. Balz and S. Schulz, eds. *Das Wort und die Wörter: Festschrift für Gerhard Friedrich.* Stuttgart: Kohlhammer, 1973. 35–46.

Lambdin, T. O. 'The *Gospel According to Thomas*' [English translation]. In B. Layton, ed. *Nag Hammadi Codex II, 2–7 together with XIII,2*, Brit. Lib. Or.4926(1), and P.Oxy. 1, 654, 655.* Vol. 1. *Gospel According to Thomas, Gospel According to Philip, Hypostasis of the Archons, and Indexes.* NHS 20. Leiden: E. J. Brill, 1989. 53–93.

Lambrecht, J. 'Jesus and the Law: An Investigation of Mk 7,1–23.' *ETL* 53 (1977) 24–79.

Laufen, R. *Die Doppelüberlieferung der Logienquelle und des Markus-evangeliums.* BBB 54. Bonn: Hanstein, 1980.

Layton, B., ed. *The Rediscovery of Gnosticism.* Vol. 2. *Sethian Gnosticism.* Studies in the History of Religions 41. Leiden: E. J. Brill, 1981.

–. *The Gnostic Scriptures.* Garden City: Doubleday, 1987.

–. ed. *Nag Hammadi Codex II, 2–7 together with XIII,2*, Brit. Lib. Or.4926(1), and P.Oxy. 1, 654, 655.* 2 Vols. NHS 20–1. Leiden: E. J. Brill, 1989.

–. 'Prolegomena to the Study of Ancient Gnosticism.' In M. White and O. L. Yarbrough, eds. *The Social World of the First Christians: Essays in Honor of Wayne A. Meeks.* Minneapolis: Fortress Press, 1995. 334–50.

Lelyveld, M. *Les logia de la vie dans l'évangile selon Thomas: A la recherche d'une tradition et d'une rédaction.* NHS 34. Leiden: E. J. Brill, 1987.

Liddell, H. G., and R. Scott. *A Greek-English Lexicon.* 9th ed. Oxford: Clarendon Press, 1940.

Lightfoot, J. B. *The Apostolic Fathers.* Edited and Completed by J. R. Harmer. Grand Rapids: Baker, 1976.

Lincoln, B. 'Thomas-Gospel and Thomas-Community: A New Approach to a Familiar Text.' *NovT* 19 (1977) 65–76.

Lipsius, R. A., and M. Bonnet. *Acta Apostolorum Apocrypha.* 2 Vols. Leipzig: H. Mendelsohn, 1891–1903.

Lord, A. B. *The Singer of Tales.* Harvard Studies in Comparative Literature 24. Cambridge: Harvard University Press, 1960.

Lorenzen, T. *Der Lieblingsjünger im Johannesevangelium: Eine redaktionsgeschichtliche Studie.* SBS 55. Stuttgart: Katholisches Bibelwerk 1971.

Lührmann, D. 'Das neue Fragment des PEgerton (PKöln 255).' In F. Van Segbroeck, C. M. Tuckett, G. Van Belle, and J. Verheyden, eds. *The Four Gospels: Festschrift Frans Neirynck.* BETL 100. Leuven: Leuven University Press/Peeters, 1992. 2239–55.

Luz, U. 'Das Geheimnismotiv und die markinische Christologie.' *ZNW* 56 (1965) 9–30.

–. *Das Evangelium nach Matthäus.* 2 Vols. EKKNT 1.1–2. Zürich: Benzinger Verlag. Neukirchen-Vluyn: Neukirchener Verlag, 1985–90.

McCue, J. F. 'Conflicting Versions of Valentianism? Irenaeus and

Excerpta ex Theodoto.' In B. Layton, ed. *The Rediscovery of Gnosticism. Proceedings of the International Conference on Gnosticism at Yale New Haven, Connecticut, March 28–31, 1978.* Vol. 1. *The School of Valentinus.* Studies in the History of Religions 41. Leiden: E. J. Brill, 1980. 404–16.

MacDonald, D. R. *There is No Male and Female.* HDR 20. Philadelphia: Fortress Press, 1987.

Mack, B. L. *Logos und Sophia: Untersuchungen zur Weisheitstheologie im hellenistischen Judentum.* SUNT 10. Göttingen: Vandenhoeck & Ruprecht, 1973.

Marcovich, M. 'Textual Criticism on the Gospel of Thomas.' *JTS* 20 (1969) 53–74.

Marjanen, A. *The Woman Jesus Loved: Mary Magdalene in the Nag Hammadi Library and Related Documents.* NHMS 40. Leiden: E. J. Brill, 1996.

Markschies, C. *Valentinus Gnosticus? Untersuchungen zur valentinianischen Gnosis mit einem Kommentar zu den Fragmenten Valentins.* WUNT 65. Tübingen: J. C. B. Mohr (Paul Siebeck), 1992.

Martin, D. B. *The Corinthian Body.* New Haven: Yale University Press, 1995.

Meeks, W. A. *The Prophet-King: Moses Traditions and The Johannine Christology.* NovTSup 14. Leiden: E. J. Brill, 1967.

–. 'The Image of the Androgyne: Some Uses of the Symbol in Earliest Christianity.' *HR* 13 (1974) 165–208.

–. 'Equal to God.' In R. T. Fortna and B. R. Gaventa, eds. *The Conversation Continues: Studies in Paul and John in Honor of J. Louis Martyn.* Nashville: Abingdon Press, 1990. 309–21.

Ménard, J.-É. *L'Évangile selon Thomas.* NHS 5. Leiden: E. J. Brill, 1975.

Meyer, M. W. 'Making Mary Male: The Categories "Male" and "Female" in the Gospel of Thomas.' *NTS* 31 (1985) 554–70.

–. 'The Youth in Secret Mark and the Beloved Disciple in John.' In J. E. Goehring, C. W. Hedrick, J. T. Sanders, and H. D. Betz, eds. *Gospel Origins & Christian Beginnings in Honor of James M. Robinson.* Vol. 1. Sonoma: Polebridge Press, 1990. 94–105.

–. *The Gospel of Thomas: The Hidden Sayings of Jesus.* San Francisco: Harper, 1992.

Meyer, R. 'κόλπος.' *TDNT* 3 (1966) 824–6.

Moffatt, J. *A Critical and Exegetical Commentary on the Epistle to the Hebrews.* ICC. Edinburgh: T&T Clark, 1924.

Montefiore, H., and H. E. W. Turner. *Thomas and the Evangelists*. SBT 35. London: SCM Press, 1962.

Morard, F.-E. 'Monachos, Moine: Histoire du terme grec jusqu'au 4e siècle.' *Freiburger Zeitschrift für Philosophie und Theologie* 20 (1973) 332–411.

–. 'Monachos: une importation sémitique en Egypte?' In E. A. Livingstone, ed. *Papers Presented to the Sixth International Conference on Patristic Studies Held in Oxford 1971*. TU 115 [= *StPatr* 12]. Berlin: Akademi-Verlag, 1975. 242–6.

–. 'Encore quelques réflexions sur monachos.' *VC* 34 (1980) 395–401.

Moreland, M. C., and J. M. Robinson. 'The International Q Project Work Sessions 23–27 May, 22–26 August, 17–18 November 1994.' *JBL* 114 (1995) 475–85.

Murray, R. 'The Exhortation to Candidates for Ascetical Vows at Baptism in the Ancient Syriac Church.' *NTS* (1974–5) 59–80.

–. *Symbols of Church and Kingdom: A Study in Early Syriac Tradition*. Cambridge. Cambridge University Press, 1975.

Myllykoski, M. *Die letzten Tage Jesu: Markus, Johannes, ihre Traditionen und die historische Frage*. 2 Vols. AASF, Ser. B 256. Helsinki: The Finnish Academy of Science and Letters, 1991–4.

Nagel, P. *Die Motivierung der Askese in der alten Kirche und der Ursprung des Mönchtums*. TU 95. Berlin: Akademi-Verlag, 1966.

Neirynck, F. *Evangelica: Gospel Studies – Études d'évangile: Collected Essays*. BETL 60. Leuven: Leuven University Press/Peeters, 1982.

–. *Evangelica II: 1982–1991: Collected Essays*. BETL 99. Leuven: Leuven University Press/Peeters, 1991.

–. 'The Apocryphal Gospels and the Gospel of Mark.' In F. Neirynck, *Evangelica II: 1982–1991: Collected Essays*. BETL 99. Leuven: Leuven University Press/Peeters, 1991. 715–22.

–. 'John and the Synoptics: 1975–1990.' In A. Denaux, ed. *John and the Synoptics*. BETL 101. Leuven: Leuven University Press/Peeters, 1992. 3–62.

Neller, K. H. 'Diversity in the Gospel of Thomas: Clues for a New Direction?' *SecCent* 7.1 (1989–90) 1–18.

The New Oxford Annotated Bible with the Apocrypha/Deuterocanonical Books. New Revised Standard Version. B. M. Metzger and R. E. Murphy, eds. New York: Oxford University Press, 1991.

Niditch, S. *Oral World and Written Word: Ancient Israelite Literature*.

Library of Ancient Israel. Louisville: Westminster Press/John Knox Press, 1996.

Noack, B. *Zur johanneischen Tradition: Beiträge zur Kritik an der literarkritischen Analyse des vierten Evangeliums.* Copenhagen: Rosenkilde og Bager, 1954.

Ong, W. J. *Orality and Literacy: The Technologizing of the Word.* London: Methuen, 1982.

–. 'Text as Interpretation: Mark and After.' *Semeia* 39 (1987) 7–26.

Onuki, T. 'Traditionsgeschichte von Thomasevangelium 17 und ihre christologische Relevanz.' In C. Breytenbach and H. Paulsen, eds. *Anfänge der Christologie: Festschrift für Ferdinand Hahn.* Göttingen: Vandenhoeck & Ruprecht, 1991. 399–415.

Osborn, E. F. 'Teaching and Writing in the First Chapter of the *Stromateis* of Clement of Alexandria.' *JTS* 10 (1959) 335–43.

Oulton, J. E. L., and H. Chadwick. *Alexandrian Christianity: Selected Translations of Clement and Origen with Introductions and Notes.* LCC 2. Philadelphia: Westminster Press, 1954.

Pagels, E. H. 'Conflicting Versions of Valentinian Eschatology: Irenaeus' Treatise vs. the Excerpts from Theodotus.' *HTR* 67 (1974) 35–53.

–. 'The "Mystery of Marriage" in the *Gospel of Philip* Revisited.' In B. A. Pearson, ed. *The Future of Early Christianity: Essays in Honor of Helmut Koester.* Minneapolis: Fortress Press, 1991. 442–54.

Patterson, S. J. 'The Gospel of Thomas and the Synoptic Tradition: A Forschungsbericht and Critique.' *Foundations & Facets Forum* 8.1–2 (1992) 45–97.

–. *The Gospel of Thomas and Jesus.* Foundations and Facets: Reference Series. Sonoma: Polebridge Press, 1993.

Perkins, P. *The Gnostic Dialogue: The Early Church and the Crisis of Gnosticism.* New York: Paulist Press, 1980.

–. 'Pistis Sophia.' *ABD* 5 (1992) 375–6.

–. 'The Gospel of Thomas.' In E. Schüssler Fiorenza, ed. *Searching the Scriptures.* Vol. 2. *A Feminist Commentary.* London: SCM Press, 1995. 535–60.

Poirier, P.-H. '*Évangile de Thomas, Actes de Thomas, Livre de Thomas*: Une tradition et ses transformations.' *Apocrypha* 7 (1996) 9–26.

Quast, K. *Peter and the Beloved Disciple: Figures for a Community in Crisis.* JSNTSup 32. Sheffield: Sheffield Academic Press, 1989.

Quecke, H. ' "Sein Haus seines Königreiches:" Zum Thomasevangelium 85.9f.' *Muséon* 76 (1963) 47–53.

Quispel, G. ' "The Gospel of Thomas" and the "Gospel of Hebrews." ' *NTS* (1965–6) 371–82.

—. *Makarius, das Thomasevangelium und das Lied von der Perle.* NovTSup 15. Leiden: E. J. Brill, 1967.

—. *Gnostic Studies.* 2 Vols. Nederlands Historisch-Archaeologisch Instituut te Istanbul 34.2. Istanbul: Nederlands Historisch-Archaeologisch Instituut te Istanbul, 1975.

—. 'The *Gospel of Thomas* Revisited.' In B. Barc, ed. *Colloque international sur les textes de Nag Hammadi.* Bibliothèque copte de Nag Hammadi, Section 'Études' 1. Québec: University of Laval. Leuven: Peeters, 1981. 218–66.

—. 'The Study of Encratism: A Historical Survey.' In U. Bianchi, ed. *La traditizione dell'enkrateia: motivazioni ontologiche e protologiche. Atti de Colloquio Internazionale Milano, 20–23 aprile, 1982.* Rome: Edizioni dell'ateneo. 1985. 35–81.

—. 'Qumran, John and Jewish Christianity.' In J. Charlesworth, ed. *John and the Dead Sea Scrolls.* New York: Crossroad, 1991. 137–55.

Räisänen, H. 'Jesus and the Food Laws: Reflections on Mark 7.15.' *JSNT* 16 (1982) 79–100.

—. 'Zur Herkunft von Markus 7,15.' In J. Delobel, ed. *Logia. Les paroles de Jésus – The Sayings of Jesus.* BETL 59. Leuven: Leuven University Press/Peeters, 1982. 477–84.

—. *Paul and the Law.* WUNT 29. Tübingen: J. C. B. Mohr (Paul Siebeck), 1983.

—. 'The "Hellenists" – A Bridge Between Jesus and Paul?' In idem, *The Torah and Christ.* Publications of the Finnish Exegetical Society 45. Helsinki: Finnish Exegetical Society, 1986. 242–306.

—. *Beyond New Testament Theology: A Story and a Programme.* London: SCM Press. Philadelphia: Trinity Press International, 1990.

—. *Jesus, Paul, and Torah: Collected Essays.* JSNTSup 43. Sheffield: Sheffield Academic Press, 1992.

Reicke, B. 'πᾶς (B.3–4).' *TDNT* 5 (1967) 892–3.

Rengstorf, K. H. 'Urchristliches Kerygma und "gnostische" Interpretation in einigen Sprüchen des Thomasevangeliums.' In U. Bianchi, ed. *Le Origini dello Gnosticismo: Colloquio di Messina 13–18 Aprile 1966.* Leiden: E. J. Brill, 1967. 563–74.

Richardson, C. C. 'The Gospel of Thomas: Gnostic or Encratite?' In D. Neiman and M. Schatkin, eds. *The Heritage of the Early Church: Essays in Honor of the Very Reverend G. V. Florovsky.* OrChrA 195. Rome: Pontificium Institutum Studiorum Orientalium, 1973. 65–76.

Richter, G. 'Präsentische und futurische Eschatologie im 4. Evangelium.' In J. Hainz, ed. *Studien zum Johannesevangelium.* BU 13. Regensburg: Friedrich Pustet, 1977. 346–82.

Riesenfeld, H. *The Gospel Tradition.* Philadelphia: Fortress Press, 1970.

Riley, G. J. 'The *Gospel of Thomas* in Recent Scholarship.' *Currents in Research: Biblical Studies* 2 (1994) 227–52.

–. *Resurrection Reconsidered: Thomas and John in Controversy.* Minneapolis: Fortress Press, 1995.

Robbins, V. K. 'Rhetorical Composition and Sources in the *Gospel of Thomas*.' SBLSP 36 (1997) 86–114.

Robinson, J. M. 'LOGOI SOPHON: On the Gattung of Q.' In J. M. Robinson and H. Koester. *Trajectories through Early Christianity.* Philadelphia: Fortress Press, 1971. 71–113.

–. ed. *The Nag Hammadi Library in English.* Leiden: E. J. Brill, 1977.

–. 'Jesus from Easter to Valentinus (or to the Apostles' Creed).' *JBL* 101 (1982) 5–37.

–. 'On Bridging the Gulf from Q to the Gospel of Thomas (or Vice Versa).' In C. W. Hedrick and R. Hodgson, Jr, eds. *Nag Hammadi, Gnosticism and Early Christianity.* Peabody: Hendrickson, 1986. 127–75.

–. ed. *The Nag Hammadi Library in English.* 3rd, completely rev. ed. San Francisco: Harper & Row, 1988.

–. 'Die Bedeutung der gnostischen Nag Hammadi Texte für die neutestamentliche Wissenschaft.' In L. Bormann, K. Del Tredici, and A. Standhartinger, eds. *Religious Propaganda and Missionary Competition in the New Testament World: Essays Honoring Dieter Georgi.* NovTSup 74. Leiden: E. J. Brill, 1994. 23–41.

Röhl, W. G. *Die Rezeption des Johannesevangeliums in christlich-gnostischen Schriften aus Nag Hammadi.* Europäische Hochschulschriften: Reihe 23, Theologie Bd. 428. Frankfurt: Peter Lang, 1991.

Rosenberg, B. A. 'The Complexity of Oral Tradition.' *Oral Tradition* 2 (1987) 73–90.

Rowe, C. J., ed. *Phaedrus: Translation and Commentary on Plato.* Warminster: Aris & Phillis, 1987.

Rudolph, K. *Die Gnosis: Wesen und Geschichte einer spätantiken Religion.* 3rd ed. Göttingen: Vandenhoeck & Ruprecht, 1990 [1977].

Säve-Söderberg, T. 'Gnostic and Canonical Gospel Traditions, with Special Reference to the Gospel of Thomas.' In U. Bianchi, ed. *Le Origini dello Gnosticismo Collocuio di Messina 13–18 Aprile, 1966.* Leiden: E. J. Brill, 1967. 552–62.

Safrai, S. 'Education and the Study of the Torah.' In S. Safrai and M. Stern, eds. *The Jewish People in the First Century.* CRINT: Section One: II. Assen: van Gorcum, 1976. 945–70.

Sandelin, K.-G. *Wisdom as Nourisher: A Study of an Old Testament Theme. Its Development within Early Judaism and Its Impact on Early Christianity.* AAAbo, Ser. A 64.3. Åbo: Åbo Akademi, 1986.

Sanders, E. P. *Jesus and Judaism.* 2nd ed. London: SCM Press, 1987.

Sasse, H. 'κοσμέω κτλ.' *TDNT* III (1965) 867–98.

Sato, M. *Q und Prophetie: Studien zur Gattungs- und Traditionsgeschichte der Quelle Q.* WUNT 2.29. Tübingen: J. C. B. Mohr (Paul Siebeck), 1988.

Schenke, H.-M. 'The Function and Background of the Beloved Disciple in the Gospel of John.' In C. W. Hedrick and R. Hodgson, eds. *Nag Hammadi, Gnosticism, and Early Christianity.* Peabody: Hendrickson, 1986. 111–25.

–. *Das Thomasbuch (Nag Hammadi-Codex II,7).* TU 138. Berlin: Akademie-Verlag, 1989.

Schmidt, A. 'Zwei Anmerkungen zu P.Ryl III.' *Archiv für Papyrusforschung* 35 (1989) 11–12.

Schmidt, C., and V. MacDermot, eds. *Pistis Sophia.* NHS 9. Leiden: E. J. Brill, 1978.

Schnackenburg, R. *Die Person Jesu Christi im Spiegel der vier Evangelien.* HThKNTSup 4. Freiburg: Herder, 1993.

Schneemelcher, W., ed. *New Testament Apocrypha.* Vol. 1. *Gospels and Related Writings.* Vol. 2. *Writings Relating to the Apostles, Apocalypses, and Related Subjects.* English trans. ed. by R. McL. Wilson. Cambridge: James Clarke; Louisville: Westminster Press/John Knox Press, 1992.

Schoedel, W. R. 'Naassene Themes in the Coptic Gospel of Thomas.' *VC* 14 (1960) 225–34.

Schrage, W. *Das Verhältnis des Thomas-Evangeliums zur synoptischen*

Tradition und den koptischen Evangelienübersetzungen: Zugleich ein Beitrag zur gnostischen Synoptikerdeutung. BZNW 29. Berlin: Töpelmann, 1964.

Schrenk, G. 'ἐκλέγομαι (C–E).' *TDNT* 5 (1967) 172–5.

Schröter, J. 'Thomas and Judaism.' Paper Presented at the Annual Meeting of the Society of Biblical Literature. New Orleans, November, 1996.

Schüngel, P. 'Ein Vorschlag, *EvTho* 114 neu zu übersetzen.' *NovT* 36 (1994) 394–401.

Schürmann, H. 'Das Thomasevangelium und das lukanische Sondergut.' *BZ* 7 (1963) 236–60.

Schweizer, E. *Der Brief an die Kolosser.* EKKNT 12. Einsiedeln: Benziger, 1977.

–. 'σάρξ κτλ. (E & F).' *TDNT* 7 (1978) 124–51.

–. *Das Evangelium nach Markus.* NTD 1. 6th ed. Göttingen: Vandenhoeck & Ruprecht, 1983.

Scott, B. B., and M. E. Dean. 'A Sound Map of the Sermon on the Mount.' *SBLSP* 32 (1993) 672–725.

Segelberg, E. A. 'The Coptic-Gnostic Gospel according to Philip and Its Sacramental System.' *Numen* 7 (1960) 189–200.

–. 'Prayer Among the Gnostics? The Evidence of Some Nag Hammadi Documents.' In M. Krause, ed. *Gnosis and Gnosticism: Papers Read at the Seventh International Conference on Patristic Studies.* NHS 7. Leiden: E. J. Brill, 1977. 65–79.

Seim, T. K. *The Double Message: Patterns of Gender in Luke & Acts.* Nashville: Abingdon Press, 1994.

Sell, J. 'Johannine Traditions in Logion 61 of the Gospel of Thomas.' *Perspectives in Religious Studies* 7 (1980) 24–37.

Sellew, P. 'Early Collections of Jesus' Words.' Ph.D. Diss., Harvard Divinity School, 1985.

Sieber, J. H. 'A Redactional Analysis of the Synoptic Gospels with regard to the Question of the Sources of the Gospel according to Thomas.' Ph.D. Diss., Claremont Graduate School, 1965.

–. 'The Gospel of Thomas and the New Testament.' In J. E. Goehring, C. W. Hedrick, J. T. Sanders, and H. D. Betz, eds. *Gospel Origins & Christian Beginnings in Honor of James M. Robinson.* Vol. 1. Sonoma: Polebridge Press, 1990. 64–73.

Silberman, L. H., ed. *Orality, Aurality and Biblical Narrative.* Semeia 39. Decatur, GA: Scholars Press, 1987.

Slusser, M. 'Reading Silently in Antiquity.' *JBL* 111 (1992) 499.

Smith, J. Z. 'Garments of Shame.' *HR* 5 (1966) 217–238. Reprinted in idem, *Map is Not Territory: Studies in History of Religions.* SJLA 23. Leiden: E. J. Brill, 1978. 1–23.

Smyth, K. 'Gnosticism in the *Gospel According to Thomas.*' *HeyJ* 1 (1960) 189–98.

Snodgrass, K. R. 'The Gospel of Thomas: A Secondary Gospel.' *SecCent* 7.1 (1989–90) 19–38.

Speyer, W. 'Religiöse Pseudepigraphie und literarische Fälschung im Altertum.' In N. Brox, ed. *Pseudepigraphie in der heidnischen und jüdisch-christlichen Antike.* Wege der Forschung 484. Darmstadt: Wissenschaftliche Buchgesellschaft, 1977. 195–271 [originally published in *JAC* 8–9 (1965–6) 88–125].

–. *Die literarische Fälschung im heidnischen und christlichen Altertum: Ein Versuch ihrer Deutung.* Munich: C. H. Beck, 1971.

Stählin, G. 'ἴσος κτλ.' *TDNT* 3 (1977) 343–55.

Streeter, B. H. *The Four Gospels: A Study of Origins.* London: Macmillan, 1924.

Stroker, W. D. *Extracanonical Sayings of Jesus.* SBL Resources for Biblical Study 18. Scholars Press: Atlanta, 1989.

Talbert, C. H. 'The Problem of Pre-existence in Philippians 2.6–11.' *JBL* 86 (1967) 141–53.

Till, W. C. *Koptische Grammatik.* Leipzig: VEB, 1978.

Torjesen, K. J. *When Women Were Priests.* San Francisco: Harper, 1993.

Trumbower, J. A. *Born from Above: The Anthropology of the Gospel of John.* Hermeneutische Untersuchungen zur Theologie 29. Tübingen: J. C. B. Mohr (Paul Siebeck), 1992.

Tuckett, C. 'Thomas and the Synoptics,' *NovT* 30 (1988) 132–57.

Turner, H. E. W. 'The Gospel of Thomas: Its History, Transmission and Sources.' In H. E. W. Turner and H. Montefiore, *Thomas and the Evangelists.* SBT 35. London: SCM Press, 1962. 11–39.

Turner, J. D. *The Book of Thomas the Contender from Codex II of the Cairo Gnostic Library from Nag Hammadi (CG II,7): The Coptic Text with Translation, Introduction, and Commentary.* SBLDS 23. Missoula: Scholars Press, 1975.

–. 'The Interpretation of Knowledge' [Transcription and Translation]. In C. W. Hedrick, ed. *Nag Hammadi Codices XI, XII, XIII.* NHS 28. Leiden: E. J. Brill, 1990.

Uro, R. *Sheep Among the Wolves: A Study on the Mission Instructions of Q.* AASF DHL 47. Helsinki: The Finnish Academy of Science and Letters, 1987.

–. ' "Secondary Orality" in the Gospel of Thomas? Logion 14 as a Test Case.' *Foundations & Facets Forum* 9.3–4 (1993) 305–29.

–. 'The Secret Words to Judas Thomas: The *Gospel* and the *Book of Thomas*.' Paper Presented at the Annual Meeting of the Society of Biblical Literature. New Orleans, November, 1996.

–. 'Asceticism and Anti-familial Language in the *Gospel of Thomas*.' In H. Moxnes, ed. *Constructing Early Christian Families: Family as Social Reality and Metaphor.* London: Routledge, 1997. 216–34.

Valantasis, R. 'A Theory of the Social Function of Asceticism.' In V. L. Wimbush and R. Valantasis, eds. *Asceticism.* Oxford: Oxford University Press, 1995. 544–52.

Vielhauer, P. 'ΑΝΑΠΑΥΣΙΣ: Zum gnostischen Hintergrund des Thomasevangeliums.' In *Apophoreta: Festschrift für Ernst Haenchen zu seinem siebzigsten Geburtstag.* Berlin: Töpelmann, 1964. 281–99.

Vielhauer, P. *Geschichte der urchristlichen Literatur: Einleitung in das Neue Testament, die Apokryphen und die Apostolischen Väter.* Berlin: Walter de Gruyter, 1975.

Vielhauer, P., and G. Strecker. 'Introduction [to Apocalypses and Related Subjects].' In W. Schneemelcher, ed. *New Testament Apocrypha.* Vol. 2: *Writings Relating to the Apostles, Apocalypses and Related Subjects.* English trans. ed. by R. McL Wilson. Cambridge: James Clarke; Louisville: Westminster Press/John Knox Press, 1992. 542–68.

Vogt, K. ' "Männlichwerden" – Aspekte einer urchristlichen Anthropologie.' *Concilium* 21 (1985) 434–42.

Vööbus, A. *History of Ascetism in the Syrian Orient.* Vol. 1. *The Origin of Ascetism, Early Monasticism in Persia.* Corpus Scriptorum Christianorum Orientalium 184, Louvain: Van den Bempt, 1958.

Vukomanovic, M. 'An Inquiry into the Origin and Transmission of the Gospel of Thomas.' Ph.D. Diss., University of Pittsburgh, 1993.

Waldstein, M., and F. Wisse, eds. *The Apocryphon of John: Synopsis of Nag Hammadi Codices II,1, III,1, and IV,1 with BG 8502,2.* NHMS 33. Leiden: E. J. Brill, 1995.

Walker Jr., W. O., ed. *The Relationships among the Gospels: An*

Interdisciplinary Dialogue. Monograph Series in Religion 5. San Antonio: Trinity University Press, 1978.

Wansbrough, H., ed. *Jesus and the Oral Gospel Tradition.* JSNTSup 64. Sheffield: Sheffield Academic Press, 1991.

Westbrook, R. 'Punishments and Crimes.' *ABD* 5 (1992) 546–56.

Williams, M. A. 'Uses of Gender Imagery in Ancient Gnostic Texts.' In C. W. Bynum, S. Harrell, and P. Richman, eds. *Gender and Religion: On the Complexity of Symbols.* Boston: Beacon, 1986. 196–227.

Wilson, R. McL. *Studies in the Gospel of Thomas.* London: A. R. Mowbray, 1960.

Wimbush, V. L., ed. *Ascetic Behavior in Greco-Roman Antiquity: A Sourcebook.* Studies in Antiquity and Christianity. Minneapolis: Fortress Press, 1990.

–. 'The Ascetic Impulse in Early Christianity: Some Methodological Challenges.' *StPatr* 25 (1993), 462–78.

Wimbush, V. L., and R. Valantasis, eds. *Asceticism.* Oxford: Oxford University Press, 1995.

Winston, D. *The Wisdom of Solomon.* AB 43. New York: Doubleday, 1979.

Wisse, F. 'Flee Femininity: Antifemininity in Gnostic texts and the Question of Social Milieu.' In K. L. King, ed. *Images of the Feminine in Gnosticism.* Studies in Antiquity and Christianity. Philadelphia: Fortress Press, 1988. 297–307.

Index of ancient references

Biblical References (including Apocrypha)

Early Jewish Literature

Early Christian Literature

Other Greek and Latin Literature and Papyri

Index of names

Meyer, M. W. 9n., 50, 51n., 54n.,
  66n., 75n., 91n., 95n., 101,
  125n., 127n., 176n.
Moffatt, J. 127n.
Montefiore, H. 23n., 108n.
Morard, F.-E. 157n., 158n., 159n.
Moreland, M. C. 147n.
Mowbray, A. R. 108n.
Moxnes, H. xi, 143n.
Murphy, R. E. 131n.
Murray, R. 158n.
Mygdonia 99
Myllykoski, M. 58n.

Nagel, P. 148
Neiman, D. 108n., 141n.
Neirynck, F. 22n., 61n., 86n.
Neller, K. 43n.
Nickelsburg, G. W. E. 82n.
Nicodemus 74
Niditch, S. 11n.
Noack, B. 37n.

Olympias 99n.
Ong, W. J. 10n., 11n., 18n.
Onuki, T. 40
Origen of Alexandria 146n., 147n.
Osborn, E. F. 21n.
Oulton, J. E. L. 146n., 152n.

Pachomius 157
Pagels, E. H. 52n., 150n., 159n.,
  160n., 161n.
Papias of Hierapolis 20–21, 87
Parry, M. 17
Patterson, S. J. 1, 8n., 9n., 20, 28n.,
  42n., 58n., 77, 78n., 90n.,
  99n., 108n., 144n., 148n.,
  151n., 151n., 154n., 171n.
  176n.
Paul 26n., 48, 60, 87, 88n., 138n.,
  150n., 161, 164–165, 174,
  178–179

Paulsen, H. 40n.
Pearson, B. A. 151n., 168, 170n.
Perkins, P. 84n., 92n., 93n., 141n.,
  160n.
Peter 24, 25, 52, 67–69, 75n., 77,
  82n., 87, 89–91, 95, 96, 97,
  99, 102–105, 119, 122n.
Philip 84–85, 100
Philo 54, 59, 70, 150, 157
Plato 17n., 100
Pliny the Younger 66n.
Poirier, P.-H. 78n.
Polotsky, H. J. 51n.
Porter, S. E. 32n.
Prodicus 163n.
Ptolemy 178, 179
Puech, H.-C. 91n., 107n.

Quast, K. 75n.
Quecke, H. 128n.
Quispel, G. 9n., 30, 37, 39, 46n.,
  91n., 107n., 108n., 109n., 140,
  145–146, 147n., 151n., 157n.,
  158n., 159n., 167–168

Rad, G. von 130n.
Räisänen, H. 3n., 25n., 26, 179n.
Refoulé, F. 24n.
Rengstorf, K. H. 95n., 102n.
Reicke, B. 60n.
Richardson, C. C. 108n., 111n.,
  141n.
Richman, P. 151n.
Riesenfeld, H. 13n.
Riley, G. J. 40, 56–57, 58n., 72n.,
  73n., 107n., 155n.
Robbins, V. K. 6n., 32n.
Robinson, J. M. 8n., 9n., 15n.,
  42n., 44n., 51n., 84n., 91n.,
  105n., 108n., 147n., 149n.
Röhl, W. G. 114n.
Rosenberg, B. A. 18n.

Index of subjects